Blocking Spam & Spyware For Dummies®

D1199979

System Maintenance

For Anti-Spam Solutions	For Anti-Spyware Solutions
Data backups daily.	Regularly read reports on what is being blocked and why. Data backups daily.
System backups monthly.	System backups monthly.
Make sure the quarantine area does not overrun available disk storage.	Automatic filter updates turned on.
Automatic filter updates turned on.	Regularly review spyware logs.
	Turn on active or on-access blocking.

User Maintenance

For Anti-Spam Solutions	For Anti-Spyware Solutions
Update whitelist entries as new contacts are made.	Update signature files regularly.
Clean out quarantine periodically (as needed).	Scan for spyware regularly.
	Report found spyware to IT.

Useful Web Sites

Web Site	Address
The Spamhaus Project	www.spamhaus.org
Coalition Against Unsolicited Commercial Email	www.cauce.org
Internet Privacy For Dummies	www.internetprivacyfordummies.com
The SPAM-L FAQ	www.claws-and-paws.com/spam-l/tracking.html
SpywareInfo Forum & other stuff	http://spywareinfo.com
Anti-spyware software and reviews	http://spychecker.com
Consortium of Internet providers GetNetWise	http://getnetwise.org
Internet Scam site	http://scambusters.org
Anti-Phishing Working Group	http://antiphishing.org

Blocking Spam & Spyware For Dummies®

Cheat Sheet

Troubleshooting the Spam Filter

If Mail Is Missing . . .	If Too Much Spam Is Getting Past the Filter . . .
Verify with the sender that the mail was sent.	Make sure that your filter updates are current.
Check the user quarantine for a false positive.	Check and see if your whitelist is too permissive.
Check spam filter logs for the mail or errors related to it.	Check with the vendor regarding the spam that is getting in.
Examine firewall and mail host logs for evidence of the mail.	See if a local rule can eliminate the problem.

What to Expect from a Spam Filter

- ✔ Some spam will make it through the filters.
- ✔ Some good mail will get filtered.
- ✔ Some mail will go missing for unrelated reasons and be blamed on the spam filter.
- ✔ Users will panic about missing mail and demand that the spam filter be removed.
- ✔ Spam that gets through will offend users, and they'll demand perfect filters.
- ✔ The filtering market will change radically, more than once.
- ✔ A larger company will most likely purchase your vendor.
- ✔ Spam will still clog up your pipes, unless you are using an ASP (Application Service Provider).
- ✔ The volume of spam you filter will increase over time.
- ✔ If spam filtering is working perfectly, nobody will notice.
- ✔ Everything will catastrophically fail, but you have backups — right?
- ✔ Net time spent dealing with spam will decrease only slightly.

A Complete Defense in Depth Checklist

- ❏ Use antivirus software on workstations and servers.
- ❏ Block spam.
- ❏ Implement firewalls on notebook computers.
- ❏ Implement strong security settings in Internet Explorer; then lock the settings so that users cannot relax them.
- ❏ Block Web access to unsavory sites known to harbor spyware (such as gambling sites).
- ❏ Remove administrator privileges from users so that they cannot install third-party software on their workstations.
- ❏ Educate users regarding safe practices and how spyware gets onto systems.

Blocking Spam & Spyware FOR DUMMIES®

by Peter Gregory and Michael A. Simon

Wiley Publishing, Inc.

Blocking Spam & Spyware For Dummies®

Published by
Wiley Publishing, Inc.
111 River Street
Hoboken, NJ 07030-5774
www.wiley.com

WILEY

About the Authors

Peter Gregory, CISA, CISSP, is a career IT guy who has worn just about every hat that could be worn in the Data Processing/Information Systems/Information Technology business. Peter has IT experience in government, banking, non-profit, legalized gambling, and telecommunications. The Usenet-E-mail-Internet bug bit him in the mid 1980s. He has spent the past eleven years in two wireless telecom companies, working in positions where he develops security policy, security architecture, and security emergency response teams, and is a security consultant in general.

His passion for computers is matched only by his dedication to helping people know how to use information systems — from personal computers to mainframes — more effectively and safely. He achieves this through his speaking appearances at security conferences, in *ComputerWorld* and other online publications, and through a security consulting company that he co-founded in 2002.

Peter lives at Alki Beach in West Seattle, Washington, and enjoys antique shopping; driving his old German car on twisty, tree-lined roads; movies; looking for beach glass; and relaxing with friends in local coffee houses.

Michael A. Simon works as a computer security consultant in the Seattle area and the northwestern U.S. with clients in banking, e-commerce, health care, and biotechnology. Mike has been working in IT security for around 20 years and wrote his first programs on punched cards for an IBM mainframe in the early 1980s. Although he doesn't get much chance to exercise his skills in COBOL or Fortran these days, he keeps a deck of blank IBM punch cards around just in case.

For the last 10 years, Mike has been working for the company that he co-founded with Corwin Low when the Internet was more innocent, and convincing people of security's importance was a difficult task. Mike keeps busy assessing new threats for his clients, lecturing at Seattle University and the University of Washington, and advancing the public service goals of Northwest Security Institute, a non-profit that he helped to found.

When he steps away from the structured electron flows, Mike can be found roaming around the Olympic Peninsula or the Oregon coast with his wife, Dawn, and dog, Coda.

Dedications

Peter Gregory dedicates this book to Laney, Lexie, and Regan. I dearly love and miss you all.

Michael A. Simon dedicates this book to Dawn.

Authors' Acknowledgments

Peter Gregory would first like to thank Melody Layne, acquisitions editor at Wiley, for her vision, guidance, and drive. Mike and I are likewise grateful for Rebecca Huehls, our project editor who knows the *For Dummies* brand and how to produce a top-notch *For Dummies* book. We are also highly appreciative of all the copy editors — Barry Childs-Helton, Virginia Sanders, and Jean Rogers — who suggested hundreds of valuable changes in the manuscript. Special thanks also go to Satnam Purewal for thorough tech editing, and to Wiley's graphics team for their great illustrations.

Just as I got this book started, a number of cataclysmic events happened in my life that made writing this book extraordinarily difficult. Melody and Rebecca were sympathetic and supportive, but we had a book to finish. We agreed that we needed to find a co-author; a local friend and security expert, Mike Simon, graciously agreed to take this project on. Mike brought great insight and experience, which improved the book markedly.

Nalleli Lopez Hosek and Janice Winsor read the entire draft manuscript and made numerous productive suggestions to make the book easier to read and understand.

And finally, I would like to thank Art, Bob, Michael, Kate, Rietta, Paul, Ron, Tina, Jennifer, Michele, and especially Elizabeth for your support in 2004.

Michael A. Simon would like to thank Corwin Low, Sara Boddy, Mark Schulstad, and Raymond Pompon, the staff at Conjungi who put up with my occasional physical or mental absence while I wrote on a deadline.

I would like to thank Peter Gregory for dealing with a co-author that hadn't written a book in 10 years, and for thinking of me when he needed some help.

Last, but perhaps most importantly I would like to thank my family, who support me in everything I do, even when they have no idea what I'm doing. If I do something good, it's because you all make it possible.

Publisher's Acknowledgments

We're proud of this book; please send us your comments through our online registration form located at www.dummies.com/register/.

Some of the people who helped bring this book to market include the following:

Acquisitions, Editorial, and Media Development

Project Editor: Rebecca Huehls

Acquisitions Editor: Melody Layne

Copy Editors: Jean Rogers, Barry Childs-Helton, Virginia Sanders

Technical Editor: Satnam Purewal

Editorial Manager: Leah Cameron

Media Development Manager: Laura VanWinkle

Media Development Supervisor: Richard Graves

Editorial Assistant: Amanda Foxworth

Cartoons: Rich Tennant, www.the5thwave.com

Composition Services

Project Coordinator: Erin Smith

Layout and Graphics: Carl Byers, Andrea Dahl, Joyce Haughey, Barry Offringa, Lynsey Osborn, Heather Ryan, Mary Gillot Virgin

Proofreaders: Leeann Harney, Jessica Kramer, Joe Niesen, Carl William Pierce

Indexer: TECHBOOKS Production Services

Publishing and Editorial for Technology Dummies

    Richard Swadley, Vice President and Executive Group Publisher

    Andy Cummings, Vice President and Publisher

  Mary Bednarek, Executive Acquisitions Director

    Mary C. Corder, Editorial Director

Publishing for Consumer Dummies

    Diane Graves Steele, Vice President and Publisher

    Joyce Pepple, Acquisitions Director

Composition Services

    Gerry Fahey, Vice President of Production Services

    Debbie Stailey, Director of Composition Services

Contents at a Glance

Table of Contents

Introduction

Spam as a luncheon meat is a fine product. Just ask anyone who grew up in Hawaii, where they consume more of the mechanically separated pork product per capita than anywhere else in the United States. The spam that arrives in our e-mail inboxes, on the other hand, is almost universally loathed (even in Hawaii), and some folks even predict that it will bring about the end of e-mail entirely. Likewise, spyware has begun to have a visible impact on businesses and consumers who are spending more time looking over their shoulders (so to speak), wondering whether their information is safe. Although businesses are unlikely to abandon the most useful communication medium since the telephone just to avoid spam and spyware, this terrible twosome is having a significant impact on any business with a presence on the Internet.

Current estimates say that somewhere between 65 percent and 80 percent of all e-mail on the Internet is spam. With those kinds of numbers, you can easily see where the doomsday predictions are coming from, but the fatalists are ignoring an important fact, which is that where there are problems, ingenious people are always ready to solve those problems — usually for a fee. Spam filtering has progressed a lot from the early days when it was looking for certain "bad" words and filtering out anything with any form of any word in the list. Modern spam filters can examine word usage in context, recognize patterns in e-mail that look spamlike, and dispose of 97 percent to 99 percent of actual spam.

Although the same kind of useful statistics aren't readily available for spyware as we write this book, a lot of people are taking notice of spyware's impact on Internet computing. Huge, faceless corporations are tracking everyone's personal Web-surfing habits through tracking cookies, scumware is replacing banner ads on Web sites, and key loggers are recording online banking and other management of sensitive corporate and personal information.

If you're not already filtering spam and spyware in your business — which seems likely since you have this book in your hand — you are still bearing the full impact of the piles of malware being sent your way. Employees are spending too much time deleting junk, your Internet connection is spending too much time delivering junk to you, your users' surfing habits are being watched, and you might even have legal troubles brewing with the accumulated gunk that's hanging around in everyone's e-mail inboxes. Read on, and prepare yourself for the battle ahead!

About This Book

Blocking Spam & Spyware For Dummies is a reference. That means you're not expected to read it, starting with Chapter 1 and eagerly turning pages late into the night until you reach the exciting conclusion. In fact, let us tell you the end right now: The butler did it — that is, if the butler is an annoying spammer in his spare time, running the operation from a laptop in the basement. The pages of this book are what computer geeks like to call "random access." You can open up to any page you like and start reading there.

On the other hand, choosing pages at random seems like a slow way to acquire the information that really interests you, so . . .

- ✔ Use the Table of Contents to find the chapter or section that you're looking for.

- ✔ If you run across a term that you haven't seen before, check out the Glossary at the back of the book to explain geek speak.

- ✔ If you have the book open and are feeling lost, look up at the top of the page, where you'll find a running head, telling what chapter and part of the book you are open to.

- ✔ If you want to find information on particular topics, troll the index and turn to the page(s) indicated.

- ✔ Dive in and out of the chapters and Glossary in whatever way makes sense to you. It's *your* book, use it the way that works best for you! (Except for propping up the corner of your couch. For that, use *Home Maintenance For Dummies,* by James and Morris Carey, published by Wiley.)

Why We Combined Spam and Spyware

Some of the chapters in this book are strictly about spam, and others are only about spyware. Still other chapters have spam and spyware sections, and some chapters make no distinction and seem to be about both. What gives?

Spam and spyware are completely different phenomena, so we use separate chapters and sections when discussing their technical details. However, some of the aspects of how you remedy spam and spyware are so similar that we talk about both in certain sections and even whole chapters. The two are even more closely related than you might think: Some spam contains spyware, and some spyware is used to decide who to spam.

The reason we combine spam and spyware in this book is simple: Both are relatively recent phenomena, they're both about security, and the anti-spam and anti-spyware product markets are both more or less in their earlier stages of development. Few people in IT organizations have experience battling either one, which is why we wrote this book in the first place.

How This Book Is Organized

This book is divided into five parts to help you find what you need quickly.

Part 1: Understanding the Problem

This part is about getting up to speed on what spam and spyware are all about, and what businesses are doing about them in general terms. You get a decent overview of what spammers and spyware writers are doing and how they affect your business. We take a look at the issues surrounding

  ✔ How spam and spyware impact business

  ✔ Why spam and spyware exist

  ✔ Choosing a filtering product

Part 11: Justifying and Selecting Spam and Spyware Filters

Money doesn't grow on trees, so in this part we talk about ways to help you sell the idea of installing spam and spyware filters to the folks who write the checks in your organization. To sell them the idea, you have to show them how much spam and spyware are really costing the organization. If you do the numbers, you find out that spyware and spam are costing your business a bundle, and we show you a few of the ways to calculate just how large of a bundle that is.

After you know how much spam and spyware are costing you, you can get a handle on how much you're willing to spend to make the problem go away, so we also talk about how to figure out what filtering solutions will work best for you. A lot of options are available, and we cover all the interesting ones, with some of the pros and cons for each.

Part III: Deploying Your Chosen Solution

This is the meat and potatoes of IT: preparing your users for the new filters, installing them, and then supporting the installed solutions. In any IT project, you can fall into a lot of common traps, and we've fallen into most of them at one time or another. Although we don't lift our shirts and show the scars, we tell you how to avoid those traps. In this part, we share a lot of good ways to prepare for the introduction of this new technology into your enterprise as well as some of the things that might seem like a good idea — until you've done it with real users or a real data center.

Although you don't need to read this part in any particular order, we organized it in the order of how we expect things will happen for your rollout to users: training, followed by installation, followed by support.

Part IV: Maintaining Your Defenses

Almost anything that has more than one moving part will break down if not properly maintained. This is where we talk about how to keep the thousands of moving parts in your defenses working at peak efficiency, what sorts of failures you should expect, and how to cope with them.

No defense is perfect, and some of the constant beating that your filters see will cause you some headaches. We try to anticipate a lot of these, which should help you cut back on the aspirin.

Part V: The Part of Tens

Are you short on time? Do you need to know as much as possible about spam and spyware filtering in 20 minutes before your next meeting? This part is written for just that sort of cramming. We talk here about ten filtering solutions, including some ASP solutions, some tips on getting your filter right the first time, and a list of the worst problems you're likely to encounter.

Following the Part of Tens chapters are three appendixes. If you're anxious to get started on your spam or spyware-blocking projects, you don't have to start with a blank sheet of paper. In the appendixes, you find detailed lists of requirements and project plans — perennial favorites of medium- and big-company project managers.

In addition, you find a glossary of terms used in this book, so you can easily look up any jargon that's unfamiliar to you. And to get hip to the lingo *really fast,* you might just read the glossary from A to Z sometime. (Discreetly, of course.)

Conventions Used in This Book

When you need to issue a command in Windows, we show a command like this: Tools⇨Options. In this example, click Tools from the menu bar at the top of the window, and then click Options, which appears in the list. If you don't see Options in the list, you might need to click the down arrows at the bottom of the list of options to make all the options appear.

We wrote the chapters in this book separately but collaborated often because we live only about a mile apart. In this intro, we say "we," but in the rest of the book, we say "I" because we're nice guys and doing so made life easier on our editors (we never could be consistent). Seriously though, even though each of us took on the main responsibility for respective chapters, we worked closely together and often the experience or opinion in these pages is collective.

Defining Spam, Spyware, and Malware

Spam and *spyware* are subjective terms. Just ask ten people for their own definitions of each and you'll probably get ten different answers.

- ✔ **Spam** generally refers to unwanted commercial e-mail that is typically sent in bulk to thousands or even millions of recipients. There are some gray areas that we hope won't trip you up: Some people may include the e-mail produced by mass-mailing viruses or Trojan horses as spam. Similarly, some people may include e-mail from a company they *have* done business with as spam. Also, if you subscribe to some e-mail list and at some time in the future you no longer want it, that might be spam.

- ✔ **Spyware,** for the purposes of this book, is an inclusive term that also includes adware and scumware. Basically, spyware is software (or software components such as cookies and browser configuration settings) that many people would prefer was *not* present on their workstations — regardless of *how* the spyware got onto the workstation to begin with. In every case, spyware gives away information about you that you didn't authorize.

- ✔ **Malware** is a generic term that includes both spyware and some forms of spam, and in some contexts also includes "traditional" malware such as viruses, Trojan horses, and worms.

Sidebars

All through this book you can find gray boxes (like this one) called *sidebars*. These contain additional useful information that may be of interest, and sometimes our opinions, interesting or not. Feel free to read them or skip them as you please. We think you'll like them.

Foolish Assumptions

We're going to do our Karnak the Magnificent imitation and try to figure out who our readers are. Because you can't see us, please hold this book up to your forehead while we concentrate. . . .

- ✔ You are a systems administrator in a smallish IT department, and some higher-up has asked you to look into your organization's spam or spyware problem.

- ✔ You might *be* the IT department in your really small company, and you know that spam and spyware are — or will be — a problem.

- ✔ You are a computer hobbyist experiencing spam or spyware problems at home.

- ✔ You are a project manager and need to get a jump on putting together a project plan or requirements on your upcoming spam or spyware project.

How are we doing so far?

- ✔ You are an IT professional and you need to find out more about how spam or spyware gets into your environment.

- ✔ You want to know how much at risk you are and whether you're properly protected.

- ✔ You want to know more about how to use your antivirus program.

- ✔ You want to move beyond antivirus software and firewalls to begin to find out about spam filters and anti-spyware.

- ✔ Your online retailer sent you this book instead of the steamy novel you wanted, and it's too late to return it before your beach vacation. What the heck?

This is who we think you're *not:*

- ✔ **You aren't a spammer:** There are *no clues here* on how to create, distribute, or profit from spam or spyware. If you are a spammer or spyware writer, you can see how helpful this book will be in stopping your kind. Give up now and save us all the trouble!

- ✔ **You're clearly no dummy:** Even if you don't know a thing about spam or spyware, buying this book shows just how smart you are.

Icons Used in This Book

If you've used Windows (or UNIX), you've seen icons. They're the little symbols that appear on the screen that have special meaning. We use icons in this book, too, and they're a lot easier to understand than the ones used in Windows:

Here is a shortcut or hint to save you time or trouble.

Get out your geeky glasses, plaid shirt, and pocket protector!

Watch out! Some trap or pitfall awaits you.

Don't forget these important points — they are well worth, uh, remembering!

Where to Go from Here

Stopping spam and spyware isn't easy, but many people have forged the trail ahead of you, and early adopters have many valuable lessons to share.

If you want to understand the big picture of spam and spyware, you can start with one of the chapters in Part I. If you are already familiar with the nature and effects of spam and spyware, then go straight to Part II. If you're even further down the road and you have chosen a solution, the chapters in Part III can guide you through implementation. If lists are your particular fancy, the Part of Tens was written with you in mind.

If you need information on related topics, pick any of the following books (all published by Wiley Publishing, Inc.) *in addition to* this book:

- *Network Security For Dummies* by Chey Cobb
- *Firewalls For Dummies*, 2nd Edition, by Brian Komar, Ronald Beekelaar, and Joern Wettern
- *Internet Privacy For Dummies* by John R. Levine, Ray Everett-Church, Greg Stebben, and David Lawrence
- *Computer Viruses For Dummies* by Peter H. Gregory

You need to stay current on security issues in this rapidly growing and changing landscape. Some sources for good information include

- *Information Security Magazine* (http://infosecuritymag.com)
- *SC Magazine* (http://scmagazine.com)
- *CSO Magazine* (www.csoonline.com)

    ✔ *SearchSecurity* (`http://searchsecurity.com`)

    ✔ *Computerworld* (`http://computerworld.com`)

    ✔ *InfoWeek Magazine* (`http://informationweek.com`)

Some of these resources publish both paper and online editions; others are online only. Most have services where they will push article summaries to you on your choice of topics as often as you like.

And the Latest Breaking News . . .

. . . is not here. As we wrote this book, we passed news articles back and forth about the latest spyware and antivirus company merger, the latest vulnerability, the latest trend, the latest opinion article, and the latest statistics. It was driving us crazy, and nearly made us miss the deadline when the publisher was to put the book into production (this is one of the very last things to be written).

Then we realized that this book isn't about the latest news or about being the most up to date. Readers (or potential readers) who are after that are missing the point. You know the phrase, "Give a man a fish, he will eat today and be hungry tomorrow. Teach a man to fish, and he will never be hungry again." We're not giving you fish in this book, but teaching you to fish. We discuss the important, timeless concepts that will make you successful if you take them to heart and apply them. And your success is our greatest desire — that's why we stayed up late, got up early, and worked weekends to write this book.

Write to Us!

Have a question? Comment? Complaint? Please let us know. Write to us at

`questions@spamandspyware.com`

We'll *try* to answer every question personally. Also, look for the Frequently Asked Questions link (and other useful information) at

`www.spamandspyware.com`

For information on other *For Dummies* books, please visit

`www.dummies.com`

Part I
Understanding the Problem

The 5th Wave   By Rich Tennant

"Wow, I didn't know an antispam solution could redirect an e-mail message like that."

In this part . . .

Here I introduce some background regarding the spam and spyware problem and sketch the outline of a battle plan to deal with the threat that they pose to your company.

If you're going to deal with the spam problem for your company, you have a big job in front of you, so I describe the steps you need to take and some of the issues that you'll run into along the way.

I also help you gain a better understanding of the enemy. Because the people behind spam and spyware are a somewhat elusive lot, I provide some insight into their business plans and some of the dirty tricks they use to accomplish those plans.

Chapter 1

Spam and Spyware: The Rampant Menace

In This Chapter

▶ Understanding how spam and spyware affect the organization

▶ Fighting back

▶ Taking stock of your business

▶ Justifying a spam solution

▶ Choosing the right solution

▶ Making the solution work

You just got on the spam and spyware rollercoaster. In this chapter, you will whiz through a lot of topics at a high level. So please remain seated and keep your arms and legs inside the car at all times. Strap in and *hang on* 'cause you'll be plunging down the hills, whipping through the turns, and rolling around the loops.

In later chapters, you get a chance to slow down and soak up the details of all these topics, but this chapter's bird's-eye view is a good place to start if you're just beginning the task of blocking spam, spyware, or both.

Knowing How Spam and Spyware Affect the Organization

Because you're reading this book, you probably have a suspicion that spam and spyware are — or may be — affecting your business. If you have e-mail, chances are that spam *is* making an impact in your organization. And while employees in your business are surfing the Net, their workstations are becoming rotten with spyware that's doing who-knows-what. Knowing *how* the impact is manifesting itself is important if you want to get the upper hand.

Increasing e-mail volume

This is an understatement to be sure. Many studies conclude that the volume of spam entering most businesses hovers in the 70 to 80 percent range. Your e-mail servers are working hard to process inbound and outbound mail, and the majority of that inbound mail is putrid filth. If you're sufficiently privileged to be able to walk up to your e-mail server, that giant sucking sound you hear is the inbound spam choking the life out of your server.

Spam is consuming network resources, CPU resources, disk and network buffers, disk space — everything. If your e-mail server is sluggish, imagine how much faster it would run if you could eliminate 70 percent of the incoming traffic. On the other hand, if your e-mail server *is* able to keep up with the torrent of filth, it's because you bought a system far larger than should have been necessary, in order to manage the relevant business e-mail *and* the spam.

Everybody is in the same situation: Either they've had to invest more capital dollars in e-mail servers to keep up with the growing tide of spam, or else their mail servers are suffering under the workload.

If you are so well organized that you have statistics on inbound e-mail volume over a period of years, I'm willing to bet that you can see that the volume is increasing at a rate that significantly outpaces any increase in the number of employees in your organization.

Draining productivity

Almost all organizations have their share of employees who are drowning in spam. Three to five hundred spam messages per day for some employees is not uncommon these days. Those employees come from every level in the organization, from executives to call center employees, and everybody in between. So what is it like for these employees? I have spoken to more than just a few; here is what some of them have to say:

> "It takes me longer to get through my e-mail because I have to weed out all the spam first."

> "I can't stand the porn — even the subject lines are lewd and offensive!"

> "My spam filter at home frequently throws away messages from friends. I can't afford to have a spam program at work toss out important messages from customers or suppliers."

> "Yyyyyyuck!!"

These comments point to some of the key problems that result from employees dealing with spam, which include the following:

- ✓ **Extra time spent sifting through all e-mail in order to identify and delete spam messages.** This becomes increasingly difficult as spam messages look more and more like ordinary messages.

- ✓ **E-mail quota problems due to spam filling up users' mailboxes.** This is especially troublesome for those who travel, unless they are able to log in almost every day and delete all the spam from their inboxes.

- ✓ **Loss of important business e-mail messages that were accidentally overlooked and deleted.** Legitimate messages often get caught in the crossfire whether or not a spam-blocking solution is in place.

- ✓ **Phishing scam messages that look like they originated within the company or from a legitimate outside source.** Sometimes, these scams result in virus infections, security breaches, fraud, and other issues.

- ✓ **Employees who are enticed to visit Web sites waste more time and increase the risk of security issues caused by the hostile code on Web sites.**

- ✓ **Increased computer support costs.** Employees who are plagued by spam and related maladies are certain to be calling the IT helpdesk more frequently than employees who receive little or no spam. You are fortunate if your helpdesk tracking data is granular enough to capture this information.

Unless you are in the upper echelon of IT organizations that measure and categorize every electron, the spam problem is more likely one that you feel in your gut. You know it's a problem, perhaps a big problem. If you're wondering how to quantify and justify a way out of your predicament, you'll find the answers in Chapter 4.

How spam got its name

Funny names are ascribed to otherwise-mundane components in the technology world. An e-mail popup in X-Windows (a windowing system like Microsoft Windows that was invented ten years earlier) was called "biff," which was the name of the programmer's dog. Those little session- or person-identifiers that your browser stores on your computer are called "cookies."

And, of course, junk e-mail is called spam. But why "spam"?

The term "spam" was first coined in the 1980s to refer to various means of sending lots of useless information to a computer in order to overload it or be annoying to its users (or both). The Monty Python "Spam" skit was new and popular among computer science students and early (now aging) computer professionals. Reportedly, those in the Multi-User Dungeon (MUD) community originally coined the term and brought it to USENET and eventually e-mail. Legend has it that someone programmed a macro to simply post the word "spam" every few seconds (like part of the lyrics from that Monty Python skit where they simply repeat the word "spam")...

```
SPAM SPAM SPAM SPAM SPAM SPAM
   SPAM SPAM SPAM SPAM SPAM
   SPAM SPAM
```

...until someone finally kicked him off.

Exposing the business to malicious code

Through the year 2003, almost no spam carried malicious payloads such as viruses, worms, and Trojan horses. Spam was just spam. This changed in 2004 (how could you *not* have noticed?) with the apparent — uh, *obvious* — growing alliance between virus writers and spammers. Theirs is a symbiotic relationship: Spammers give virus writers the means to distribute their wares, and now spammers can do more than just send junk mail — they can control their victims' computers. I discuss this topic at length in Chapter 3.

Organizations with a sound antivirus infrastructure can take some consolation in the fact that their antivirus software will strip the malicious code from most inbound spam messages. Mail servers that are configured to strip executable attachments from incoming e-mail messages are contributing to the defense.

Worse yet, antivirus programs have been "looking the other way" when it comes to spyware. Spyware isn't stopped by most firewalls, mail servers, or antivirus programs, and often the flaws (in configuration, as well as vulnerabilities in design) let the spyware just waltz right in to end-user workstations to listen, snoop, and sometimes send data back to the hacker's home base. Spyware also raises support cost because much of it makes browsers unstable, and some spyware makes changes to Web browser configurations that users notice — like changing the default home and search pages.

But is it safe to assume that 100 percent of end-user workstations are adequately protected? You can fool yourself, but you can't fool me. Sobering lessons from the past should certainly convince IT professionals that a few viruses — and a *lot* of spyware — are getting through the defenses.

Face it: Spam is clogging the pipes and it has *attitude,* and spyware is just a little too nosey for most people to tolerate. An antivirus solution only handles one small aspect of the spam and spyware plague: It strips malicious code (*most* of the time), but does nothing about the growing volume of inbound e-mail, and it often lets spyware right through.

Creating legal liabilities

Aside from being among the unfortunate ones whose inboxes are hammered by spam every day, most legal departments have not yet addressed issues of corporate liability in connection with spam or spyware. That, however, is changing.

Subjecting employees to offensive language and images

An appreciable amount of spam is pornographic in nature, and this naturally means that employees who receive spam are going to get messages that contain content that is offensive to many people. And this is not just in the content of messages: Spammers are becoming more brazen and are including suggestive and offensive messages right in the subject lines. This is an irritant to many, but it's insulting and distressing to others.

Some spammers have been sending messages containing *only* graphic images as one method to dodge spam filters. For spammers in the business of distributing promotional messages for porn sites, this usually means that these images contain pornographic pictures. Depending upon how an organization's choice of e-mail clients, their default configuration, as well as how employees use them, this can mean that employees who get flooded with spam will be subjected to pornography and other offensive images.

In many instances, porn spam is sending some employees "over the top," resulting in grievances and even threats of lawsuits. Organizations that are doing little or nothing to stop spam probably do not have much of a defense, I am sorry to say. Employees who are distraught because of the offensive nature of spam have a strong case for relief. They also have my sympathy — I don't like the stuff either.

Leaking corporate information via spyware

Spyware collects information as relatively harmless as a user's surfing habits, and as harmful as key logging (spyware that records your keystrokes and sends the record to someone else). A corporate user's workstation with a working key logger can create liability if it captures a user accessing sensitive information, *and* the key logger's owner subsequently compromises that data.

Downstream liability if spam originates from company computers

Figuratively and literally speaking, spam messages have no return address, so it is difficult to pin the blame on those who originate the messages. However, if a company's own e-mail server or one of its end-user workstations was being used as an e-mail relay (a system that spammers use to "originate" their hordes of messages), other individuals or companies being subjected to this spam could build a legitimate grievance against the company whose computer is being used to relay spam.

A spammer can use a company's e-mail server as a relay if the e-mail server is still using old e-mail server software. In the old days, relaying e-mail through an e-mail server was a common practice for moving legitimate mail, but now only spammers utilize this now-antiquated function in order to cover their tracks.

An organization ought to know how to prevent its computers from becoming spam relays. Any organization that fails to fulfill its due diligence in this regard can be found negligent and be subject to civil lawsuits. Organizations that forward spam (or propagate other security threats) cannot completely escape culpability.

No Silver Bullets: Looking for Ways to Fight Back

Malware (which includes spam and spyware, but also viruses, Trojan horses, and really anything that you don't want running on your computer and would prevent if you could) is a complex problem that comprises threats and issues on many levels, and no single remedy can eliminate it. Your best defense against spam and spyware is *defense in depth,* which is much like the multiple layers of defense of a medieval castle.

A castle may have a moat (a body of water surrounding the castle), with a hungry moat monster swimming around. The castle also has a drawbridge, heavy gates, high walls, and places where archers can shoot arrows at attackers and others can pour boiling liquids on would-be attackers who make it across the moat. This castle has many layers of defense. Should any one or more of these layers fail, other layers continue to provide protection.

Similarly, you can best stop (it would be more accurate to say "slow down") the harmful and annoying effects of spam by using a variety of remedies, which I introduce in the following sections. Chapter 13 is dedicated to this topic and offers even more details.

By themselves, some of the remedies I discuss will, to some degree, hinder the effectiveness or penetration rate of malware. Together, they represent a multilayered defense that provides a good level of resistance against spam and spyware.

Adding a spam blocker

A key component of your defense is a spam blocker, more often called a spam filter, which you purchase from an outside vendor. These solutions all use the same basic features to identify and weed out spam:

- ✔ **Vendor-supplied filtering rules and signatures:** Computer code and a list of known spam patterns (like fingerprints) that the spam-filtering software uses to identify messages as spam.

- ✔ **Enterprise filtering policies:** Centrally managed configurations that reflect the company's needs.

- ✔ **User preferences:** User-definable settings that tell the spam filters about spam that individuals find especially irritating, as well as options on how the product behaves on users' workstations.

✔ **User blacklists and whitelists:** Lists of known bad addresses (that go in the blacklist), and addresses from outsiders whose incoming messages should never be tagged as spam (whitelists).

✔ **Quarantines:** The holding places where spam messages are stored until individual users can look to see if any good messages were accidentally blocked by the spam filter.

Figure 1-1 shows how a typical anti-spam application works. Exactly *how* each application performs these functions varies considerably from vendor to vendor. The following steps explain what's going on in Figure 1-1 in more detail:

1. **Inbound e-mail arrives at the anti-spam application.**

2. **The anti-spam application examines the message and compares its contents with enterprise filtering policies, vendor-supplied filtering rules, end-user preferences, blacklists, and whitelists.**

3. **The application uses the comparison to decide what to do with the message:**

   - **If the message is permitted to pass,** the application forwards the message to the enterprise mail server, which will in turn route it to the recipient's mailbox.

   - **If the message is not permitted to pass,** the anti-spam application will check to see if the recipient has a quarantine. If the recipient does have a quarantine, the anti-spam application will put the message there. If the recipient does not have a quarantine, the anti-spam application will delete the message.

4. **When the end-user logs in and runs her e-mail program, she will look at messages in her inbox.**

   If there are any messages there that *should be* classified as spam, the spam application usually provides a way for the user to specify that fact so that similar messages will be rejected in the future.

   I discuss wrongly identified messages (false positives and false negatives) and how to handle them in Chapter 11.

5. **If the end-user has a quarantine, she will also have to examine it from time to time to make sure that there are not any messages there that should not have been blocked.**

   If there are any desired messages (false positives) in the quarantine, the user tells the anti-spam application that any messages from the sender should be accepted; that e-mail address will be placed in the user's white-list. Usually the anti-spam application will also forward the message to the user's normal mailbox so that she may open, read, reply, and store it using her e-mail program.

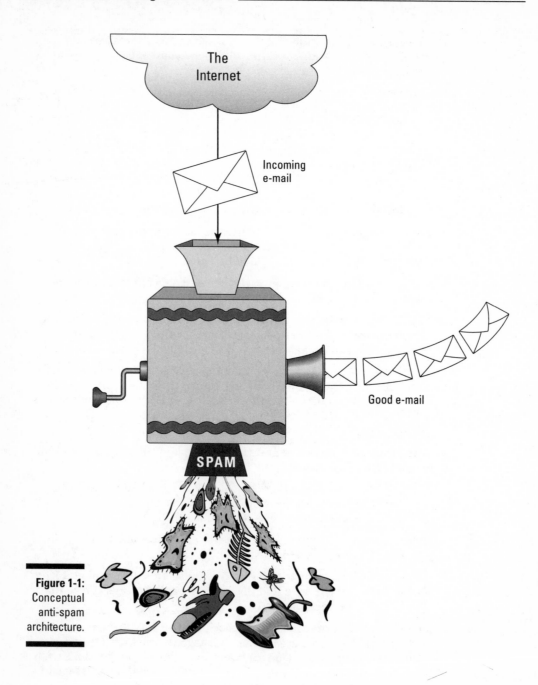

The
Internet

Incoming
e-mail

Good e-mail

SPAM

Figure 1-1:
Conceptual
anti-spam
architecture.

Resisting the urge to counter attack

Some suggest that everyone should take up arms and form nineteenth-century style vigilante squads, or perhaps hire bounty hunters, to hunt down spammers. I'm sorry to tell you, Sheriff, but until you figure out *who* the spammers are and *where* the spammers are, you should leave your torches and axes in the back shed.

Some suggest that retaliation or counter-attack wouldn't be such a good idea anyway. The hacker and spammer crime families have recently intermarried, and so I think that any retaliation against spammers (supposing that you would be able to identify them) would be met by fierce retribution. After that, a lot of spam wouldn't seem nearly so bad.

Most anti-spam applications have several other characteristics in common:

- Anti-spam applications generally keep pretty good statistics as a way of tracking how many messages are being blocked, as well as other details.

- Many anti-spam applications permit the administrator to specify which users will have a quarantine and which will not. Inbound messages identified as spam can be "tagged" (usually by adding the word [SPAM] to the subject line, or they can just be deleted.

- Users can edit their whitelists, blacklists, and other preferences as often as they wish.

- Anti-spam applications will have not only simple filters containing key words, but also one or more complex algorithms that are used to differentiate spam messages from non-spam messages.

When you understand these principles and characteristics, you'll be in a position to talk with vendors (as well as people in other companies who are using anti-spam solutions), ask the right questions, and understand the answers. Then you can begin thinking about how you might block spam in *your* organization.

Because an anti-spam solution is essential to keeping as much spam as possible out of employees' inboxes, I spend a lot of time explaining them in more detail throughout this book. I explain what you need to know about your business in order to choose an anti-spam solution in the section, "Taking Stock of Your Business," later in this chapter. In the "Choosing Anti-Spam and Anti-Spyware Solutions" section, later in this chapter, and also in Chapter 5, I offer more details about the different models and features.

Keeping spyware away from workstations

There has been serious debate about the links between spyware and spam. Nonetheless, most Internet users dislike the very idea that companies are tracking their movements. At this level, spyware is an affront to privacy, and people feel better when they know that spyware is being blocked or, at least, periodically scanned for and removed.

But spyware doesn't just stop there. Some forms of spyware attempt to do more than just track users' movements: They also change Web browser settings by changing the home page, the search page, inserting bookmarks, and other intrusive pranks. Some of this spyware digs in deep: Last year I was searching for something, went to a Web site, and my PC was injected by Xupiter spyware — and it was a real pain to remove.

The most insidious spyware is the *key logger:* Software that records keystrokes and mouse clicks in the hopes that a user will type in user IDs and passwords to financial services Web sites, so that the key logger's owner can later use the captured user ID and password to vacuum out the poor user's account.

Good anti-spyware tools are available: Some for a fee, some for free. But by the time you read this, spyware blocking will be a part of most antivirus companies' portfolio of products, perhaps even built right in to antivirus software.

If you are concerned about spyware, you're already in the right place. The book that you are holding is devoted to spam *and* spyware — what they're about and how to get rid of them.

Walking through protocol holes

Spam represents one of the more recent methods used to smuggle worms and viruses into organizations. Gone are the days when a hacker could scan selected organizations (or randomly chosen ones) to look for open and vulnerable protocols that could be exploited for fun and profit. As organizations began to implement firewalls and close off all unnecessary ports, hackers had to find other ways to get inside.

Anymore, those methods include sending malicious code to millions of office workers via spam. The other popular method is to attack a Web-based application using buffer overflow or SQL injection attacks, for instance.

These attacks have been successful because they travel through ports that are left open to facilitate needed services such as e-mail and Web. They are also successful because some firewalls are not designed to perform "deep inspection" — that is, to examine the *contents* of a network packet to determine whether it contains malicious or potentially damaging code.

The methods of attack are growing more complex and difficult to stop. Despite advances in firewalls, antivirus, anti-spam, anti-spyware, anti-this, and anti-that, attackers will continue to be cunning and creative, keeping everyone ever vigilant and watchful.

Do Not Spam list

CAN-SPAM legislation in the U.S. requires that the FTC (Federal Trade Commission, the government bureau that oversees and regulates commerce) study the feasibility of creating a national Do Not Spam list that would be similar to the Do Not Call list that telemarketers are required to conform with. However, the FTC has thus far recommended against the creation of a Do Not Spam list. Unlike telemarketers, who are relatively easy to find, spammers send their spam through thousands of open relays (e-mail servers with older versions of software that permits mail to be relayed through them in order to hide spammers' tracks) and *zombified* computers (a technical term meaning home users' computers that are possessed by hacker-spammers' Trojan horse programs, permitting spam relaying). Further, spammers frequently operate — or relay their messages through — overseas connections, which is one means to distance themselves from the long arm of the law.

Thus, it is thought that a Do Not Spam list would actually become a Do Spam list, because spammers are accustomed to operating outside of the law.

Other good defense-in-depth practices

In addition to blocking spam and spyware, you need to employ the following remedies to keep your company secure (I discuss each of these in turn in Chapter 13):

- ✔ Attachment filtering at the e-mail server to remove potentially harmful executable files
- ✔ Antivirus software at the mail server *and* at users' workstations in order to stop known harmful malware
- ✔ Popup blockers on users' workstations that block this irritating and sometimes-harmful pest
- ✔ Firewalls — on laptops as well as at the enterprise perimeter — to block the entry of self-propagating worms

Understanding the role of legislation

Those of you who have been tracking the volume of spam in relation to United States regulation of CAN-SPAM (Controlling the Assault of Non-Solicited Pornography and Marketing Act of 2003) can attest to the effectiveness of legislation thus far: Nil. Nada. Zilch. By now, anyone who was hoping that legislation would have any effect on spam has realized that spammers have taken no notice of the change in the law, primarily because most of them have already developed methods that make it difficult to trace any spam to them. One need only look to drug trafficking or Prohibition-era liquor smuggling to realize that those who make their livings working on the wrong side of the law are not easily deterred or discouraged by additional legislation.

In response to citizen outrage against spyware, some U.S. state legislatures have introduced and passed anti-spyware legislation. But don't think this will make spyware go away anytime soon, either. Some spyware writers sneak in their wares with what appears to be legitimate software, and *tell* you on page 50 of the end-user license agreement — in microscopic type — that they will be spying on you. In these types of circumstances, it may be difficult to make a law that hinders their spying ways.

As I write this chapter, several known spammers have been apprehended and charged with spamming under state or federal laws. Many others have been arrested and charged with crimes, or sued by ISPs in civil court. But it's too soon to tell whether there will be enough successful prosecutions to make a dent in spam.

Taking Stock of Your Business

I'm not sure of your mindset, but I figure (shhh, I'm concentrating) it is one of these: You *know* that malware is an issue in your organization, or you *suspect* that spam or spyware may be an issue, but you aren't sure how to find out for certain — or how to find out how big an issue it may be.

I don't know very much about your organization, so I'm going to throw out a bunch of general ideas. Your job is to take those that make sense in your situation and refine them as much as you think you need to.

Before you get started, remember that you can make measuring spam as scientific as you like, but the effects of spam, such as degraded network performance or lost productivity, are about as fuzzy as you can get. Measuring the impact of spyware is a bit more difficult in that it's trying to stay well hidden, and the costs can be harder to assign because they may include public relations risks (from spyware exposing customer information) or the loss of confidential information (such as where certain researchers in your organization are browsing on a regular basis). Assigning dollars to these losses is about as much fun as taping jelly to your window. But still, you gotta start somewhere — how about here?

Talk with people

For some of you, this is painfully obvious, but I include this here anyway because of its vital importance. You cannot (and should not) assess spam or spyware's influence solely by crunching numbers your computer. There's no substitute for getting out and talking with people. Here is a list of different people you need to talk to, in no particular order:

- ✔ **PC helpdesk:** The helpdesk folks can tell you whether they get many calls about spyware or spam. Most users in an organization have the sense to call the PC helpdesk if malware is making them crazy, even if all they can do is complain. If the helpdesk tracks these calls, this would be good information to have. The more detail you can get here, the better (to a point).

- ✔ **Malware victims:** You can likely get the names of these people from the helpdesk. How long have they had the problem? How many spam messages per day do they get? Rough orders of magnitude are fine here — do they get 10, 100, or 1,000 spam messages per day? Is spyware installing when they visit Web sites or click on installers that they believe are benign?

- ✔ **Other people you work with:** I'd venture a guess that if you know ten people in the organization, one of them gets more than just a few spam messages every day. In the current IT environment, I'm certain that you know someone with spyware that he or she can't seem to get rid of.

If you're like most IT people, you don't have a lot of time to do this, and even less to spend an appreciable amount of time trying to cook up estimates on the number of spam messages that your entire organization receives on an average day. To get a broader perspective on how spam is affecting users, a survey can be a more time-efficient approach, as I explain in the next section.

Conduct a survey

A useful way to get information in a consistent format from larger numbers of users is to survey them. You can develop an online survey, or use e-mail, or even paper. But to attain statistically significant results, you need to survey more than a handful of users. Regardless of your survey medium, the following list provides some questions that you can start with. Add more of your own if you want to. Remember to ask for each respondent's name, department, extension, and e-mail address so that you can follow up if you need to.

- ✔ About how many e-mail messages do you send to Internet users per day?

- ✔ About how many e-mail messages do you receive from the Internet per day?

- ✔ How long have you worked in this organization? And (if appropriate), How long have you had e-mail in this organization?

- ✔ Have you received any spam messages in the past month? (If the answer is no, users can stop here.)

- ✔ About how many spam messages do you receive per day?

- ✔ Does your e-mail address appear on the company Web site?

- ✔ Does your e-mail address appear on other Web sites, or in newsgroups, online communities, or other locations?

You could ask more questions and get more detail, but I think you would overburden yourself making sense of the survey results. Two thoughts: First, you can always follow up with a more detailed survey for users who get a lot of spam, and second, I think you should talk with a number of the victims in person in order to better understand the spam problem as they perceive it.

If you can survey and talk to enough people, you should be able to extrapolate (guess) how many people in your entire organization get spam, and how much. Rough estimates are all that you need. Don't go overboard by asking everyone to count, unless you want to be run out of town.

Understanding your architecture

The size and makeup of your technical infrastructure will influence your approach when you begin looking at various types of spam-blocking solutions. You need to resist looking at specific solutions until you have a good understanding of your organization's architecture: size, geography, network design, and how e-mail is moved around.

Before you can begin thinking about any specific spam-blocking solutions, you must have a thorough understanding of how your present e-mail system — and by "system" I mean *everything*: Servers, clients, and every component in the enterprise that stores, processes, or transmits e-mail, from the Internet router to users' workstations, and everything in between.

Several factors contribute to the size and type of anti-spam solution that you should consider. These factors include

- **Number of e-mail users:** It is convenient to speak about the size of an organization's workforce in terms of orders of magnitude: Are there 10, 100, 1,000, 10,000, or 100,000 users in the enterprise? Solutions ideal for organizations with 10 or even 100 workers are probably infeasible for organizations with 10,000 or more people.

- **Network architecture:** This isn't so much about hubs, switches, or VLANs. Instead, focus on a few basic items such as how many Internet connections your organization has. If your company has more than one Internet connection, does e-mail enter by more than one Internet connection?

- **Geographic makeup:** Are your users and e-mail servers are located in the same building, or are they scattered all over the country or the world? Some anti-spam solutions fit best when they are very near (both physically and logically) to the e-mail servers. Other spam solutions are installed in the e-mail servers themselves, so you'd better figure out where they are.

- **E-mail architecture:** There are so many different ways that organizations can — and have — put together their e-mail environment. One organization might have one or more Microsoft Exchange servers (large organizations can have dozens), another may use Lotus Notes, another may have open-source POP servers, and another may have its e-mail hosted by an ISP. It is also important to know — in detail — how e-mail gets into the organization in the first place. Perhaps it first hits a UNIX-based SMTP server and gets routed to the appropriate internal server, or maybe inbound SMTP sessions are terminated directly on one or more internal Exchange or Lotus Notes servers. If your organization is lacking detailed diagrams of its e-mail architecture, it's time to sharpen your pencils and get drawing.

Taking users' skills and attitudes into account

As I often say, if you need new technology in an organization to be successful, you must have not only a deep understanding of the underlying and surrounding technology, but also a keen insight into the people who will use it. Here some human factors to consider:

- **How much training will users need, and how much training can you provide?** Some anti-spam solutions incorporate changes in users' e-mail interface. In all but the smallest organizations, this means that users will need some level of training in order to understand the new controls and how they work. This can be a challenge in large, distributed organization where many users may be located in remote offices, retail locations, or even overseas. You need to find out what types of training have been successful in the past, and see if you can use those methods here. Chapter 7 covers training in detail.

- **What is the attitude toward technology?** Do the organization's e-mail users embrace new technology, or do they whine about it? This is important because any new technology project will be successful only to the extent that it is accepted and used. If the people in your organization are stubborn and resist new technology, the project may be in danger of failing. The better you know your users, the more familiar you will be with their attitudes. If you don't know many of your users (those inside IT don't count, if that's where you work), now is a good time to get out there and meet people.

- **Will you have executive support?** Closely coupled with what I call "technology attitude" is the extent to which the organization's senior management openly embraces new technology. If senior management rejects a new anti-spam tool, so too may many — or most — of the employees in the rest of the organization. You (or your manager) need to find out what executives are thinking about spam — whether they perceive it as a problem or not. In Chapter 4, I cover how to financially justify your filtering project by calculating the return on investment (ROI) for the project, which may help garner executive support.

If you are purely technocentric and don't like to deal with the human side of technology projects, then you need to find a manager, project manager, business analyst, or someone with similar project-management skills in your organization to deal with the human side of things so that your anti-spam project can be successful. Or you may need to get in touch with the right side of your brain — you never know who you might meet.

Evaluating available skills in IT

Few, if any, anti-spam solutions are truly easy to install and maintain, but instead require some level of expertise so that someone in your organization can keep the fires burning, so to speak. An effective, although complex, anti-spam solution is no bargain if no persons are available to train on it. Here are some pointers:

- ✔ **E-mail administrator:** How skilled is your e-mail admin — did this person design and build the infrastructure, or does he just manage user accounts and groups? A deep knowledge of e-mail message processing is needed, because the anti-spam solution will likely change it in some major way.

- ✔ **Network engineer:** Did the current staff build the organization's network, or have they made any significant changes to it? A spam-blocking solution may require expertise in DNS, firewalls, and DMZ architecture.

- ✔ **Helpdesk/PC support staff:** Good people and training skills are needed here, because many people will get frustrated or won't understand what is going on. Remember, success is in the eyes of the beholder: Regardless of the technical beauty of the solution, if the users don't understand how to use it, your project may be labeled a failure.

Other positions and functions in IT may also be affected, but probably less so. But you need to keep this concept in mind: Training will be needed not only for users, but also for many in IT who play a part in designing, implementing, maintaining, and supporting a spam filter.

Working within your budget

Money, of course, is always a factor in what you can do. When you start looking at anti-spam solutions, knowing your price limits can help you find the right one. I suggest you contact a few vendors (you can find a list of several in Chapter 14) and get some rough pricing for your organization. Then you will have a vague idea of product cost; next, you need to take a stab at how much, if any, professional services or consulting you will need for design, implementation, rollout, and training. If you aren't experienced at this type of resource planning, find someone who is and ask him or her to help you.

Size is everything when estimating costs. In a smallish organization (say, less than 200 users, all in one location), it will be possible to make rough estimates of consultant and contractor hours you need to complete the project. But larger organizations (hundreds or thousands of users, possibly in many locations), implementation and training will take considerably more planning before you will have even an order-of-magnitude estimate of total project cost. Again, someone with experience in such project planning and budgeting is needed to sketch out a rough total project cost.

Justifying Spam and Spyware Control

By the time you get to justifying spam control, you are pretty sure that your organization will be better off with a spam-blocking solution than without one, despite the potentially high cost (both time and money) required to put a spam-blocking solution in place. It will take a little more sleuthing to justify blocking spyware, because for most users, it is an invisible problem that you'll need to ferret out.

Justifying investment in security projects is often tricky and slippery business. Calculating a return on investment (ROI) for a solution that *prevents* an event's occurrence is especially tricky to calculate. Partially, this is because it may be difficult to estimate the impact and true cost of an occurrence — in this case, a spam message that a user receives and now must do something about.

Spam affects an organization in several ways, including

- **Productivity:** Spam wastes peoples' time — maybe a little, maybe a lot. Users have to sift through messages and delete them (and sometimes they read them, and maybe even visit the spammers' Web sites, oh my!).

- **Support costs.** Many users call the helpdesk to complain about spam and to ask that it be stopped.

- **Liability:** All the lewd material filling up employees' mailboxes may create a situation where employees feel badgered and abused, particularly if the organization is doing nothing about it. A different angle on liability may result when employees find themselves victims of phishing scams that were delivered to their inboxes.

- **Overhead:** The additional volume of spam is filling up networks, servers, and mailboxes. Much of the continued investment in the capacity to process e-mail is used to process spam, like it or not.

- **Malware:** An increasing percentage of spam contains malicious code (viruses, worms, Trojan horses), some of which might just sneak by other defenses and disrupt the business.

In some organizations, you (or someone else) will need to turn one or more of the problems in the preceding list into dollars and cents that can be measured before and after the spam filter is in place. In other organizations, a qualitative justification may be more compelling.

Spyware's effect on an organization is usually less complex than spam: It gunks up workstations and causes more helpdesk calls, usually about unstable browsers or mysterious home page and search page configuration changes. I haven't yet met a user who called the helpdesk to complain about the key logger that was installed by a Trojan horse. How is a user going to notice *that?*

If you're not sure which approach is right for your organization, you need to start talking with your managers or others to better understand what kinds of approaches for justifying projects (especially security projects) have worked best in the past. In Chapter 4, you can find more about calculating ROI and quantitative and qualitative justifications.

Choosing Anti-Spam and Anti-Spyware Solutions

After you understand how anti-spam and anti-spyware solutions work and spend time getting to know your business and its needs, you're ready to start shopping around.

If you like choices, then an enterprise anti-malware project is going to hold your interest, because several types of solutions are available for enterprises. Anti-spam solutions come in four basic setups: software, appliance, ASP, and client-only. Each setup handles the key features of an anti-spam solution a little differently. Anti-spyware is widely available for workstations, but by the time you read this, I would not be surprised if one or more anti-virus appliances or gateways also blocked spyware.

If you spend time understanding your business, you'll save time in the long run. This understanding helps you quickly rule out options that won't work. Compare the list of needs that are important to your business with the key features of a spam solution. Here, I help you understand what those features are and how the different models compare.

Types of anti-spam solutions

As I mention earlier, anti-spam solutions come in four varieties:

- **Software model:** Several software-based anti-spam solutions are available that you load on a dedicated server or right on your e-mail server.

- **Appliance model:** In anti-spam solutions, the appliance acts as sort of an e-mail firewall, in that it logically is placed between the Internet and enterprise mail server(s). The anti-spam appliance examines every incoming mail message and, using a list of filtering rules, makes a pass or block decision for each message. I'll grant you that software and ASP solutions *also* are e-mail firewalls — it's just that an appliance solution also *looks* like one.

- **ASP model:** ASP stands for Application Service Provider, meaning the application resides on a computer located elsewhere, and what you're buying is essentially a *data service,* in this case e-mail filtering. Anti-spam companies offering the ASP model perform all the spam filtering on their physical (or logical) premises, and deliver only the clean e-mail to you.

- **Client-only model:** Anti-spam software that is wholly contained on the end-user workstation is definitely worth considering if you have a small number of users (exactly how small is up to you). That's because you could install it on workstations one at a time as users complain about spam, and you can control how that spam is filtered based on individual needs. However, this solution has its downside, too. Most client-side solutions offer no centralized management or reporting capability, and these solutions don't keep the spam off your mail servers, because they don't filter messages until they reach the desktop.

If you're in a medium or large organization and are fortunate enough have only a few users with spam problems (tell me your secret!), client-only might also be for you. Just remember that it won't scale (if you change your mind and decide that all 5,000 users should have it — trust me when I tell you that you'll likely regret installing client-only spam filters on that many workstations), but that may be okay for you for now.

Chapter 6 explains the different types of solutions in more detail.

What are the key features?

All anti-spam solutions offer some of the same basic features (they block spam, of course, but you knew that). Here are some questions to ask about those features when you look at any anti-spam solution:

- ✔ **Administration of underlying operating system:** Relevant only for a software-based solution. Whether UNIX or Windows, someone will have to spend some time maintaining the operating system: installing patches, making configuration changes from time to time, and monitoring resource consumption and performance.

- ✔ **Enterprise policy administration:** Centralized spam blockers, whether software, appliance, or ASP, require some amount of company-level administration, including whitelist management, quarantine management, and adjustments to the degree of filtering, should too many or too few messages be tagged as spam.

- ✔ **Need for performance upgrades:** As the organization and/or the volume of e-mail grows, someone needs to watch resource utilization over time so that any upgrades to server hardware and network capacity is anticipated and dealt with proactively.

- ✔ **Signature and algorithm updates:** In order to stay effective, a spam filter must have the latest *signatures* (characteristics of known spam messages) and rules (ways to calculate whether a message is spam or not). Spam filters accomplish this by periodically downloading updates from the spam filter's vendor. Someone needs to watch this diligently to ensure that this always works properly.

- ✔ **How much server space does this solution require:** If you need to purchase additional hardware to run your spam-blocking solution, do you have the room (floor and/or rack space, power, cooling, and so on) required to accommodate it?

- ✔ **Directory harvesting attacks:** Spammers and hackers use some techniques to coax e-mail addresses out of an e-mail server — or at least they try.

- ✔ **Your level of control:** Only you can determine how much control you will have: Do you want the power and flexibility to be able to manage the OS that is "under" a spam filter, are you content with a "black box" appliance, or do you prefer to let an ASP filter your e-mail on its premises?

Choosing the right model

Personally, I love side-by-side comparisons and offer one for you in Table 1-1. For each of the features I cover in the preceding section, you can see how each model measures up. For more details on choosing an anti-spam solution, see Chapter 6.

Table 1-1	Side-by-Side Comparison of Anti-Spam Solutions			
Feature	*Software*	*Appliance*	*ASP*	*Client-Only*
Administration of underlying operating system:	Up to you.	Little or none.	None. This is why you out-sourced it.	Not fun, because you have dozens, hundreds, or even thousands.
Enterprise policy administration:	Centralized.	Centralized.	Centralized.	Practically impossible.
Need for performance upgrades:	Up to you.	Work with your vendor.	Hopefully, the ASP takes care of this so that it always runs fast.	Variable.
Signature and algorithm updates:	You have to make sure they work.	You should make sure they work.	Little, if any-thing, to worry about.	Difficult and out of your control.
Space in your data closet:	Depends on whether it runs on your e-mail server or a stand-alone server.	Very little.	None.	None.
Prevention of directory-harvesting attacks:	You may still be subject to this.	With the right architecture, this problem goes away.	Nothing to worry about.	Still a potential problem.
Your level of control:	You have abso-lute control. You can turn it off or remove it any time you wish.	You have a lot of control. You can turn it off, but you prob-ably cannot tinker with its its insides.	You have very little control. By-passing the ASP may take hours or or days.	Ha! Little or none.

Sizing for now and the future

In all matters of technology, you're wise to plan with not only today in mind, but also next year and the year after that. In this regard, you need to consider the following when pondering your potential anti-spam or anti-spyware solutions:

- ✔ Plan for not only the headcount growth of your organization, but also of e-mail volume in general. The volume of e-mail to and from the Internet is roughly proportional to the number of users, but the volume of e-mail *inside* the organization is more exponential. Are there any plans for expanding the role of e-mail to support business processes?

- ✔ Anti-spam applications will have to work harder to filter spam. Forklift upgrades (physically moving applications to a larger server, which you may need to bring in with a forklift, hence the name) are disruptive, so plan with extra capacity (for higher volumes of spam, as well as more complex and computation-intensive filtering algorithms) in mind, particularly if you are considering a software solution that will exist on your hardware. Think *easily upgradeable without having to replace the server.*

- ✔ Spam will likely get worse before it gets better (if it *ever* gets better). The techniques that spammers use will grow ever more sophisticated. They have a lot at stake and will continue to be creative and devious in order to reach as wide an audience as possible. The general rule is that whatever capacity you think you'll need in three years, double or triple it and buy enough hardware today to handle that future workload.

- ✔ The anti-spyware market is still an emerging market. You can expect the solution you buy in 2005, as I write this book, to be out of date in a year or two as certain solutions gain dominance and larger companies buy up smaller solutions and generally improve and consolidate the available options.

You have many other factors to consider when making a choice: If you're at or near that point, skip over to Chapters 5 and 6 for the low-down on choosing a solution.

Making the Solution Work

Stepping back a little bit, you can have a look at the factors that will determine both short-term and long-term success. In this section, I discuss the importance of planning, planning, and more planning. And, because blocking spam is a disruptive undertaking, you should seriously consider a trial prior to pushing the solution out to the entire organization. (Although spyware blockers aren't as disruptive — you don't put them in between incoming e-mail and the end-user, like a spam filter — I suggest a trial for spyware blockers, too, in case you run into unknown interactions with some of the other software your business runs.) This section discusses other vital issues that you should be familiar with if success is important to you.

Creating a good plan

An IT project with little or no planning has little chance for success. Filtering spam is a disruptive and invasive change to make in an organization: A new and slightly unpredictable component is being placed right in the critical path of e-mail. Users' e-mail experience will grow more complicated, especially if they have quarantines. Managing a spam blocker requires constant attention to ensure that updates are flowing regularly and that users are continuing to update whitelists and marking false negatives (spam messages not marked as such) to train the spam filter.

On top of this, many different IT (and non-IT) people are needed to pull off such a project: system, network, firewall and e-mail administrators, the helpdesk staff, a project manager, and someone from the legal and human resources departments. You (or someone else) will need to figure out who needs to do what, how long each task will take, and the dependencies there are among tasks.

And that's the easy part. You'll have to make sure that all of these people will actually be *available* when you need them.

I go deep into planning in Chapters 5 and 8, and you'll find a sample project plan in Appendix A. If you need to get up to speed on project management, I recommend you get a copy of *Project Management For Dummies* by Stanley E. Portny and *Software Project Management Kit For Dummies* by Greg Mandanis (both published by Wiley).

Setting up a trial

In IT-speak, a *trial* is test run of new software, limited in some way (such as to a small number of users). Even though anti-spyware is practically invisible to end-users, an anti-spyware trial will help to shake out any installation or operational glitches that will be more difficult to solve after the solution is installed on everyone's workstations.

Something as intrusive as a spam filter needs to be carefully tested first, ideally with a small number of users. The principle reasons for this are

- ✔ **To verify that incoming e-mail still works.** Because a spam filter is directly on the critical path for inbound e-mail, you've got to know whether everything can be set up correctly so that e-mail from the Internet still reaches users' mailboxes.

- ✔ **To verify the appropriateness of the spam filter's settings.** You want to filter out all the spam, and only the spam, and allow all other messages through unscathed. Spam filters are less than 100 percent accurate, so it's important to test the spam filter in your environment to make sure it's filtering appropriately.

- ✔ **To verify capacity.** In a trial, you're only dealing with a fraction of the entire organization, but it's still important to gauge how much effort the filter takes to block spam. Then you might make some educated guesses as to whether the filter can take on the entire organization's inbound e-mail workload.

- ✔ **To verify operational procedures.** A trial is the time to get all the operational procedures such as updates, backups, restarts, and so on figured out while only a small number of users are affected.

- ✔ **To get install procedures right.** It's important to make sure that any software installs or configuration changes on user workstations are done properly so that installations are quick and trouble-free.

- ✔ **To find out how users learn and use the spam filter.** In order to train all the users in the organization, it's important to see how initial users' experiences go, so that any changes in teaching or training can be made.

Many technology implementations run into trouble because the right users weren't chosen for early testing. I can't stress enough the importance of choosing wisely. I recommend looking for test users who

- ✔ Are inquisitive and persistent. These are the people who will not balk at the first low hurdle, but will try to find their way around it.

- ✔ Are unafraid of change.

- ✔ Take responsibility and ownership of a project.

- ✔ Understand why the project is important.

- ✔ Are unafraid to offer constructive feedback, whether positive or negative. Correspondingly, you must be unafraid to receive constructive criticism.

- ✔ Have ample time to do the testing and communicate results and issues with you.

- ✔ Are articulate and able to explain the issues.

- ✔ Will help you "sell" the solution to co-workers.

- ✔ Have full appreciation for the importance of testing.

- ✔ Respect the need to refrain from "bitching and moaning" about any problems experienced in the test, but instead will be discrete with you because they understand that bad publicity isn't good for the project.

The intention of a trial is to test everything when the stakes are low, and to avoid unpleasant surprises after you've rolled it out to the entire organization. In Chapter 8, you can find more details about how to prepare for and conduct a trial for both spam filters and spyware blockers.

Training users

For something as vital as e-mail, users need to know how to operate their e-mail after you implement an anti-spam solution. You might consider putting your test users through the training first, just to make sure that the training is effective and makes sense.

You need to pull out all the stops and do whatever is needed: Schedule brown-bag sessions well in advance of implementation. Explain what you are doing and why, and what changes users can expect. Listen to their feedback, positive or negative. You need your users' backing if you are to succeed.

And as important (but similar to) training users, you need to keep them informed. Whether you're scheduling outages, changing configuration settings, or doing anything else that affects users, let them know what they need to know.

Similarly, you need to consider what — if any — training is required for users and their new anti-spyware program. If users will be required to periodically perform any tasks, then you need to train users to do those tasks. (Note that only some spyware blockers are fully automated, and there may be some reason for you not to choose one of those.)

I talk a lot more about training in Chapter 7.

Taking your solution live

After you have completed a successful trial and have trained users, you're almost ready to turn your malware filter on for the entire organization.

I say *almost,* because I don't want you using Chapter 1 as a shortcut. There are many details involved and many paths to failure if you aren't prepared. I describe as much detail as you need in Chapter 9.

Maintaining the system

Malware filters require some level of maintenance and observation. As important as malware blocking is, you've got to make sure it's working properly and do your chores. The major tasks include

- **Managing quarantines.** These are the directories that contain e-mail messages that the spam filter tagged as spam. Here you must make sure that there is sufficient disk space. At first, this will be a tuning issue, as you figure out how many days' worth of spam can be stored in the quarantine for the entire organization.

- **Manage whitelists.** A *whitelist* is the list of e-mail addresses that the spam filter will let through, no matter what. This is the company's way of making sure that e-mail from known senders won't accidentally get caught in the spam filter.

- **Manage filter rules.** Depending upon which spam- or spyware-filtering product you're using, it may be necessary to add, tweak, or remove specific rules, particularly if your organization's e-mail correspondence regularly contains keywords (such as "Viagra," if you work for a pharmaceutical company) that your filter would otherwise block. However, as products improve, this will become less and less of an issue.

- **Manage updates.** In order to be effective, the filter must download new filter rules periodically, as often as several times a day. Here, you have to make sure that these updates are working properly. In addition to rules updates, the filter software itself gets periodically updated, so you've got to be sure these updates are working too.

In order to keep your users happy, someone has to pay attention to these issues. I provide significantly more detail on maintenance in Chapter 11.

Chapter 2

The Spyware Who Loved Me: Stopping Spyware in Its Tracks

An old Chinese saying (or is it a curse?) goes, "May you live in interesting times." Certainly the Spyware Wars, as folks may come to know these times, will be interesting and memorable.

Ridding users' computers of spyware is not a trivial task. It's similar to — but a little harder than — battling viruses, mostly because spyware comes in so many different forms, and because many of the spyware-blocking programs available still lack enterprise features such as central management, logging, and configuration.

However, not many of us can just walk away from the spyware fight. If you've been tagged with solving the spyware program in your organization, you're going to earn your stripes — or your spots if your company is a bit odd.

What Is Spyware?

Spyware is software or a software configuration that gathers information about a person or organization without permission or knowledge. Spyware does this often by just peeking, but other times, it spies by changing the configuration of the victim's computer.

I admit that the preceding is a highly general definition (open to as much interpretation and subjectivity as the definition of *spam*). However, spyware takes many forms, and if the definition was any more precise, I might accidentally exclude some new scheme that most people would consider spyware. In the following sections, I elaborate on this definition a bit so that you can see what the most common forms of spyware are all about.

An information collector

Spyware can collect information from a user's computer and periodically transmit it to a specific location — usually a server someplace. The method used to collect information may be a built-in feature of the Web browser, a downloaded ActiveX control, a Web browser plug-in, or a standalone executable program.

The type of information collected by spyware may include the following:

- **Tracking Web sites:** You may have heard the term *adware,* which many consider as a *subset* of spyware. Marketing companies and banner ad providers (many of which are totally legitimate companies) use adware solely to track which Web sites a user visits and whether the user patronizes banner ads. Such information is generally used by marketing companies, which are always trying to separate folks from their money. Some spyware may do more than just track Web site visits, however.

- **Logging keystrokes:** Among the diabolical types of spyware are *key loggers,* vile beasts that actually record every keystroke on a user's computer and transmit them to a hacker's lair. Users who perform online banking and other electronic commerce on computers with key loggers are bound to have their highly sensitive user IDs, passwords, credit cards, and bank account numbers recorded and sent to unsavory individuals.

I discuss *how* spyware collects information in more detail later in this chapter.

An information transgressor

Spyware can alter information on a user's computer, such as the browser's default home page, search page, and the *HOSTS file* (a text file that contains the IP addresses corresponding to specific host names).

Among the types of spyware that change information on your computer is *scumware,* which is a term describing browser plug-ins that alter the appearance of Web sites, often substituting the Web site's banner ads with its own ads. A Web site might include a banner ad that takes viewers to the Web site owner's Amazon.com affiliate pages, for instance, but the scumware inserts *its own* banner ads (and those of its advertisers) in place of those that the Web site intended the viewer to see.

Scumware also creates hyperlinks within the text of Web pages that take users to advertisers' pages. For instance, a user may be viewing a Web site for a local merchant. The scumware inserts hyperlinks on certain keywords on the merchant's page (as viewed by the user whose PC has the scumware installed) that lead the viewer away from the merchant's site, perhaps leading to competing Web sites. Usually an ActiveX control, scumware alters the content of a Web page, and it does so by changing (in real time) how the user's browser displays the page.

Figure 2-1 illustrates how scumware works.

One personal spyware battle that I recall vividly is Xupiter. As I was searching for information one day, I visited some Web sites that appeared to contain something I needed. After visiting those sites, I noticed that my default search page had changed: When I searched for information on the Web, I'd end up at `xupiter.com` whenever I mistyped a domain name. Xupiter was a pain to remove from my computer, too, because it installed new browser helper objects in Internet Explorer, installed DLLs, and changed Registry settings. Unless I cleaned out *all* of Xupiter's gunk from my computer, it would reinstall itself, and I'd have to start all over again. Fortunately, I found a Web site (one of several) that contained precise and accurate instructions on removing Xupiter and many other pests.

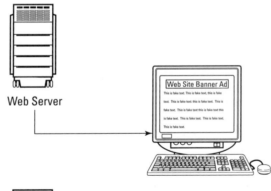

1. Web site pushes Web page to user's browser.

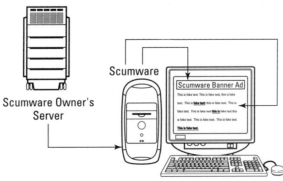

Figure 2-1:
Scumware alters Web content by inserting its own banner ads and hyperlinks from within the browser.

2. Scumware retrieves its banner ad from the Scumware owner's server and creates links in Web page's text.

3. Scumware replaces Web site's banner ad with its own, and creates links in the Web site's text.

4. Result is an altered Web page with different banner ads and new text links.

If you search for instructions for removing spyware, make sure you are following accurate instructions on a trusted Web site. I list some good sites in Chapter 18.

How Spyware Gets In

Spyware infiltrates a user's computer via a number of methods. The most obvious sources are the other scum that are designed to wreak binary havoc: Some viruses, worms, and Trojan horses are designed to install spyware on victim computers either by carrying the spyware directly as a part of its payload or by downloading it after the virus has successfully implanted itself.

Other sources aren't so obvious to the untrained or unsuspecting user. The following sections explain what these common methods are and how they work so that you understand how your network and users are vulnerable.

Finding holes in the Web browser

The spyware taking up residence in a computer may be an ActiveX control, a browser snap-in (intended to extend browser functions), a browser helper object, or a standalone executable that is loaded into the user's computer when he or she visits a Web site that contains the spyware. The spyware may load because of a security setting that is too lax, such as permitting the downloading of unsigned ActiveX controls.

Spyware can also install itself via one of many vulnerabilities that have been discovered in recent years. For instance, it could be an ActiveX control that is specially designed to fool the browser into thinking that the control is coming from a Trusted Sites Zone or Intranet Zone instead of the Internet Zone.

One example of a vulnerability involves a cleverly coded Web page, loaded from a site on the Internet, that is designed to fool a user's computer into thinking that the page is in the My Computer Zone or the Trusted Sites Zone, instead of properly classifying the page as the Internet Zone. If this malicious Web page has embedded scripts, the victim's computer will execute those scripts as though they originated in a Trusted Sites Zone. This can result in a script performing almost any imaginable function on the user's computer.

Antivirus software and security patches are the best defense against vulnerabilities; I discuss patches and other defenses in Chapter 13.

Tagging along in e-mail

E-mail programs that display HTML e-mail (such as Outlook, Outlook Express, and Mozilla Thunderbird) are often subject to the same vulnerabilities that have beset Microsoft Internet Explorer in recent years. Often, just *displaying* a mail message is sufficient for the spyware to get loaded in the user's computer. This is because Outlook is using the same vulnerable DLLs to display HTML as is used by Internet Explorer. I cover more about display vulnerabilities in mail clients in Chapter 12.

Hiding in software downloads

Many downloadable software programs — and programs that you can purchase online or over the counter — contain spyware programs that are silently installed when you install the software. Sometimes (but not always), the software's End User License Agreement (EULA) states that "other programs may be installed." How many people read the fine print? I must admit that I don't always read the EULA before installing software. Maybe you should add "carefully read all license agreements" to your list of New Year's resolutions, no matter what time of year it is now.

Is spyware Microsoft's fault?

In the late 1990s, when Microsoft belatedly discovered (**Note:** I did not say *invented*) the Internet, Microsoft's software products were feature-rich and permitted software programs of many types to communicate with one another by using existing and new standards and protocols. You could say that Microsoft's programs were network extroverts — after installation, they would strike up conversations with other programs and always "keep the door open" in case some other program wanted to talk.

The openness of Microsoft's software products was on a collision course with the gritty culture of the maturing Internet. Microsoft was unprepared for the tidal wave of exploitation that resulted. Many mass-mailing viruses and Internet worms flourished and crippled business and government worldwide solely because of specific features of Microsoft software that existed *by design*.

Microsoft is the company that spammers, spyware writers, vxers (virus writers), and many others love to hate. But if Microsoft's fate was different and everyone used Linux, would there still be as much of a virus, spam, and spyware problem today? In Microsoft's defense, I think the company is targeted as much for its sheer size, its corporate image, and for the fact that its software is ubiquitous.

Organizations that adopt a defense-in-depth strategy are better able to defend themselves. Read Chapter 13 for more on this topic.

Peer-to-peer file sharing

Although nothing is inherently wrong with peer-to-peer file sharing, almost all its actual uses are illegal, and as the saying goes, "If you play with fire, you will get burned." The predominant use of peer-to-peer file sharing is to share music files and other protected or copyrighted content, typically illegally, with others on the peer-to-peer network.

Legal problems aside, the software for these peer-to-peer networks leaves a computer or network open to spyware in the following ways:

- ✔ The software doesn't limit the files that might be shared to just music, so frequently what comes down the peer-to-peer pipe is spyware.
- ✔ Some peer-to-peer programs themselves have spyware bundled with them that gets installed when the peer-to-peer program is installed.

The result is a pretty ugly situation. Not only does the peer-to-peer software poke several holes in your system, enabling spyware to seep in, but some software also contains vulnerabilities that allow people to retrieve any file they choose to from the peer computer. Is it any wonder, then, that many companies forbid the use of peer-to-peer sharing programs?

How Spyware Gets Information from Your Computer

Spyware creators have an arsenal of tricks for extracting information from a user's computer. Most utilize a Web browser as a coconspirator, but spyware can also sneak in when other programs are installed, as well as if a virus or worm successfully lodges itself in a user's computer.

The following sections explain the key ways spyware extracts information from your computer. Before all the gory details make you inordinately paranoid (a little paranoia is probably appropriate, but the spyware can't access your brain or anything like that, at least not any that I've heard of), keep in mind that I explain how to prevent and remedy spyware problems later in this chapter, in the section "Fighting Back."

Hijacking cookies

A Web site can attempt to access a cookie that is associated with *another* Web site (in case you're not familiar with how cookies work, one Web site is not *supposed* to be able to access any cookies except for those it left there earlier). For example, if you're visiting www.scumads.com (not a real site . . . at least, not when I wrote this book), that site may try to retrieve your Yahoo! or Google cookie by impersonating the original Yahoo! or Google site in particular ways.

Why would this be useful to a hacker?

Well, for starters, if you use Yahoo! or Google e-mail and you configure that mail to automatically log you in, having your cookie might be enough for the hacker to log into your e-mail too. Whoever does this can send mail from your account, receive your e-mail, and view all your stored e-mail. That includes e-mails with your résumés attached, notes to and from your friends, and forgotten passwords that your financial services Web sites sent you. Oh my!

At the very least, a hacker can use a hijacked cookie to track what Web sites you've visited and when. Remember that much of what's going on with spyware is about advertising, and knowing what sites you're visiting is quite valuable to advertisers. I have a feeling, however, that the types of spyware and malware that hijack cookies are not used by the big uptown marketing companies, but by those shady operations in the bad part of town.

Executing programs

Running a program on your computer might be what's needed to install certain spyware, but running a program could also be what the spyware *does* after it's installed.

A vulnerability in Internet Explorer can permit a Web site to download and execute a malicious ActiveX control that, in turn, can do pretty much anything it wants on a user's computer, including run other programs or download additional programs and files to the user's computer. In keeping with the theme in this section (how spyware gets information from your computer), these programs could snoop around in a user's computer, permitting a program to do pretty much whatever it pleases.

Any hacker with a decent imagination can wreak all kinds of havoc on victim computers, including (but not limited to) destruction of the user's information, transmission of a user's sensitive documents to others, and denial of service attacks (sending thousands of packets to a server in order to cripple or disable it).

Reading the Clipboard

Another one of those supposedly *friendly* features of Internet Explorer is its ability for Web sites to read the contents of your Clipboard. (See the sidebar, "Is spyware Microsoft's fault?" for details on the origins of the friendly features.)

Although I can imagine the potential usefulness of sharing the Clipboard, in my mind this also spells trouble. Who knows what could be on your Clipboard at any given time? Do you ever copy pathnames, URLs, user IDs, passwords, or paragraphs of confidential information? I can smell the potential danger, and I hope you do, too.

Accessing the hard drive

An ActiveX control on a Web page can not only access the user's hard drive, but also read and write data on that hard drive. Combined with other vulnerabilities, scripting on a Web page can cause *any* data on a user's hard drive to be moved, altered, destroyed, or copied over the Internet to any location.

Spoofing well-known Web pages

A cleverly (or, I should say, diabolically) coded Web page can impersonate a well-known Web page, including the URL in the browser's address bar! The vulnerabilities that permit this gave rise to many successful phishing scams. (A *phishing* scam is typified by official-looking e-mail messages that lure unsuspecting victims to Web sites where they are asked to surrender sensitive information, such as financial institution user IDs and passwords, or perhaps credit card or bank account numbers.)

A lapse in the user's judgment leads him or her to visit the Web page referenced in the message. A vulnerability in the user's browser permits the page to fake the URL in the browser's address bar, making the user believe that he or she is visiting the site that is actually being impersonated. However, many times a phishing scam will take a user to a Web site where the URL only *resembles* the real thing, hoping that the user won't notice the difference.

After the spoof fools the user into believing that he or she is on a trusted site (say, a bank's site), the user is coerced into providing information to the attackers or potentially even downloading and running even more harmful software.

Logging keystrokes

A *key logger* is a program that is designed to record every keystroke on a user's computer. Some key loggers even record all mouse movements and button clicks. Although they're potentially useful as diagnostic or corporate surveillance tools, hackers often use key loggers for illegitimate purposes, such as stealing user IDs and passwords from unsuspecting users.

In some well-publicized cases, people have installed key loggers on public-access computers in public libraries or Internet cafes. But most likely, many thousands of key loggers are running on unsuspecting users' computers around the world.

Fighting Back

Spyware prevention requires several actions that, in combination, minimize the opportunity for spyware to wriggle its way into your company's computers. The following sections outline the steps you need to take in order to win the spyware wars: You need to rid your system(s) of vulnerabilities and use tools to scan, detect, and block spyware. You can also bookmark this page and read Chapter 13, where I discuss a more thorough defense in depth.

Testing for vulnerabilities

Be sure to know whether a user's computer contains any of the technical vulnerabilities that permit a Web site (or HTML-coded e-mail message) to illicitly access information, make changes, or implant one or more programs on that system.

Many free and fee-based tools can scan networks and identify specific vulnerabilities on servers and workstations. Some of the more sophisticated tools in this category can even install the appropriate patches on those systems if needed.

Some of the tools available for this task are

- ✔ **Microsoft Windows Update:** This is the friendly, free, Web-based patch installation site, found at `http://windowsupdate.microsoft.com`.

- ✔ **Microsoft Baseline Security Analyzer (MBSA):** Just go to `www.microsoft.com` and type **MBSA** in the search text box. This free tool scans for vulnerabilities but does not install patches.

- ✔ **Microsoft Automatic Update:** This is the free set-it-and-forget-it tool built into Windows 2000 and XP that lets Windows automatically download and install security patches.

- ✔ **HFNetChkPro:** This is a scanning and patching product available at `www.shavlik.com`. Interestingly enough, Shavlik wrote the scanning engine for this product and also for Microsoft MBSA.

- ✔ **GFI LANguard:** Available at `www.gfi.com`. This is another scanner-only tool that does not install patches. This is a fee-based tool, but you can get a trial version to see whether it fits your needs.

- ✔ **Patchlink:** Available at `www.patchlink.com`. This is another commercial software product; an evaluation version is available.

The size of your organization should influence your choice of tools. Small organizations can consider Windows Update or Automatic Update, but larger organizations should consider bulk scanning and patch installation products.

Patching vulnerabilities

Companies have discovered that unpatched servers and workstations are nothing but trouble and cause costly, disruptive security incidents if left unpatched for long.

Patching systems — whether you're talking dozens or thousands — is costly and time-consuming, but it's nowhere near as expensive and disruptive as doing nothing and risking the infiltration of worms, viruses, and spyware. Every organization, whether it has 1 or 100,000 workstations, needs to develop procedures for keeping its system(s) up to date with the latest security patches. Although this can be a daunting task, tools and products are available to help you out, regardless of the number of workstations.

Most of the scanning tools described earlier in this section also install patches.

Scanning and removing spyware

The original — and still the most popular — means for identifying and removing spyware is to run a spyware-scanning program that will search a workstation or server for spyware, list the spyware found, and remove it if the user so desires. But software that *blocks* spyware before it can be loaded is becoming more popular.

A thorough spyware scanning and removal program must check for spyware in many places, including

✔ **Cookies:** Although cookie-based spyware is the most benign of spyware, many people are concerned about the Web-tracking capability that such spyware facilitates.

✔ **ActiveX controls:** As I mention earlier in this chapter, ActiveX is Microsoft's proprietary technology whereby scripts (short computer programs) can be dynamically loaded from a Web site and executed on the user's computer. ActiveX is a "client-side" scripting language similar to JavaScript.

✔ **Java and JavaScript:** Java is a structured computer language introduced in the 1990s; JavaScript, a scripting language similar to Java, is often used as a "client side" scripting language used to execute instructions via a user's Web browser.

✔ **Browser Helper Objects (BHOs):** Executable code that Internet Explorer loads into memory and has complete access to everything the browser does and displays. BHOs are used by spyware to track what you are doing and where you are going.

✔ **Registry entries:** Spyware often creates distinctive Registry entries that facilitate and configure its execution. Registry entries also control a browser's home page and default search page, among many other settings that spyware often utilizes.

✔ **Standalone programs:** Computer programs that operate entirely on their own. In the Windows world, a standalone computer program has all of the access privileges of the user who runs it. This applies not only on the computer it's running on, but to any network resource (such as files on a file server) that the user is able to access.

A typical spyware program scans a computer on demand, and some permit automatic scanning to take place at system startup or on a set schedule. Some of the newest spyware programs will perform on-access scanning, just like a virus scanner. If you have more that just a few workstations to manage, you'll greatly appreciate automatic downloads, scanning, and blocking. Expecting users to remember to update or scan is unrealistic in most situations, and you probably don't have time to do it for them.

Isn't spyware just another form of malware?

Antivirus software has been around for years (decades, almost). The scope of coverage by antivirus software has slowly grown to include worms and other annoying stuff creeping into your computer, but until recently, virus scanners pretty much ignored most forms of spyware. Now that companies are starting to make some real money selling ways to prevent and eliminate spyware, the major antivirus software vendors are all taking notice and either buying up anti-spyware software vendors or adding new spyware-prevention code for their own product lines. The original line drawn between viruses and spyware was pretty artificial to begin with, and it will soon disappear almost entirely.

For a spyware scanner's scans to identify all the latest spyware, it must periodically update its database of known spyware. Typically, you accomplish this by manually downloading the latest signatures from the spyware company's database over the Internet.

When a spyware scanner locates specific spyware on a computer, it either prompts the user, asking whether it should proceed to remove all the spyware, or it may automatically remove all spyware that it found.

I doubt you're alone if you're thinking that the preceding description resembles the mechanisms found in antivirus programs. Read on — this gets even more interesting.

Preventing spyware from getting a foothold

Some of the newer and more advanced spyware tools don't just scan and remove spyware that is already on a user's computer; they can actually block spyware's attempt to install itself in the first place.

Like the spyware scanners, you must regularly update spyware blockers with the signatures of all known spyware.

If this talk about scanning for spyware, blocking it, and updating signatures is beginning to sound familiar, you may have already read *Computer Viruses For Dummies* (written by Peter Gregory, one of the authors of this book, and published by Wiley Publishing, Inc.). If not, pick it up and give it a read. You can find many of the same ideas discussed there, but discussed in far more depth and detail.

Choosing and Using Spyware Blockers

You have a significant challenge right now: You need to choose a good spyware-blocking program. As I write this chapter, standards for what good spyware-blocking software should do are still taking shape, and few good reviews comparing the products are available. In fact, this market is so young that the terminology is still pretty fluid, and different products may refer to the same feature with different names.

Because there's such variance in terminology and function at this point, you need more than the typical one-page, product-feature glossies to figure out what each product is doing. Most likely, you need to demo each product to understand the features they tout and whether the features are meaningful to you.

Chapter 17 covers ten major players on the spyware-blocking market today. You can find details about their features, costs, makers, and more. You can use this chapter to begin your search for a spyware blocker that will suit your business needs and budget.

Understanding the changing market

The spyware-blocking market is changing rapidly. Not long ago, spyware-blocking programs were the fruit of a new cottage industry. Literally dozens of so-called spyware-blocking programs have been available for free, and some of the better programs have fee-based models with even more features.

Still, as I write this, few spyware blockers have true big-company features, such as central control and management, reporting, and hands-free operation for users (so you won't need to remind them to download new updates or manually scan for spyware). By the time you read this, the stronger spyware-blocker programs, such as Ad-Aware, SpywareBlaster, and Spybot-S&D, may have been purchased by antivirus software companies.

The larger your organization, the greater the risk you're undertaking by making a large investment in what is still a pure, mostly unmanaged, client-side solution. No matter how you solve the spyware problem, you'll be solving it again in a couple of years because the product market will mature and spyware blockers will catch up with antivirus products in terms of management capability.

I'm not advising you to sit on the sidelines, however. Spyware is a serious problem in many environments. It's a problem that you may need to solve even though the tools for dealing with it are still relatively immature.

Training users and getting their help

Unless you're deploying one of the very few mostly hands-off spyware-blocking products, you're going to have to get your users' help. You may need to ask them to do a variety of chores regularly, including

- **Updating signatures:** Every two to four weeks, users should update signatures. Like antivirus software, anti-spyware software isn't very useful if it doesn't have up-to-date signatures.

- **Performing scans:** Users need to manually perform scans on spyware blockers that lack a scan-scheduling capability.

- **Reporting anything that the scan comes up with:** Most spyware blockers work by reporting the presence of spyware after the fact, so if they find something, the machine may have been infected for a while, and you need to know about that in case sensitive information was exposed.

Developing a network and Internet usage policy

Speaking of bad user habits — if your company doesn't already have an acceptable usage policy for your network and the Internet, you may want to consider writing one up. If not, at least give your users the basics:

- Web browsing using company computers and networks is intended for business use only. Use care when visiting Web sites: Do not download software unless approved in advance by IT. At no time may any employee visit Web sites containing sexually offensive, gambling, hate, or illegal content.

- Don't download *anything* from the Internet and open it unless you know *exactly* what it is and you have approval for this action.

- Don't open e-mail attachments unless you both know the sender and were expecting the attachment.

- Don't load or run any software on your company computer that isn't specifically approved by IT.

- Only company-owned computers may be connected to the company network. At no time may any personal or third-party computer or other devices be connected to the network without advance permission from IT.

Rather than just closing your eyes and adopting the above language for your acceptable use policy, you need to consider your organization's culture, business activity, and tolerance for risk.

In many environments, personal Web browsing, downloading activities, and general non-business-related activities are considered so dangerous that workstations are made available that have no connection to the company's network and their own private (firewalled) Internet connection. These are frequently made available in public areas for employees that need to use the Internet for non-business-related activities.

You might also discover other chores that your users need to perform from time to time until the spyware-blocking products do these automatically.

You also need to remove the stigma that goes along with getting infected by spyware. Users tend to not report getting infected because they think it reflects badly on them and their Internet usage. In fact, sometimes it does, but you really need an amnesty policy for the first few times someone becomes infected because otherwise, users won't tell you about it. If the user doesn't 'fess up, you have a company machine that's sharing information with someone on the Internet, and you don't have a clue about it. I'd rather forgive bad user habits any day than have the problem go undiscovered. In exchange for this amnesty, ask users to review your user policy and explain that following it can help prevent future problems.

Chapter 7 covers training users in more detail.

Finding a product that deploys easily

Unless you're deploying a spyware-blocking solution to a very small number of computers, you need to consider the ease with which you can deploy it to all your users' systems without installing it yourself on each one. You may want to consider several other factors so that you can deploy the blocker more easily, including the following:

- ✓ **Default settings:** What settings do you want your spyware-blocking program to have on all of your users' systems? Can you automatically deploy the program with the settings you need? Can you "lock" the settings so that users cannot change them?

- ✓ **Browser-protection settings:** Some spyware-blocking programs have features that provide added protection for browsers, such as preventing configuration changes. Are such settings appropriate for your site?

- ✓ **HOSTS file protection:** Some spyware-blocking programs can prevent the HOSTS file from being modified. Is that appropriate for your environment?

- ✓ **Browser and OS versions:** Before you install your chosen spyware blocker on everyone's computers, make sure that it plays well with all the versions of Windows (and Mac OS and Linux) installed on your users' computers. Also, test it with different versions of Internet Explorer and even other browsers such as Firefox and Opera if that applies to your environment. More important than just *behaving,* does your spyware blocker continue to provide protection with different browsers and versions of Windows?

IT veterans will advise you to perform plenty of testing before pushing your spyware blocker out to everyone. The larger the organization, the more important testing becomes.

Using spyware blockers

Until anti-spyware programs mature and include more enterprise features, you may be flying blind in terms of knowing how your spyware-blocking programs are performing on users' systems. Not all programs that block spyware in real time have event logs. Must you rely on faith alone to know whether your spyware-blocking programs are doing anything? Until event logging is commonplace, you may have no choice. You may need to rely upon month-to-month helpdesk statistics to see if spyware-related calls decrease over time.

Keep in mind that spyware blocking is relatively new, and to some degree, imperfect. For an example of this, find a spyware-infected machine somewhere (any machine that's been operating without a blocker for a while should do) and run a spyware-blocking tool of your choice, eliminating everything that it complains about. Now, repeat the process on the just-cleaned machine with a different blocker. There's an excellent chance that the second program will still find something. Just because you're running a spyware blocker doesn't mean that your users are spyware-free. It really means that they're *mostly* spyware-free.

Chapter 3

Understanding the Enemy: What Really Spawns Spam

In This Chapter

▶ Understanding how spammers get e-mail addresses

▶ Directory service attacks (DSAs)

▶ Sneaking it in: How spammers get through the defenses

▶ Understanding the spam economy

▶ Taking a look at the unholy alliance of spam and viruses

*I*f you want to have a chance at beating spammers at their own game, you need to understand how they play. They have one rule: Take no prisoners. Spammers are highly motivated to get their messages into everyone's mailboxes, no matter what it takes: deception, dishonesty, subversion, trickery, or lies.

In this chapter, I explain the various methods that spammers use to acquire e-mail addresses and to get their messages through spam defenses. Although this book focuses on issues and solutions for businesses, the information in this chapter applies to home computing as well. Whether you are in the market for a spam-blocking solution, or you already have one and just need to understand more about how spammers do what they do, this is the chapter for you.

Understanding How Spammers Get E-Mail Addresses

Spammers employ a variety of methods to acquire e-mail addresses. Some methods take advantage of the e-mail addresses readily available on the Internet, whereas others employ different levels of trickery, from harvesting to outright stealing. I discuss the common — and not so common — methods in the sections that follow.

Harvesting from the Internet

Spammers (and their assistants) utilize a technique called *harvesting* to acquire e-mail addresses. While harvesting requires a lot of bandwidth, it is ingeniously simple: Simply download the right pages from select Web sites and extract the e-mail addresses that are there for the picking. Some of the tools and sources employed in harvesting e-mail addresses from the Web include the following:

- ✔ **Web spiders:** Spammers employ Web crawlers and spiders that harvest e-mail addresses from Web sites. It's common for Web sites to include `mailto:` URLs as well as unlinked `user@domain` addresses. Put your e-mail address on a Web site, and you're spam bait.

  These spiders are not unlike the spiders and Web crawlers used by Yahoo, Google, and others that scan the Internet's Web sites in order to keep Web search indexes fresh. Except that e-mail address harvesting spiders are up to no good. And where do these spiders get domain names? With over 90 million `.com` domains in existence, it's easy enough to just *guess* domain names in order to come up with quite a few.

- ✔ **Newsgroups:** It's a straightforward task to harvest e-mail addresses from Usenet newsgroups: Just pull in a big newsfeed and extract the e-mail addresses with a simple shell or Perl script. Newsgroup volumes are still increasing exponentially — as I write this chapter, at a rate of at least several gigabytes per day. This means lots of e-mail addresses are there for the taking. Any spammer with enough bandwidth can slurp up all those bits and just sift out the e-mail addresses.

- ✔ **Groups, blogs, and discussion boards:** Yahoo! and Google have their groups and mailing lists, many of which make their members' e-mail addresses available. There are thousands of blogs and discussion boards out there, too, that contain easily acquired e-mail addresses.

- ✔ **Test messages:** In this method, which I've observed firsthand, spammers send test e-mails to recipients whose addresses they simply guess. I have seen so-called test e-mail messages sent to addresses like `service@`, `info@`, `test@`, `marketing@`, `security@`, at one of the domains that I own. I can't think of any legitimate explanations for these messages other than that they were spammers or *e-mail address brokers* (people who buy and sell e-mail addresses for spamming purposes) trying to discover more real e-mail addresses.

  Spammers at one time could reliably conclude that, if they receive no "bounce-o-gram" back from the domain, the e-mail address must be legit. This is because e-mail servers used to routinely send nondelivery receipts (NDRs) back to the sender of a message sent to a nonexistent address. But that ain't necessarily so any more: More servers are opting to stop sending NDRs for this and other reasons; I discuss this in more detail in Chapter 12.

✔ **Malware:** Spammers sometimes use Trojan horses, viruses, and worms to extract e-mail addresses from individual users' computers. As creative as spammers and vxers (virus writers) are, I would not be surprised if they have not only thought of this, but also used it on more than one occasion.

If mass-mailing worms can extract the contents of a user's e-mail address book for the purpose of propagating spam, then it's going to be easy to perform the same extraction and simply send the list back to the hacker's lair. This would probably be easier, in fact, because this activity is far less likely to be detected than a mass-mailing worm.

✔ **Unsubscribe requests:** A good number of spam messages contain "unsubscribe me" links that a user clicks to opt out. However, many spam operators actually continue to send spam to e-mail addresses submitted to "unsubscribe me" links. When a user submits such a request, the spammer knows that the address being sent is a valid e-mail address. Do you think they'll actually stop sending spam to a known valid address? Not on your life!

Buying and stealing addresses

Among spammers and e-mail address brokers, e-mail addresses are a traded and sold commodity. If you know where to look, you can purchase CDs and downloads containing e-mail addresses by the hundreds of thousands or millions. I've even seen them sold at a major, well-known computer warehouse chain. I've also been spammed with offers of these lists.

The old whois trick

whois is a network protocol that is used to query whois servers about domain names. Before domain registrars such as Networksolutions.com constructed a Web interface for querying domain names, using whois was the only means available for getting information about a domain.

Although doing high volumes of whois queries used to be pretty easy, most (if not all) of the domain registrars and other whois operators have put a stop to this. Most now employ a combination of distorted-image challenges (where they display a graphic containing a word that is fairly easy for humans to read, but difficult for software, and you must type in the word in a form field) and session quotas (where they permit only so many queries from a single IP address before they start blocking further queries). Perhaps there are legit whois servers that still permit high-volume mechanized searches, but I don't personally know of any.

And of course, everyone has heard the stories of Web sites that collect your e-mail address and promise not to sell it (ha!). But they sell, trade, or give away e-mail addresses anyway, even when their privacy policy says they won't. A few high-profile companies have been prosecuted and/or fined for this practice.

Business and service provider e-mail lists are also stolen and sold to spammers. In mid-2004, a former AOL employee was charged with stealing 90 million screen names and 30 million e-mail addresses from AOL and selling them to a spammer for $100,000. This is not an isolated case, but it is a noteworthy one because of the size of the heist. So much for privacy, eh?

As you may have guessed, the buying and stealing of addresses is closely tied to the black market that's emerged from the business of spam. I discuss this in more detail in "The Economics of Spam" section, later in this chapter.

Directory service attacks

One type of attack uses VRFY requests to get e-mail addresses from a mail server. A VRFY request is one of the commands in the SMTP protocol that is used to verify whether a given e-mail address is valid or not. Using a technique unforeseen by the inventors of SMTP, spammers pound an organization's inbound SMTP server with continuous VRFY requests in order to extract by brute force an organization's e-mail list from its e-mail server. This kind of an attack is called a *directory service attack (DSA)* because it is attacking the directory service feature of an SMTP server, very much like a dictionary attack attempting to guess a user's password by trying every available password combination.

The following steps show you how a VRFY request works:

1. **Open a command prompt window by choosing Start➪Programs➪ Accessories➪Command Prompt.**

2. **In the command prompt window, open up a telnet connection on port 25 to your e-mail server by typing the following:**

   ```
   telnet mailserver.somedomain.com 25
   ```

   After you press Enter, telnet opens a connection to your e-mail server on port 25 — the SMTP port on which it receives incoming e-mail. The e-mail server will respond to your connection request with a brief salutation like this:

   ```
   220 mailserver.somedomain.com ESMTP Sendmail
           8.11.6/8.11.6; Fri, 28 Jan 2005 22:53:58 -0800
   ```

The e-mail server you connected to will wait for a HELO command like the following:

```
HELO someotherdomain.com
```

The e-mail server will respond in kind, like this:

```
250 mail.somedomain.com Hello
        207-207-91-186.ip.someisp.com [207.207.91.186],
        pleased to meet you
```

Now it's time to try the VRFY command, like this example:

```
VRFY peter.gregory
```

If you see a response like the following, your site doesn't support VRFY. Just enter `quit` and be content, knowing that you have one less thing to worry about.

```
220 warning ESMTP, Malicious use will be prosecuted.
```

3. **At the command prompt, enter a VRFY request for an existing e-mail address on your site by typing the VRFY command and then the address name. For example, for the e-mail address** `peter.gregory@ yourdomain.com`, **you'd type the following:**

```
vrfy peter.gregory
```

If you see a response similar to the following ones, then your site doesn't support VRFY; all is well:

```
250 User not local
252 VRFY un-implemented, send e-mail to verify
```

However, if you see a response like this next one, then your server *does* support VRFY, and your company e-mail addresses are an open book for spammers everywhere:

```
250 2.1.5 <peterg@servername.somedomain.com>
```

You can see from this example that any SMTP server that still has VRFY enabled offers up the e-mail address `peterg@servername.yourdomain. com` to anyone who wants it, as well as the name of your mail server.

An e-mail server that still supports VRFY is likely to also verify group addresses, even large ones like `employees@`, `everyone@`, `legal@`, `it@`, and so forth, yielding long lists of legitimate e-mail addresses for the spamming market.

If your mail server or firewall is capable of turning off e-mail to group addresses, don't allow group e-mail from the outside. There's little chance that someone on the outside has a legitimate need to send mail to `all@ yourcompany.com`, and spammers will frequently try to use addresses like *all, everyone, employees,* and *staff* to reach all of your users.

Even *unused* e-mail accounts can get spam

Before I learned about directory service attacks (DSAs), I truly believed that people who received spam got it because they were a little too careless about giving out their e-mail addresses at one time or another. I think that this is the common misperception.

But I quickly became a believer when I learned about DSAs. I am now certain that you could create an e-mail account in a domain, and before long, that e-mail account would receive spam, even if you had *never even used* that

e-mail account. That account could eventually receive spam, even if you *never* typed that account's e-mail address, anywhere.

The next time you talk with someone — perhaps one of your colleagues — who receives a lot of spam, try not to be judgmental. Before you look down your long nose at those unfortunate souls who get a lot of spam, remember that it may be a result of DSAs, and have nothing at all to do with whether they were ever careless with their e-mail addresses.

If you have discovered that your own e-mail server still supports VRFY, don't get into a lather, thinking that you have to turn it off right away before a spammer gets it. It's too late — they've already gotten you, probably dozens of times. But yes, you still *do* want to turn off VRFY. Put it on your to-do list. You can read about how to turn off VRFY in Chapter 11.

If you're still not convinced that directory service attacks are an issue, let me leave you with this thought: According to Postini, one of the ASP spam-filtering service providers, fully *half* of all SMTP connections to organization e-mail servers are established for illegitimate purposes, such as directory service attacks. Half. This figure sure got *my* attention.

Giving Filters the Slip: How Spam Messages Seep into Your Inbox

Practically everyone with a spam filter still sees *some* spam messages sneaking through the filters. How do they do it? I discuss various techniques that spammers use in this section.

If you've been paying attention to the text content of spam lately, you've probably noticed some unusual content in spam messages. I mean besides whatever marketing the spam contains, there's also a lot of text: Sometimes gibberish, sometimes text from some dime store novel. The spammers are putting this text there *deliberately* in order to get through the filters. Read on to see why they do this.

Poisoning Bayesian filters

Bayesian filtering, which I explain in more detail in the nearby sidebar, "How Bayesian filtering works," has been an effective means for filtering spam, but its usefulness has been eroding. Spammers have figured out how to make it more difficult for Bayesian filters to distinguish spam from legitimate mail by inserting blocks of irrelevant text before or after the actual spam content. I pulled an example of such a message out of my spam quarantine and present it in Listing 3-1 (e-mail headers not shown).

Listing 3-1: A Spam Message Designed to Trick Filters

```
During all crime investigations, it is necessary to visit a
        strip club at least once. I never get hungry.
        Should you wish to pass yourself off as a German
        officer, it is not necessary to speak the
        language. You grind your coffee beans in your
        mouth.

   Order from Canada and sa ve mo ney.

***We are running hot specials***
Meds starts at only $60

Just look at some of our prices...
- 30 Valium = $90
- 35 via gra = $87.50
- 20 cialis = $80
- 50 vioxx = $60
- 30 xanax = $66

- Meds are 80% less than regular price
- No doctor visits or pre.scription required.
- Quick delivery to your front door

To order starts here....

<many blank lines deleted>

Candidate fell and broke arm during interview. The farm was
        used to produce produce. Once a week, I usually
        feel hot all over. The soldier decided to desert
        his dessert in the desert. We must polish the
        Polish furniture. A job applicant challenged the
        interviewer to an arm wrestle.
```

The narrative before and after the main message was *deliberately* inserted into the message in order to confuse the Bayesian filter into thinking that this is a legitimate message. This is achieved by diluting the actual spam content (the part about the prescription drugs for sale) with correct — but meaningless — content.

How Bayesian filtering works

English mathematician Thomas Bayes (1702–1761) developed a theory of "probability inference," published posthumously in the paper *Essay Towards Solving a Problem in the Doctrine of Chances*. Bayes's ideas began to take hold in the early nineteenth century, when scientists and philosophers needed to better understand matters of "forward probability," or the chances of the occurrence of some future event based upon known prior events. For example, how many socks must I pull out of the drawer before I can be sure that I have at least one matching pair?

Bayes's theorem has been used as the basis to determine the probability that a given e-mail message is spam, based upon the presence of certain words in the message. This is keyword filtering at a completely different, and higher, level.

Users must interact with the Bayesian filter in order to *train* it to recognize new forms of spam. Essentially, a user tells the anti-spam program about its failure to correctly classify incoming mail as spam or not. This feedback tunes the Bayesian filter, keeps it up to date, and helps it to better predict whether future messages are legitimate or not. Continual training keeps a Bayesian filter smart.

This attack is successful because it skews the Bayesian filter by statistically making spam messages more closely resemble legitimate mail. And if this technique allows the spammer to get at least *some* of his messages through to the end-user, then he will consider this a success. The ultimate test, of course, is still based upon the number of suckers — er, customers — he is able to hook.

Hash busting

Hash busting is another technique that spammers use to sneak their messages by the spam filter. What spammers do is deliberately misspell or insert characters or spaces into words in order to cause the spam filter to not recognize the keywords and tag the message as spam.

In the example in Listing 3-1, the spammer has inserted characters into the words *prescription* and *viagra* and the phrase *save money* in order to avoid being identified by the keyword filter.

Anyone who has used the older PC-based spam filters, which filter messages only on keywords, knows how useless those filters are today. I know: I chased the variations in keywords for a while until I realized that the spammer won't stop at *pre.scription*, but also *pre,scription*, *prescripti0n*, *pr3scription*, *p.r.e.s.c.r.i.p.T.i.o.n* . . . you get the idea.

Not long ago, Microsoft Outlook attempted to filter spam by scanning for keywords in the content of messages and by rejecting messages if the originating e-mail address was found in a "junk senders" list. Both of these techniques are all but useless anymore. The junk senders list is ineffective because spammers don't use real `From:` addresses, but instead they generate addresses at random. Much of the time, you won't get more than one spam message from the same `From:` address. So much for the junk senders list!

Snowflaking messages

Spammers have become more sophisticated over time (as you probably have already guessed). When they started sending messages in large volumes, they sent identically formed messages, which weren't all that difficult for larger organizations and ISPs — with thousands of recipients — to identify and block.

But then the spammers started making every message different — sometimes radically different, using a technique called snowflaking. With *snowflaking,* the spammer automatically tweaks each message so that no two spam messages are exactly alike, just like — you guessed it — snowflakes. When every message is unique, centralized spam filters have a difficult time blocking large volumes of messages the way they used to.

All it takes to snowflake a batch of spam messages is a little extra programming. On the way through the assembly line, the spammer just needs to sprinkle a few hundred random words from a dictionary, or a few paragraphs from some cheap romance novel, into each message. Gag on *this,* spam filters!

Forging From: and Received: headers

I'm pretty sure you all know that a spammer is *not* going to use his or her real e-mail address when sending spam. Even those spammers who *mitnicked* (did something dumb enough to get caught more than once) aren't *that* foolish.

However, it's not just the `From:` header that's often forged, but also many other elements in a message's headers. Spammers may plant fake `Received:` headers (each mail server that processes a mail message stamps it with a `Received:` header, which when put together can help someone trace a message's path from origin to recipient) to throw spam filters off the scent.

But — like snowflaking the actual message text — to be effective, the spammer needs to vary the contents of the e-mail headers in each message. This is particularly true for the `Received:` headers. Otherwise, it will be too easy to detect the phony `Received:` headers and simply throw them out. You can find an example of `Received:` headers in Chapter 12.

Relaying to hide message origins

Spammers don't originate their messages on their *own* server. Even with fake `From:` and `Received:` headers — which, like the breadcrumbs in the fairy-tale *Hansel and Gretel,* are used to trace a message's path back to its point of origin — you'd still be able to trace those messages back to the spammer by reading all the other `Received:` headers. And of course, spammers don't want you to do that.

To make it far more difficult for you to trace their messages, spammers *relay* their messages through another system in a way that causes the message to look like it originally came from the relaying system.

Older versions of sendmail supported a once-common method for re-originating mail — sending a message to a mail server that was not the destination server, but an intermediate server. For example, you could initiate an SMTP connection to `elroy.somedomain.com` and send it a message that is being sent to `george@otherdomain.com`. The sendmail program would happily accept and forward the message on to its final destination. This is what is called *relaying*. With relaying, it is possible to re-originate a message and completely hide the true origin of a message. (For some odd reason, spammers don't want people to be able to find them so easily.)

Today, most system admins will have upgraded their sendmail with a version that no longer permits relaying: Newer versions of sendmail will only accept messages intended for its own domain and no other by default.

Figure 3-1 illustrates how messages are relayed.

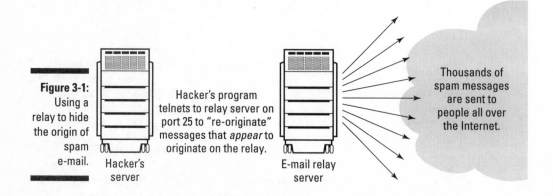

Figure 3-1:
Using a relay to hide the origin of spam e-mail.

Hacker's server

Hacker's program telnets to relay server on port 25 to "re-originate" messages that *appear* to originate on the relay.

E-mail relay server

Thousands of spam messages are sent to people all over the Internet.

You may be wondering how relaying differs from legitimate mail origination. Well, when you or I send an e-mail message, we create it in an e-mail program such as Outlook or Lotus Notes. In relaying, the program sending a mail message to the SMTP server isn't a program like Outlook, but a special program used to originate spam. Basically, instead of actually typing e-mails, this program connects to the relay server (a mail server with an older or mis-configured version of sendmail that still permits relaying) and then creates e-mails on that server. The program that spammers use need not be complicated — it could be a simple script.

To illustrate how this works, Listing 3-2 shows an example I used in the 1990s to demonstrate how easy it was to forge a completely genuine-looking mail message. All it takes is telnet and a cursory understanding of the SMTP protocol. In Listing 3-2, the commands that I typed to relay a message from the Vatican to my friend John appear in bold.

Listing 3-2: Hiding a Message Origin with a Relay

```
% telnet mail.vatican.va 25
220 mail.vatican.va SMTP Sendmail 8.11.6/8.11.0 here
HELO
250 mail.vatican.va Hello wbar7.sea1-4-4-021-163.sea1.dsl-
   verizon.net [4.4.21.163], I'm listening
MAIL From: pope@vatican.va
250 pope@vatican.va... sender ok
RCPT To: jwalters@a6.com
250 jwalters@a6.com... recipient ok
DATA Subject: I haven't seen you in a while
354 Enter mail, end with "." on a line by itself
John,
You haven't been to confession in a while. Please come
and see me soon. I don't want you to end up in purgatory.

Signed,
The Pope
.
250 HAA19816 Message accepted for delivery
quit
221 closing connection
%
```

A few minutes after I created the relay message, a mail message would show up for my friend John (and he always knew it was really from me). The message appeared to have *actually* originated on the vatican.va mail server — *because it did!* I used to do this demonstration for people to show them that you shouldn't assume that a message is genuine despite outward appearances. By the way, vatican.va turned off mail relaying several years ago (good for them — they probably discovered that their mail server was being used to relay spam). **Warning:** Don't try this at home — I'm quite sure that this is illegal these days.

If spammers can't *find* a mail relay, then they *make* one. That's right: The world is full of computers just waiting to be taken over, while their clueless owners browse the Internet with a false sense of complacency.

Briefly, here's how it works: Many viruses and worms actually plant an SMTP relay on infected systems. Well, not a *real* SMTP relay in the truest sense of the word, but something that *functions* as one. If you want to discover more, turn to the next section, where I describe this in greater detail.

The Economics of Spam

Ever since DARPA (the Defense Advanced Research Projects Agency, which funded the research into and the construction of the early Internet) withdrew funding in the late 1980s, capitalism has driven the growth of the Internet. There is money to be made and money to be saved in ways that boggle the imagination. Online banking, shopping, research, music, video, news, travel, sights and sounds, financial services, entertainment, learning, sex, messaging, publishing, broadcasting, surveillance, reading, and of course, spam.

Spammers *are* making money. Send enough messages and you *will* get some suckers — er, customers. A 21-year-old online casino operator, allegedly connected with the AOL e-mail theft case (see the section, "Buying and stealing addresses," earlier in this chapter), was reportedly making $10,000–$20,000 per *day*. Good Lord Almighty. Figure 3-2 illustrates the basics of the spam supply chain.

In this section, I discuss the market for e-mail addresses and the capabilities required to distribute spam. As you read this section, think about why I regularly advise people not to open spam messages and not to buy from spammers.

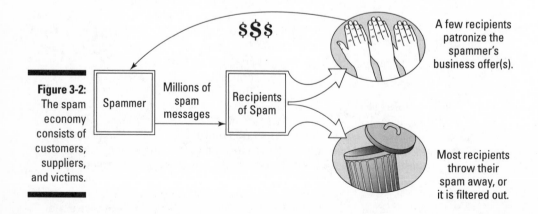

Figure 3-2:
The spam economy consists of customers, suppliers, and victims.

$$$

Spammer → Millions of spam messages → Recipients of Spam

A few recipients patronize the spammer's business offer(s).

Most recipients throw their spam away, or it is filtered out.

Making money with spam e-mail

If you crunch the numbers in the AOL stolen e-mail case, those 30 million e-mail addresses sold for $100,000, or about $0.003 (one-third of a cent) per address. Makes you feel cheap, doesn't it? But this was a bulk deal, and it sounds like the seller didn't have any other buyers, so the buyer probably got an especially good deal. I have a hunch that e-mail addresses typically sell for between $0.02 and $0.10 each, in some healthy quantities, of course. This is just a guess. Honest.

This should tell you that spammers are figuring that a pretty low percentage of spam messages result in real business, probably less than 1 percent. But when they're sending out hundreds of thousands of messages, that could still mean that one batch of spam could result in hundreds of transactions.

It's all a numbers game. Big numbers.

If you're a spammer, having lots of e-mail addresses is nice, but you also need a way to distribute your message. You need bots.

A black market of bots for relaying spam

Bot is a technical term (short for robot) that is used to describe a computer that is used to relay spam. A computer becomes a bot when it's infected with a virus, worm, or Trojan horse that is specially designed to install a *backdoor program* — a program used to provide remote control of the system and relay spam, for instance. But a bot could just as easily be functioning as a spyware component — see Chapter 2 for a discussion of bots and spyware.

Methods vary, but usually the backdoor program is designed to respond to specially coded messages sent to specific TCP or UDP ports. The originator of a particular virus will, after releasing it, either scan the Internet to find the systems that have become infected with his virus, or his virus's backdoor program will send an "I've found a new victim at IP address 4.160.44.209" message back to the virus owner's lair. Then he'll have his list of bots to which he can later send commands, such as spam relay requests, or bombard a particular IP address with packets as part of a distributed denial of service attack.

A well-organized individual can, as a result of his backdoor-installing virus, amass a sizeable collection of bots that can deliver quite a volume of spam. The enterprising person can use them for himself, or he can rent, trade, or sell his spam-relaying bot army to others.

As a result of the masses of bots, a new class of business entities known as Spam Service Providers has emerged. Who'd have thought that cottage industries would provide a spectrum of services, including

- ✔ Writing the viruses
- ✔ Brokering and selling those viruses
- ✔ Releasing and distributing the viruses
- ✔ Collecting and controlling the bot armies
- ✔ Sending the spam through bot armies

There is a complete and complex supply chain of such companies, each with customers and suppliers, each looking for new markets to exploit.

Spam's New Attitude: The Convergence of Spam and Viruses

Through the 1990s, spam laced with malicious code of any kind was a rarity, but now it shows up in over 4 percent of all spam. What's the deal?

Cyber-godfathers: Organized crime in the digital era

The presence of the Internet, with its myriad money-making opportunities (both legitimate as well as illegitimate), has not escaped the eyes of organized crime. The capabilities of cyber-thugs have spawned a new generation of extortion, protection rackets, and cyber-terror of other sorts.

For instance, in East Asia, gangs of cyber-lords routinely launch *denial-of-service attacks* (floods of TCP/IP packets intended to knock Web sites and mail servers off the air for hours or days at a time) on smaller Web site operators who are unable to protect themselves, and then extort money out of them in order to stop the attacks. This is really nothing more than a 21st century version of the infamous protection rackets that the Mafia ran in 1920s American cities.

Another scheme that has been in the news is one where office workers receive threatening e-mail messages that say, "Unless you pay us $50, we'll hide porn on your computer and you'll lose your job because of it. Fill out this convenient form; we take MasterCard and VISA." A surprising number of people have paid up for fear that the claims are true (and sometimes they are).

And, of course, you've got to figure that organized crime is going to be in the business of brokering e-mail addresses. Where there's money to be made in an underworld economy, organized crime is sure to be there in force.

The newly emerging combination of spam and viruses is deliberate and represents a new direction for virus writers and spammers. Several factors account for this, including the following:

- ✔ **Spam gives viruses "legs" to go further.** A virus writer who wants his menace to reach as many people as possible can hire a spammer to let his virus hitch a ride on batches of spam.

- ✔ **Virus writers are new customers for spammers.** In order to grow their business and pay the kids' dentist bills, spammers have found virus writers to be eager customers.

- ✔ **The joined forces of spam and viruses help expand the reach of the spam market.** People who are in the business of acquiring, controlling, or using bot armies can hire the right talent to produce and deliver malicious code to legions of new systems.

Whatever you call it — deadly embrace, unholy alliance, or a pair of sixes — the spam-virus combination gives everyone all the more reason to build and maintain a defense against both.

The days of mass-mailing worms are numbered. Microsoft Outlook blocks executable attachments by default. Antivirus programs keep an eye on — and can stop if necessary — large volumes of outgoing mail. Personal firewalls (even though the adoption rate is still low) block outgoing e-mail generated by implanted executables. So it makes sense that other ways are needed to get malicious code into as many users' systems as possible. Spam is a logical avenue, and this is why the incidence of malware in spam is rising fast.

Advancing the War to New Fronts: Instant Messages and Text Messages

With each new communication medium come new possibilities for interacting with others over time, distance, and new devices — and, not far behind, spam. There's always a spoiler to ruin the fun.

Since the turn of the century (2000, not 1900!), a number of nasty tricks with instant messages and cell phone text messages are conspicuously similar to those perpetrated through spam e-mail. These tricks include

- ✔ Trojan horses sent to cell phones that caused them all to dial the U.S. equivalent of 911.

- ✔ Worms and spam transmitted over major service providers' Instant Messaging services.

- ✔ Worms and Trojan horses that exploit weaknesses in the operating systems of new sophisticated cell phones and/or PDAs.

- ✔ Spam sent to vast numbers of cell phones over SMS (Short Message Service, in other words, cell phone text messages). Most cell carriers charge for SMS text messages sent and received; these are costing subscribers money.

There are few, if any, defenses in place to slow down attacks on Instant Messaging programs and cell phone/PDAs, even though they're both becoming more sophisticated and widely used by individuals and businesses. It may be only a matter of time before spam appears in intolerable volumes on the new, smaller devices.

The virus, spam, and spyware wars are far from over, and the enemy will continually take the war to new fronts. If you utilize instant messaging or cell phone text messaging (or any other emerging technology) as part of your infrastructure, you'll need to tap in to regular and reliable sources of good information so that you'll be well informed as technologies — and exploitation — mature. Both authors of this book maintain an extensive list of such sources at www.spamandspyware.com.

Part II

Justifying and Selecting Spam and Spyware Filters

The 5th Wave   By Rich Tennant

"This isn't a quantitative or a qualitative estimate of the job. This is a 'wish-upon-a-star' estimate of the project."

In this part . . .

*I*f you could just run down to the local Compu-Mart and buy an enterprise anti-spam or anti-spyware package off the shelf with petty cash, this part wouldn't be necessary. Unfortunately, it's not quite that easy. You have to figure out exactly what you want to do, get others to agree with you, justify your plan to various people at your company, and decide what product, vendor, or ASP will work best.

In this part, I discuss some accounting techniques to help you justify your project to the bean counters, some ways of creating and evaluating specifications to help choose the proper solution, and ways to make the purchasing ordeal a bit easier. Or, if you happen to be a bean counter, you can find out how hard IT people work to convince you to let them have more stuff.

Chapter 4

Calculating ROI for Your Anti-Spam and Anti-Spyware Measures

. . . .

In This Chapter

▶ Doing the ABCs of Activity-Based Costing

▶ Working with fixed and variable costs

▶ Looking at security in terms of e-mail volume, employee productivity, and risk avoidance

▶ Justifying anti-spam measures in qualitative terms

▶ Justifying anti-spyware measures

. . . .

*I*n the modern business enterprise, few things are as controversial as calculating a return on investment (ROI) for any investment in information security. That topic is known as Return on Security Investment (ROSI).

Here are some reasons why such a return is hard to calculate:

> ✔ **Did it happen?** Security expenditures don't often save money directly; instead, they're geared to *prevent* the occurrence of costly incidents. Unfortunately, if the organization *isn't* attacked, you can't very well put incidents that didn't happen in the financial statement — even though *spending* for security has to be accounted for. Businesses hate to pay for things (most things) that don't happen.

> ✔ **Is the prevention measure effective?** It can be difficult to prove that a given security mechanism (for instance, anti-spyware software) has actually *prevented* any particular security incident. Even if it *was* possible to prove, it would still be difficult to quantify the expense of the incident had it occurred.

> ✔ **How vulnerable is the company?** The decision to invest in information security has more to do with risk management than with return-on-investment decisions. Risk-management methods vary from business to business — from highly structured and quantified to qualitative measures and assessments of probabilities to gut feel.

✔ **What did that security incident cost the company?** The cost of a security incident in terms of time spent (even if accurate data is available) represents cash that the organization would have spent anyway. For instance, suppose an employee who earns $50 per hour spends four hours handling an incident. The organization did not have to fork over another $200 out of its treasury. The organization was going to pay the employee anyway, but he or she would have been doing something else instead — maybe some task that had nothing to do with security, but which the organization already considers productive (and would rather pay for). For that matter . . .

✔ **Do these security measures hurt productivity?** Productivity in the information systems and technology business is really hard to measure, especially over short periods of time. Anyone who has attempted to build an Activity-Based Costing model is familiar with the struggles involved in trying to determine the cost of any employee's time — not to mention the *value* of the employee's time!

Okay, maybe your organization doesn't attempt to justify security investments — or *any* investments. Spam is costly even if the costs are hard to pin down. This chapter still gives you needed insight, even if you aren't the person who signs the checks.

The next several sections look at suggested models for estimating the cost of spam in your organization. You are not bound to choose one at the exclusion of all the others. Do what works. You are free to pick and choose whatever you think will accomplish your goal of justifying an investment in something — software, hardware, really big flyswatters, anything! — that will effectively block spam and spyware.

Firewalls and fire extinguishers

My good friend Scott Jackson and I had a conversation about Security ROI several years ago, and he asked me a simple question that has stayed in the forefront ever since: *What is the ROI of a fire extinguisher?* In many heated debates on ROSI since then, I have asked this question, and it nearly always silences the crowd.

Granted, fire extinguishers are required by law in most localities, but if they weren't, most businesses would have them anyway. Few executives would argue about purchasing fire extinguishers, but why do they put up resistance when it comes to investment in information security? I can think of two reasons:

✔ Fire is tangible, and it causes direct, devastating, and immediate damage to the business.

✔ Security incidents are intangible. In fact, to a great degree, the information systems that security mechanisms are protecting are also intangible.

Understanding Activity-Based Costing

Before you can get into any in-depth discussion on the cost of spam, you need a methodology that can turn statistics into cost estimates. Here's one: Activity-Based Costing, or ABC. You start with the total cost shelled out for a given resource (usually a *human* resource, but it could be a technical infrastructure, too), and then make reasonable estimates of how much time the (ahem) resource spends performing specific activities. Tweak, bash, and otherwise adjust the estimate till it fits your reality pretty well. Then you can come up with fairly good numbers for estimating the cost of each activity. A few common examples show how ABC works. . . .

Helpdesk example

Suppose you need to find out how much it costs the IT helpdesk to answer user questions that have to do with getting rid of excessive popup windows.

Four employees, who earn an average of $18 per hour, staff the helpdesk. The HR department has provided a "fully loaded" (taxes, benefits, and so on) factor of 1.36 for the business. This means you multiply the average salary of $18 per hour times 1.36 to factor in taxes, benefits, vacation time, the executive washroom, and so on, to arrive at a more accurate cash expenditure for an employee.

Of the 6,440 incoming phone calls that the helpdesk received last month, 484 were related to popup windows. So how much did popups cost the helpdesk last month? A little fast arithmetic tells the tale:

1. **Calculate the total helpdesk labor cost:**

   $18/hr × 40 hrs/week × 4.33 weeks/mo × 4 employees × 1.36 (factor)

   Total helpdesk Labor cost for four employees comes to $16,959.74 per month.

2. **Calculate the portion of the total cost just for calls that deal with popup window complaints:**

   $16,959.74 × 484 / 6,440

   For four employees, it comes to $1,274.61 per month. This is how much it costs the company to deal with popups.

Sounds like a story problem, doesn't it? Okay, I grant you that it may seem simplistic as an approach to the real world. But it's adjustable: You can make Activity-Based Costing as simple or as complex as you can tolerate.

Activity-Based Costing is a model

The point of Activity-Based Costing is not to calculate *direct* expense for an activity, but to arrive at a better — and quantitative — understanding of how much various activities cost the organization. Like weather forecasting and risk analysis, ABC is a *model* that helps to make something abstract a little more tangible, namely the *allocation* of the cost of an activity.

Cost-of-e-mail example

Suppose a department's general manager wants to know the cost associated with e-mail traffic on the company's Internet data circuit.

Not a bad idea — after all, the company in this example coughs up $8,640 a month for that data circuit. It gets a lot of use — inbound Web traffic to a public Web server, outbound Web access by company employees, e-mail, and other traffic.

A network engineer puts a sniffer program on the Internet connection and has it count packet types over a three-day period. The results look reasonable enough:

E-mail	48 percent
Inbound Web traffic	29 percent
Outbound Web traffic	18 percent
Miscellaneous	5 percent

The general manager calculates that the e-mail's share of the circuit cost is 48 percent of $8,640, or $4,147.20.

Upon seeing those same figures, however, the network engineer remarks that the cost of e-mail is probably *more* than 48 percent if you base it on the byte count instead of on the packet count. Out goes the sniffer again, for three more days; some different results come back:

E-mail	54 percent
Inbound Web	22 percent
Outbound Web	12 percent
Miscellaneous	12 percent

Calculated this way, e-mail's share of the circuit is 54 percent of $8,640, or $4,665.60.

Which is the correct figure? Arguably, either could be approximately correct. But you could also tweak the answer by taking time into account in other ways — for example, these:

- ✔ **How about a longer time to check?** You could run that sniffer for a week or more to see whether you get a statistically different result. (Maybe the general manager had only three days to get an answer.)

- ✔ **Was the time of year relevant?** During the holidays (for example), the cost could be greater or less, depending on how many employees take vacations, as well as whether business use of e-mail during the time of the measurement was representative of average use over the entire year. You may want data from a more "typical" time of year.

As simple as ABC?

With these examples, you see that Activity-Based Costing is little more than taking the total cost of a resource and calculating the proportions of the cost, function by function. This is, however, often easier said than done. It's more typical to see an ABC exercise done over a large department that has a great number of complex costs associated with it — such as leasing, depreciation, reserves, and stock on hand (for starters). ABC can become complex in a hurry.

Understanding Fixed and Variable Costs

In the cost-of-e-mail example in the preceding section, someone might erroneously argue that reducing the volume of e-mail will have an impact on the cost of the data circuit. Estimating the cost of activities requires an additional dimension, the understanding of fixed costs and variable costs.

Fixed costs are those costs that do not vary from one period (say, a month) to the next. Some examples of fixed costs are

- ✔ **Data circuits:** Telco circuits such as T-1s and DSL are usually billed at fixed costs regardless of usage.

- ✔ **Depreciation:** Generally, this is a fixed amount each month over a period of time, although from one year to the next the amount may vary. Still, most consider depreciation a fixed cost. It's predictable.

- ✔ **Equipment leases:** You generally pay a fixed rate per month for leased computers and network equipment, whether you use them or not.

Variable costs are called that because, well, they vary. They go up or down in response to how you use a resource. Examples of variable costs for resources (other than human) are

- **Electricity:** You pay only for the electrons that you permit the public utility to pump through your lights and equipment.
- **Water:** You pay for what you use.
- **Downloadable ring tones:** Ditto.

For instance, if you have a T-1 circuit connecting your organization to the Internet, its cost is the same whether you use it as your Web server's primary and highly used Internet connection, or if it's the seldom-used backup connection. For some higher-speed connections, you might be paying extra for sustained high activity, in which case the data circuit becomes a variable cost associated directly with how much you use it.

Understanding fixed and variable costs is important. You need to know the difference between the two so that you can better understand the cost of spam, spyware, or almost anything else.

Volume-of-E-Mail Model

A common method used to calculate the cost of spam is to determine the total cost for processing inbound Internet mail, and then figure out spam's share of that cost.

Using industry statistics

There are reliable and consistent statistics available for the volume of e-mail on the Internet that is spam. Whether or not the stats surprise you, they're fairly disgusting:

- According to Postini, Inc., about 77 percent of the e-mail messages that businesses receive are spam. That is an average figure, based on actual numbers of messages counted over a long period of time for thousands of their corporate clients.
- Gartner reports that 60 to 75 percent of its clients' incoming e-mail is spam.
- Other organizations cite similar numbers, usually between 60 and 80 percent. Because this is all an approximation anyway, these numbers are adequate for the moment.

So what can you do with this (besides hold your nose)? For starters, if you know how many inbound messages you get from the Internet every day, then you can estimate how many of those messages are spam.

You should be prepared to explain whether your organization's numbers are different from those cited here, and why. That difference may depend on the role of e-mail in your organization — and whether you're in a type of business that might skew the statistics way up or way down. Some businesses attract spam just by being what they are and doing what they do (for example, Microsoft — in particular, Bill Gates — gets quite a lot of spam messages a day).

Surveying your users

To be on the safe side, you may want to get empirical data on your organization's inbound spam volume before you bet your career on a particular percentage. If you go to management and proclaim that your company's percentage of incoming spam is exactly 80 percent (or 70 percent, or whatever), your figures may get sneered at (whether or not the skepticism is well founded). It may be best to do some sleuthing on your own, collect some hard facts on the volume of spam, and have them ready when you argue for spending hard cash.

Of course, if your organization has no anti-spam capability in place to use as a measuring tool, it's hard to gather the facts you need. But you don't want to just *guess*, do you? Some people are comfortable with guessing about important things, but I'm not (and I don't think you are). One possible solution might be to download some evaluation copies of a desktop-centric spam filter for a randomly chosen set of individuals, and let the program run on their systems for a month. Then collect the data, sharpen your pencil, and see where your organization stands. (Hey, I didn't say it would be easy. But if you're starting to think you should have paid more attention to those story problems in your high school algebra class, you're on the right track.)

Estimating your e-mail costs

Your organization's total cost of e-mail probably includes most of the following:

- ✔ E-mail server hardware
- ✔ E-mail server software
- ✔ A portion of the costs associated with network devices (installing, maintaining, upgrading, replacing, and so on)
- ✔ A portion of a system administrator's time

You could (of course) dig deeper into the details, and calculate things like rack space in the data center, backup media, and utility costs. I can tell you, it's easy to go overboard with this task. You've got to balance accuracy against the time it takes to figure out the most reliable numbers. The following general steps can get you started:

1. **Use Activity-Based Costing (explained in the earlier section, "Understanding Activity-Based Costing") or another model to estimate overall e-mail costs.**

   There is one rub: Your total cost of e-mail probably includes three processing chores the server has to do:

   - E-mail arriving from the Internet

   - E-mail being sent *to* the Internet

   - E-mail being sent among individual accounts inside the organization

   The latter two aren't part of the volume of spam (I hope). If spam *is* originating from your organization, you'll need to identify the source and put better protective measures in place such as stronger firewall rules, more reliable antivirus software, spyware filters, and intrusion detection. A good defense in depth is so important that I devote an entire chapter to it — see Chapter 13.

2. **Distinguish between fixed costs and variable costs.**

   For instance, if you have a T-1 circuit connecting your organization to the Internet, you can't very well claim that you'll save on circuit costs (which are fixed) if you block spam. There are two reasons for this:

   - You're paying a flat rate for your T-1, whether you use 10 percent or 80 percent of its capabilities.

   - You're probably going to be blocking spam at *your* end of the T-1.

   This second item is probably less obvious — but it means that blocking spam won't help ease your T-1 workload unless you install a device for that purpose at your telco or ISP — on the *far* end of the T-1 — incurring more cost (yikes). This was a trick question (sorry) but it shows how twisty this topic can get.

3. **Take into account the volume of storage that your server must provide for incoming e-mail.**

   You could work out the numbers and argue that, at the very least, you could *defer investment* in additional e-mail server storage capacity if you could just eliminate all that incoming spam. (Just be prepared to say for how long.)

Employee-Productivity Model

Employee productivity in many companies is about as easy to grasp as a wet, wriggling fish. There is often disagreement on the *meaning* of employee productivity — especially when you're dealing with salaried, project-oriented employees. Still, I offer arguments for two well-understood scenarios: the cost of wasted time and the cost of additional IT support calls — both arguably caused by spam and spyware.

Estimating wasted time

When an employee receives spam, it's going to sit there in her inbox until she can take the time necessary to perform a cursory examination and determine whether it's spam or a real message. This assessment may take place in the blink of an eye, or — more likely — it will take at least a few moments or longer. (How long depends a lot on what part of the country you're from.) However you look at this, cleaning up spam does take a finite period of time for the average employee.

Estimating how long takes some real guesswork (or "chainsaw math" as my friend Karl calls the result of multiplying two SWAG numbers together). Before you fire up that chainsaw, you've got to get some sort of handle on the total volume of incoming spam; have a look at the earlier section, "Volume-of-E-Mail Model," for pointers on estimating e-mail costs.

To take a good shot at estimating employees' wasted time, I prefer to use a model that has two, or even three, types of responses to spam:

- **Quick delete.** Employee looks for a few seconds and decides that the message is spam and quickly deletes it. Say this takes ten seconds per message. You *could* talk me down to five, but let's say ten.

- **Let's look at this a minute.** Employees are either confused or intrigued. The employees might think the spam is for real (and if it's a sophisticated fake, can you blame them?), or perhaps they're seriously considering buying something from a spammer (there's no accounting for taste). Figure one minute of time spent in this case.

- **I'm mad as hell and I'm not going to take it anymore.** Employee is fed up with spam and calls the helpdesk, or gets up out of the cube to go strike up a BWM (B(ahem), Whine, Moan) conversation with a co-worker. Scientific estimates suggest that this ventilation takes about ten minutes.

Okay, how often are those responses stimulated? Here's where you have to figure out your company's volume of spam. (Jump back to the previous section and get some numbers; then come back here.) The number you're after is just a total volume of spam messages in a day, week, or month.

I'm going to do more of that chainsaw math — and get completely arbitrary here for the sake of argument. Say that 0.1 percent of spam messages are going to cause "I'm mad" responses (and maybe 0.1 percent is high), 5 percent will cause "Let's look," and the rest (95 percent, I'll be optimistic, okay?) get the "Quick delete" response.

Okay, with this how-many-do-what figure in hand, say you've estimated that your organization gets 80,000 spam messages per month. Assigning the percentages gives you these results:

$80,000 \times 0.1\% = 80$ messages in the "I'm mad" category

$80,000 \times 5\% = 4,000$ messages in the "Let's look" category

$80,000 \times 94.9\% = 75,920$ messages in the "Quick delete" category

Next, multiply the number of messages times the minutes that each category consumes, like this:

80 messages $\times$ 10 minutes = 800 minutes

4,000 messages $\times$ 1 minute = 4,000 minutes

75,920 messages $\times$ 10 seconds = 12,653 minutes

Adding up these figures gives you a total of 17,453 minutes of wasted time per employee, or about 290 hours of wasted time per month. That's 37 days, or about six weeks of one full-time employee's time!

Turning hours into dollars

In the past, I have taken this estimate one step farther and turned the figure from hours into dollars. If your HR department likes you, perhaps they'll provide you with a "fully loaded average monthly compensation" figure, an average for the entire company. If they don't, you'll have to make an educated guess.

No, *fully loaded* doesn't mean somebody was estimating compensation after staying too long at the bar; I'm talking about all the costs that an organization incurs from direct payroll and benefits (tax withholding, medical coverage, and so on). If you have to guess at this total, here's a way to get a shot-in-the-dark figure: Take your average monthly compensation figure (wherever you got it from), and multiply it by 1.35. What you get is close enough for this purpose. (Remember, I'm talking about wasted time: The 1.35 factor is probably the most accurate figure in this entire calculation.) Say you think the average employee's monthly compensation is $2,400. Multiply that times 1.35, and the average fully loaded compensation comes to an estimated $3,240.

Cost and value are not the same

Remember that productivity is considered a *soft cost* — you won't actually see the bank account shrink or grow by the amount of dollars used to describe it. On the other hand, an executive knows that the *value* of an employee's total compensation exceeds her salary figure — it had better, or else the company is losing money.

Okay, go back to the 290 hours — roughly 37 days, or 1.68 man-months. To turn the man-months into dollars, multiply 1.68 times that fully-loaded-compensation figure ($3,240). What comes up is $5,443 in lost productivity per month. That's $65,316 per year.

Additional support calls because of spam and spyware-induced problems

If your IT helpdesk is equipped with the tools needed to generate statistics — and if your helpdesk people are properly categorizing support calls — then it should be pretty simple to get a tally of the number of support calls related to spam and spyware.

You're not out of the woods yet, though. It would also be helpful if you had some idea of the average amount of time needed to handle each common type of support call. Example: 2 minutes for a password reset, 23 minutes for a virus, or 46 minutes for "Is the power cord plugged in?" You're almost done.

Finally, you can use Activity-Based Costing (described earlier in the chapter) to turn "How much does it cost me to run the helpdesk every month?" into "How much do spam and spyware calls cost?" You can perform this magic by calculating the proportion of time spent for spam and spyware calls and comparing them against everything else the helpdesk has to do.

Aha — so *this* is why you had to do story problems in school. (Just don't get nostalgic for them, okay?)

Risk-Avoidance Model

This section describes a rather more slippery — but still vital — part of estimating the impact of spam on your organization. Here I talk about the secondary effects of spam: things that can result if spam does manage to infiltrate.

Some may consider this fear mongering, but that is not my intention. As all well-rounded, think-out-of-the-box security professionals do, I must be mindful of all risks — the real risks — that organizations face if they fail to stop spam (or viruses, hackers, spyware, and similar beasties). This is rather like Ebenezer Scrooge asking the Ghost of Christmas Yet to Come, "Is this what *may* happen, or is this what *will* happen?" That's largely up to you. What I point out here are additional risks associated with spam. Take a closer look at those that fit your situation and recycle the rest.

You can do a similar exercise for spyware, although it may be a little trickier because of spyware's stealthiness. I concentrate on spam in this section because its risks are more tangible and visible.

Risks from chronic exposure to obscene, violent, and hate material

Many people object vigorously to the content of pornographic, violent, and hate spam. Many porn spam messages contain explicit words in their subject lines and graphic photos in their contents. Just imagine them showing up on somebody's screen in the average cube farm — even once. And how about more than once?

Let's face it: Repeated exposure to this material is bound to offend, embarrass, and anger some employees to the point that they complain — especially if the organization is doing too little to block spam. Especially offended employees (all it takes is one) may resort to the civil legal system for relief, on the grounds that they should not have to be frequently subjected to material they find offensive (you may recall the story line behind the famous phrase, "I'm mad as hell, and I'm not going to take it any more!").

An organization that doesn't do enough to stop spam may find itself as a defendant in a lawsuit, on the grounds that the workplace has become a place of hostility or harassment. (I can picture the cross-examination now: "Mr. Thompson, as IT Director, isn't it true that your department did *nothing* to stop the pornographic spam that was arriving in Ms. Winter's inbox every day?") Personally, I would never want to face this kind of a cross-examination.

Risks from Web-site-borne malicious code

Of all risks associated with spam, that of malicious payloads (viruses, worms, Trojan horses) is probably best understood. Viruses have been around for many years, and nearly all technology-savvy folks and businesspeople clearly understand that malicious code must be blocked, and why. (For openers, it increases downtime and threatens ongoing business operations — which, in turn, can easily jeopardize profitability and efficiency.)

This is probably one of the best approaches to take for justifying the investment in anti-spyware as well as anti-spam.

How deep a defense is needed?

But if an enterprise has antivirus software on all end-user workstations — even on the e-mail server — why would it also need to block spam to prevent viruses?

The answer may surprise you: With infection rates under 10 percent, it does *not* make good business sense from a purely financial perspective to acquire a spam-blocking solution if your main objective is to eliminate malicious code. On the other hand, viruses and their Trojan horse and worm cousins are so damaging and disruptive that a defense in depth is the only sane strategy worth adopting. Defense-in-depth disciples should read Chapter 13 for a more complete discourse on the topic.

Well, okay, perhaps this is sort of a trick question. But I bring up the link between spam and malicious code here to help you prepare for the variety of questions you are bound to receive from businesspeople. They are just trying to understand the problem.

Blocking Web-site-borne malicious code

I have to bring up another topic that may not be popular, but then, viruses are unpleasant in the first place. I want to make sure you have an accurate understanding of the spam problem as it relates to malicious code present on Web sites.

Here's the story: A spam-blocking solution will block most spam messages that are trying to entice users to visit Web sites that contain malicious code. (That's the upside.) Unfortunately, that spam-blocking solution can't prevent a user from accessing a Web site cited in any spam messages that *do* sneak through — and if that site contains malicious code, look out.

To effectively reduce this risk, most enterprises must implement an antivirus, anti-spyware, and a spam-blocking solution. Together, these solutions will block most of the risk associated with malicious code in e-mail and on Web sites — but that's only a partial solution to this problem. You also need to consider phishing scams, as I explain in the next section.

Risks from phishing scams

Phishing scams are diabolically clever messages that look like official notices from financial institutions and other organizations. Whether they seem to be bullying, wheedling, warning, or notifying, these messages have a common theme: They are trying to trick the recipient into visiting a Web site that asks for sensitive information — in particular, information (such as credit cards, bank accounts, PINs, passwords, and tax identification numbers) that mean easy money for somebody dishonest.

The method of enticement varies, but common themes include

- ✓ **Fraud prevention:** (Hah!) The phishing-scam message will tell the recipient that some fraudulent activity is suspected on his or her credit card or bank account, and that the recipient must log into a special Web site to "verify" the account information (by *providing* account information).

- ✓ **Mortgage application:** Phishing-scam messages claim that the recipient's mortgage has already been "approved," and hey, all you have to do is provide some "simple" information.

- ✓ **Low-rate credit cards:** Messages claim that the recipient "qualifies" for a low-rate credit card, and all they have to do is furnish some verification information.

Spam-blocking solutions are effective at blocking most scam messages, but probably not *all* of them. This is true of this and other types of spam, but you knew that.

Qualitative Justifications

Here's where I discuss more of the touchy-feely justifications for blocking spam. Put your slide rules (slide rules?) and pocket calculators away, and put the left side of your brain to sleep: This is a right-brain section.

The justifications here are useful, but trickier to present to some organizations. They play more to the emotions of the organization's decision-makers than to their pocketbooks.

My suggestion is that you find a *quantitative* means for justifying investment in a spam-blocking solution, and rely primarily on hard facts to underpin your presentation. Use these qualitative ideas more as "talking points" — things to bring up in conversations and stimulate discussion. Keep 'em out of print. At any rate, here they are . . .

Executive frustration

If any of the folks in Mahogany Row are getting spam, you may be able to appeal to one or more of the C-level victims and have them lobby the CIO (or whoever you think will foot the bill) for a spam-blocking solution. If you don't associate directly with the executives in your organization, I'm not suggesting you begin now. Talk with your boss or with someone else who you think can work this angle for you.

If you're a little unsure of how to approach the executive management in your organization, I suggest you look around for a used copy of *Office Politics For Dummies* by Marilyn Moats Kennedy (it's out of print) or *Gray Matters: The Workplace Survival Guide* by Bob Rosner, Allan Halcrow, and John Lavin (both books published by Wiley).

Employee grumblings

If your company is especially hard-hit by spam, then it might be easy to arouse grassroots support for doing something about the onslaught. By itself, rabble-rousing may not actually win you anything, but you may be able to enlist the support of spam victims to build a qualitative justification (or even get their permission to observe incoming spam at their workstations, which can help you generate numbers).

While I'm *not* suggesting that you whip up an employee frenzy or lead a torch-light parade to the boardroom, you may be able to get the support you need to build a solid case for blocking spam.

Learning through networking

One of the best ways to learn more about spam (and spyware) problems is to network with IT professionals in other organizations. What problems are *they* having, and how have they addressed it? There is almost always someone who is farther ahead of the curve than you, from whom you can learn from by stories of his or her successes and failures.

Don't wait for a major conference to network with your peers: Find ways to network in your local community — at local chapter meetings of national or international organizations such as ISSA, ISACA, and IEEE, you might find colleagues facing many of the same problems as yourself. You might also consider joining a virtual community at `http://groups.yahoo.com` or `http://groups.google.com`, to name just a couple.

Models for Justifying Spyware Filters

There are many reasons that can be used to justify investment in spyware filters; I describe some of them in the following sections.

Helpdesk support calls

Several forms of spyware are disruptive in nature: They interfere with Web browser settings such as helper page configuration (the sites that the browser visits for searching and other functions), the default home page, and unwanted toolbars. Spyware can also make Web browsers unstable, causing them to crash or exhibit other unexpected behavior.

All of these phenomena cost the organization in the form of additional helpdesk calls. It's not just the number of calls, but also the time spent on each one until the problem is solved. A PC support team lacking tools and knowledge might spend a disproportionately high amount of time solving spyware problems. This takes time away from solving routine support issues. The result is that either the PC support team takes longer than before to solve problems, or the cost of PC support increases because of the additional support staff required to handle the increased workload.

The key to identifying and quantifying helpdesk support calls due to spyware is a good trouble-ticket application, or other effective means for tracking all support calls. You can use Activity-Based Costing to develop a reliable figure for "how much do spyware support calls cost" by calculating the proportion of time spent for spyware calls against everything else.

Potential loss of corporate information

Though rarely seen, spyware can take the direct approach to compromising corporate data, and just start e-mailing documents back to the place that spawned it. While this isn't as common as other methods, I do see it in situations where a specific company or industry, usually banking, is targeted by some spyware. Rather than just send documents out at random, the spyware even looks at filenames or contents for things that look interesting, such as `Q4PnL.doc` or `SECsomething.doc`.

Some spyware, such as a key logger, is designed to capture keystroke and mouse activity for the purpose of giving the key logger's owner access to sensitive information, generally for financial gain. In the corporate environment, users enter plenty of user IDs and passwords in order to access sensitive information inside the company itself as well as information in other locations. Some examples include

 ✔ **VPN user ID and password.** When a user accesses the corporate network via remote access/VPN, the key logger's owner can use the recorded user ID and password to also access the internal network.

✔ **ASP Web sites.** ASP, or Application Service Provider, software is a popular alternative to an organization developing custom software or hosting off-the-shelf software. Typically, corporate users must log in to the ASP site using a user ID and password. The ASP software could be just about anything, from financial analysis to project planning to exchange of marketing or engineering information — in other words, potentially the most sensitive corporate secrets.

✔ **E-mail.** Any e-mail sent from a user to anyone else inside or outside the organization would be captured and sent to the key logger's owner.

✔ **Internal applications.** Virtually anything a user would do inside of a corporate or government entity is subject to being recorded by a key logger. Everything from financial results to corporate mergers to potential scandals may be recorded by the key logger and sent to its unsavory owner.

Potential loss of custodial data

In some cases, your company may be in custodial possession of information that doesn't belong to you, but to your clients or partners. The compromise of this information in many cases is far more damaging to your company than just losing your *own* corporate data to a spyware program. In some cases, such as health care and banking, this third party data is protected by law, and the exposure results in direct civil liability, while in other cases such as patent law firms, the data itself could be worth hundreds of millions of dollars.

In every case, if the data wasn't yours to lose in the first place, the customer or associate isn't going to be very pleased when it gets mailed to them along with an extortion letter. At the very least, it will cause the end of the business relationship, at most some pretty serious fines and weeks or months in court.

Potential loss of employees' private information

If you just read the preceding section on the potentially damaging result of a key logger in revealing sensitive corporate information, then you may have also thought, what about employees who do their online banking, purchasing, or casino wagering using their employer's computer? Well, the key logger neither knows the difference nor cares, but instead just records everything and sends it all home to be exploited in the comfort of the hacker's living room.

Add to that one additional risk: An employee whose sensitive information is recorded by a key logger and subsequently exploited might have cause to sue the employer for damages for failing to detect or prevent the key logger's activity.

This alone is reason enough for an organization to stress in its corporate security policy that all information on corporate workstations is the property of the corporation, and privacy of employees' personal data is not guaranteed. Further, employees' personal use of corporate workstations could put corporate data at risk of compromise.

Chapter 5

Developing the Battle Plans

. . . .

In This Chapter

▶ Assessing your situation

▶ Knowing your business objectives

▶ Developing and refining requirements

▶ Re-engineering business processes

▶ Defining roles & responsibilities

. . . .

This chapter describes a step-by-step process that you can follow to get from "We need to solve our malware problem" to "We've got a plan." By that point, you'll have a good understanding of your present architecture and be able to identify viable solutions, roles, and responsibilities, as well as which business processes the plan will affect.

As in other parts of this book, I suggest this approach because it has worked for me and for others. If it looks promising, you can opt to borrow some of these ideas and integrate them into your own process. If, after reading, you wonder whether I was working in some alternate universe when I wrote this chapter, well, you can still benefit from other chapters in this book. And what's here still works.

Assessing Your Situation

"Know thyself," said the ancient Greeks — and it's even truer of modern information systems: Before you can begin considering solutions to your malware problem, you need to be familiar with what you already have — specifically, in these areas:

> ✔ **Architecture:** This concept includes not only how your computing machinery is laid out, set up, and configured, but also how information flows through it.

✔ **Workload and capacity:** This concept involves knowing how much work your system can handle, how much data it can store, and what it's handling now. The usual techie word for this ever-elusive quality is *bandwidth*.

✔ **Your organization's business objectives:** What is it working toward? How do you get there from here? What's in the way?

Know these and you can expect to make informed choices — and successfully combat spam in your enterprise.

Knowing thy present architecture

A keen understanding of your organization's e-mail architecture begins with the underlying network architecture, down to the nuts and bolts. A reasonable way to get there is to create good, up-to-date diagrams of the entire organization's e-mail environment — both logical and physical. Why?

Call it a philosophy: Before you go tweaking an information system, you have to understand it thoroughly. And adding a spam-filtering layer is a major tweak. Installing anti-spyware is not trivial either. Philosophy aside, know how the systems work before you start hanging new stuff on them, and you're less likely to break something.

When it comes to blocking spam and spyware, you need accurate and complete logical and physical diagrams that describe the system from end to end — from the Internet (and other entry/exit points) through firewalls to mail servers, and from there to end-user workstations. It's also a good idea to know where your antivirus solutions are placed. Your spam- or spyware-blocking solution *may be* integrated with your antivirus solution as one program that performs multiple functions. If not, you have to make sure the programs work well together.

Logical architecture

A *logical architecture* is, in effect, a diagram that illustrates a system's functional components and how information flows among them. It's the kind of diagram one would draw for someone who listens to your description of the information system and then asks, "How does it work?"

You'll need the logical architecture for a number of reasons. Try these for openers:

✔ It's probably the most effective way for you to gain a solid understanding of complex environments such as e-mail.

✔ It's a convenient baseline by defining today's architecture, which you can preserve for posterity.

✔ It's a handy point of reference during conversations with colleagues and vendors, which helps get everyone on the same page, as it were.

✔ It's a starting point for the creative process of imaging various solutions at the logical level. That exercise gives you a preliminary feel for which of the potential solutions look viable.

Figure 5-1 shows a logical architecture for a typical medium-size corporate e-mail infrastructure. Yours, of course, will probably vary from this.

Figure 5-1:
A logical architecture that illustrates how the system architecture functions.

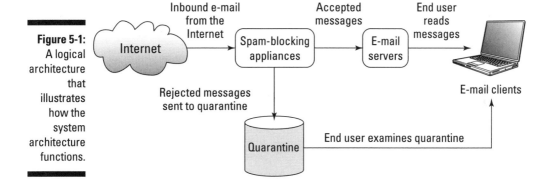

Physical architecture

A *physical architecture* is a diagram that takes the logical architecture to a level of greater detail by adding three important elements:

✔ **It identifies the actual components in the system.** That means (basically) specifying whether the components are servers or other hardware components, software components, networks, or other workings.

✔ **It shows *how many* of each component actually exist to perform certain functions.** For instance, a logical diagram may include a component labeled "e-mail server," which physically is two front-end logic processors and two back-end database servers. This is a detail that may be unnecessary in the logical architecture, but essential in the physical architecture.

✔ **It points out *where* each component is located.** In larger organizations where offices exist in several cities or countries, it is relevant to know with greater precision where all of the components are located.

Not to say that a logical diagram will gloss over these specifics, but a physical diagram *must* include them — in detail.

As with logical architecture, you must have a detailed physical architecture in order to be able to properly understand your environment and make sound decisions on possible solutions. Without it you're bound to hit snags during or after implementation.

Figure 5-2 shows a sample physical architecture, which is actually a mapping from the logical architecture shown in Figure 5-1.

Figure 5-2:
A physical
architecture
provides
additional
details of an
information
system.

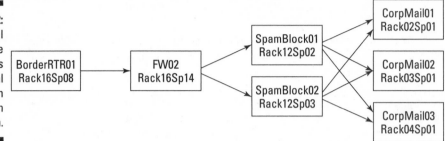

Knowing thy bandwidth

In addition to having good logical and physical diagrams, you need to be familiar with two other important characteristics of your e-mail environment: workload and capacity. These may sound the same — they are related aspects of a system's bandwidth — but what each one measures is quite different.

This whole concept gets complicated if you begin to think about measuring workload and capacity. Today you'e getting some known or unknown volume of spam, and in addition you may also be suffering under the load of Directory Service Attacks (DSAs), both of which are sapping away your Internet connection's strength.

By having this information about bandwidth, you can find a solution that's just the right size for your needs. You want to avoid overspending (on a larger solution than you need) or underspending (on a too-small solution that can't do the job) — and not discover the bad news until after implementation. Neither mistake is particularly palatable.

Workload

How much e-mail and other information flows through your organization — and which bits flow through what parts of the environment? That's the *workload* of the e-mail system. It is especially important to know the volume of e-mail that is flowing into the organization from external sources such as the Internet, as well as any direct (physical or logical) connections to other organizations. The more information on e-mail volume you have — over time — the likelier you will choose a solution of the appropriate size.

Your e-mail server should have some basic statistics available, such as number of messages processed per day, and perhaps also characters processed (usually expressed in KB or MB) per day. If you start kicking the tires with spam or spyware products, make sure you do any numerical comparisons "apples to apples" — in other words, using the same units of measure.

Capacity

You need a handle on how much information (mostly in the form of e-mail messages) your system can both transmit and store — throughout the entire environment. This is most important if you're dealing with network elements (servers, storage, or communication) that are already operating near their capacity. If you're in such a situation, you'll need to thoroughly understand the impact that a given spam-blocking solution will have on those elements: Will the elements be overloaded, or will the spam solution relieve the element of some of its workload? If you fail to take these issues into account now, your project runs a greater risk of failure, schedule disruption, or budget overruns.

Growth

Capacity is knowing what you are capable of handling right now. *Growth* is knowing your capacity at a given time in the future. Hopefully, you are measuring capacity at regular intervals so that you can make rough predictions on the capacity you will need in the future.

Knowing Your Business Objectives

Without a thorough understanding of your organization's activities and goals, you run the risk of creating more problems with a spam or spyware filter than you are solving. The bottom line here is that someone — you or someone else — needs to decide what constitutes spam or spyware in your organization. There are a few issues at stake here, including

- ✔ **Industry-related content.** If your organization is in the home mortgage business, for example, then a spam-blocking solution that relies upon common spam keywords (such as *home mortgage*) may block legitimate business messages that would clearly be spam for the rest of us. Likewise, a pharmaceutical company or medical office may be sending and receiving many business-related messages with the words *Viagra* or *Cialis* contained in mail messages.

- ✔ **E-mail from netizens.** If your organization implements a spam-blocking solution that relies heavily on *whitelists* (lists of known individuals who send real mail to you), anyone who isn't on the list can't send a message in. Persons who receive e-mail from citizens on the Internet may find that many of their messages are being blocked.

> ✔ **Personal e-mail.** Almost universally, organizations permit their employ-
> ees to conduct a minimal amount of personal communications using the
> organization's e-mail system. Arguably, this is preferable to higher-risk
> alternatives, such as Web-based e-mail, because many Web-based e-mail
> providers don't scan incoming messages for viruses.
>
> ✔ **Spyware or useful utility.** Some of the spyware out there actually bun-
> dles itself with a useful utility of some sort, to make it attractive to
> download and run. Most folks will forego the utility if they are actually
> informed of the real nature of the spyware, but it's best to be clear about
> this.

Without knowledge of the potential impact that a malware-filtering solution
will have on your business, you risk dooming your project to failure. It has to
do the job right for the system you have if it is to perform to the satisfaction
of your end-users.

Developing Requirements

Blocking malware at the corporate level isn't just a matter of marching off
willy-nilly to buy a slew of hardware and software. First you have to convince
your organization's powers-that-be of three things: That the problem exists,
that you know how to solve it, and that they can afford to solve it. When
you are familiar with your current environment, you can begin to develop
requirements — a list of must-have characteristics that define the ideal solution for your organization. I discuss both functional and technical requirements in this section. All of which leads to something you're (ahem) required
to know. . . .

What is a requirement?

Setting requirements is an essential skill; project teams have to have a
common understanding of what they're looking for in a solution to a technical problem. (Hey, if you want to block spam, you've got to get assertive. . . .)

"Mr. Scott, what *is* a requirement?"

"Aye, Captain. A *requirement* is an imperative statement that describes a
desired characteristic of a system."

Here are some typically terse examples:

✔ The solution must accommodate delegated administration, so that administrators can manage data associated with their respective business units.

✔ The solution must permit individual users to choose the desired level of spam filtering.

✔ The solution must provide buttons in Microsoft Outlook clients for functions such as Mark as Spam, Mark as Not Spam, and Manage Spam Preferences.

As you can see, these statements are pretty specific. But what are they *for* (besides making an I-mean-business impression)? There are four main practical reasons:

✔ **Consensus among team members:** Stakeholders and decision-makers have to agree on what they need in a spam-blocking solution, select it, acquire it, and make it work. These folks have a legitimate interest in developing and agreeing to requirements (whether they know it or not). Getting them involved helps ensure that everyone has the same expectation. For more about requirements, check out Appendix B.

✔ **Vendor selection:** You send requirements to each candidate vendor, who will respond to each requirement in writing. This exchange of paper helps the project team choose a solution with confidence.

✔ **Testing and verification:** During the testing and acceptance period, you need to verify each requirement to confirm that a vendor's product performs as expected.

✔ **Keeping sight of the goal:** Requirements help you avoid wasting time on ideas that don't contribute to stated business objectives, or that even wander away from the original intent.

This brings up an important point about requirements. Rather than break into song, I decided to list what good requirements are:

✔ **Specific:** A requirement should clearly define only one characteristic, or even just a single perspective of a single characteristic.

✔ **Verifiable:** A requirement must be objectively verifiable. For example, a badly written requirement might read, "Solution must have a good user interface." (Uh, yeah. And what's *good,* exactly?) A better requirement (actually, a list of requirements) would describe the desired details of the user interface.

✔ **Unambiguous:** Anyone who reads the requirement must have the same understanding on the *meaning* of the requirement. For example, a badly written requirement might read, "Solution must run on Windows." (Okaaay — which *version?*) A better requirement would nail the version(s), as in, "Solution must run on Windows NT4 SP6a and Windows Server 2003."

✔ **Realistic:** A requirement must be rooted in what is *possible*. But even more importantly, it should represent a feature or capability that one or more candidate vendors actually *can* deliver. You ensure requirements are realistic by becoming familiar with many different solutions, and also by getting several people in your organization to read them and provide feedback.

✔ **Required:** Some requirements are less negotiable than others, but hopefully not too many, or else you'll have a difficult time finding a vendor who can meet them all. Don't expect any vendor to meet all of your requirements, unless you asked one of your vendors to write your requirements for you. Otherwise, what's important is identifying the few vendors who meet *many* of your requirements.

✔ **Optional:** Many requirements will be optional, or "nice to have."

There are several typical categories into which you will want to organize your requirements. I describe these categories in detail later in this chapter. You can find an entire collection of example requirements, as well as a little more discussion, in Appendix B.

Collecting and organizing requirements

Many enterprise projects have *hundreds* of requirements. Such a collection would be Mishmash City unless the items were grouped into a hierarchy, much like the chapters and sections of a book (or the "outlines" you may remember from grade school). When you have that hierarchy in place, all parties involved can work with the requirements more easily, regardless of their roles in the project.

Functional requirements

Functional requirements describe the details of how a product or solution should work, regardless of the technology. Well-written functional requirements will be completely technology-agnostic (that is, neutral to anything but what works). Examples of functional requirements look like these:

✔ The solution must provide a quarantine for each user who wishes to use one.

✔ The solution administrator must be able to specify which users are permitted to have a quarantine, and which may not.

✔ The solution shall update spyware database automatically using a user-defined schedule.

How much detail do I need?

Those of you who are new at developing requirements for big projects may be wondering, *How many requirements is enough? How many is too many?*

For openers, the answer depends upon the size of the organization and how much money, time, and effort are going into the project. The bigger the system, the bigger the project. Big projects, where the impact of even a small "surprise" may be significant, require more planning and requirements development than smaller projects.

There is no magic number of requirements that will do the job for all organizations. However, all desired functions in a malware-blocking solution must be clearly documented, one at a time, in whatever level of detail your organization requires. That could mean 10, 100, 1,000, or even more requirements! Just how big is your outfit getting here? (Opening an office on the moon, you say? You're gonna be busy.)

Remember, too, that you have to ask each vendor to respond to your requirements. A vendor may balk at responding if the number of requirements is large compared to the size of the project. It may take an engineer several hours to respond to an RFP (Request for Proposal), but if the potential business is small, the vendor may decide it's not worth the time.

Your best bet is to find an experienced project manager who has done one or more RFP or RFI (Request for Information) projects in the past — and who has a good feel for the amount of effort that is appropriate for your project.

> ✔ The solution must have the capability to create canned reports containing message statistics that include total message volume, total number of messages filtered, types of filtering used, and number of messages filtered by user.

You can see that each of these requirements neither mentions nor implies anything about Mac, PC, UNIX, or any other specific technology.

Technical requirements

Technical requirements describe characteristics of a solution in terms of what will run on the operating systems and hardware that the organization has chosen as its standard. These requirements help limit the operating cost for the solution (solutions on nonstandard platforms tend to require costly workarounds). Here are some examples of good technical requirements:

> ✔ The solution must run on Windows 2000 Server or Windows 2003 Server.
>
> ✔ The solution must run on SQL Server version 2000 or newer.
>
> ✔ The solution must support external authentication using Microsoft Active Directory.
>
> ✔ The solution should support 100MB or 1GB Ethernet.

Did you notice that the last requirement used the word *should* instead of *must?* This is a distinction that you need to recognize: Some requirements are "must have," others are "nice to have." Reserve the use of *must* and the like for components that your system can't get along without.

Business requirements

Business requirements define the characteristics you are looking for in a vendor itself. Given that spam and spyware aren't going away any time soon, your vendor has to have some staying power. Business requirements can help you objectively eliminate those vendors whose long-term viability is questionable. Another way to look at vendors' viability is to assess how well they can give (okay, sell) you what you need. Typical questions to ask include these:

- ✔ **Does the product do the job?** For that matter, will it evolve to meet the conditions of a changing online environment?

- ✔ **Does the vendor really support the product?** Often that means talking to a real person; voicemail (or e-mail, or online chat) alone just won't cut it.

- ✔ **Can the vendor customize the product or provide training when your people need it?** Different businesses have different needs, and even those needs change over time.

Be sure you include these issues in your business requirements — along with the fine-tuned requirements described in this section. Your mission, should you choose to accept it, is to zero in on a vendor with market maturity, a robust product, and outstanding support.

Sorry, I can't tell you the answer that will work for you. What your particular organization needs is highly dependent upon its size, the expertise of its IT staff, the technology already in place today, and how much risk it's willing to assume. I can, however, offer some pointers on quantifying risk and sharpening the detail of your business requirements. Read on.

Pricing requirements

There is more to pricing than unit cost. Here's where you get to have your say on the way pricing works. Perhaps you want to pay one price for users without quarantines, and other price for users with them. Or maybe you need to sublicense the solution to customers.

This is one of those creative areas where you find out how much a vendor is willing to work with you on a custom-built business deal. However, unless you truly have unique cost needs, don't make this requirement a deal-breaker. Otherwise you risk eliminating vendors that could provide a decent solution.

Support requirements

Here, again, is an opportunity to voice specific or unusual tech-support needs that may or may not be part of a typical vendor's offering. For instance, if many of your users are on the Indian subcontinent and your home office is on the other side of the planet, you still need "daytime" support for those users. Or perhaps a subset of your organization's users has a crying need for rapid response from a living, breathing engineer to accommodate them.

High-profile users who need some technical handholding are *not* "spoiled brats" (okay, not *always*). Even if they are, you still have to make sure the solution works for them.

Past performance

When you check out a vendor's past performance, you're looking for much more than references. Here's one place you can get quantitative. Some good measures for past performance include

- **Number of years the vendor has been in business:** Do you want to be the vendor's first customer, or are you more comfortable buying from a company that has been in business for a number of years? One advantage of buying from a vendor with few customers is that they are more likely to kiss your feet and wipe your windshield. Metaphorically speaking.

- **Number of existing customers:** Newer vendors (or solutions) may not have a large installed user base — yet — but may be attractive for other reasons. Again, you may or may not be averse to becoming an "early adopter" of some new bleeding-edge solution — it's a question of whether it fits your organization's culture. If it fills the bill, consider it. But get as much of a line on the solution's track record as you can.

- **How long the present product has been on the market:** Are you willing to take on a brand-new product, or would you rather purchase/use a product that has a proven track record? I can't tell you what you want, but you can probably come up with a good idea of your own here.

In addition to these specific requirements, you need to identify — and have frank conversations with — two or more reference clients.

Checking references

Done right, this part of the process isn't as easy as it sounds — but the information from references can add tremendous value to your vendor-selection process. The key to making good use of references is consistency. Here's a quick checklist of must-dos:

- Get more than one reference from each vendor.

- Get references from two or more vendors.

✔ Ask all the same questions of each reference.

✔ Thoroughly document the answers you get during reference calls.

✔ Reach the person at the reference client's site who can answer your questions.

I suggest building a chart to help you compare the answers you get from various vendors and clients. Side-by-side comparison makes it far easier to zero in on the nuances of your reference-check data.

Just like with requirements, you need to be well organized in order to make the best use of your reference calls. You need a list of specific questions made out in advance, or you'll end up talking about baseball, members of the opposite sex, or *real* computing "back in the day" of PDP-11's, punch cards, and — well, you know where *my* weakness is.

I am constantly amazed at how often a reference that a vendor thinks is good turns out to be not so good. Favorable reference calls are always nice to have — but if you are fortunate enough to have a reference who will tell you about the problems they've encountered, you get a more balanced picture. Use such information to discern a vendor's weak spots; take those into account.

Vendor profile

Some organizations are a little wary of purchasing an enterprise-class product from a company that made 2 million dollars last year. In my opinion, that is not taking risk-adversity too far. The reality is that most businesses (or individuals for that matter) need to purchase a product from companies that are big enough and have been around long enough to give you confidence that they'll still be in the game next year and the year after that. Whether the company still stands alone or has been acquired by or merged with one of the big boys, you have some assurance that it'll still be there.

Here's a start on your vendor-evaluation checklist:

✔ **Years in business.**

✔ **Number of enterprise customers and number of customers in the same vertical industry as your own.**

✔ **Annual sales.** It's reasonable to ask what a company's sales were for the previous year. However, there are two gotchas: First, you may be dealing with a private (not publicly held) company that does not otherwise disclose its annual earnings. You may have to settle for a ballpark value here.

✔ **Number of licensed users.** This is the aggregate total of N users from Company A, N users from Company B, and so forth. This gives you an idea of whether the vendor is selling to companies that are close to your size or not. It also tells you whether a customer deployed the vendor's product in its entire enterprise, or just 12 users in a lab. (The vendor is unlikely to volunteer the latter if that's the case.)

✔ **Size of largest customer.** It is important to have this data available so that you can see if you are a vendor's largest customer or not. If you are, you run a higher risk of reaching scalability or performance issues. Either of these two factors is likely to have impact on your budget, schedule, or both. Another consideration: Does the vendor have the capacity to support you?

✔ **Profiles of company officers and directors.** Here you are trying to ascertain the career maturity of the people in charge of the vendor company. You're looking for a confidence-builder here.

These requirements are a little less important if you are considering only larger companies as vendors, but far more important if you are considering newer, smaller companies.

Developing or Updating Policy

The addition of spam or spyware-blocking solutions may prompt you or others in the organization to consider adding new policies that both heighten the visibility of spam and spyware, and also define boundaries of "acceptable use" for e-mail and Internet usage. Remember, user behavior to some degree influences the degree of risk of spam and spyware. Just because you are implementing a solution to block spam or spyware (or both), users still need to know where the boundaries are. Just as the use of seatbelts in a car does not eliminate the need to drive responsibly, the addition of spam or spyware blockers should not give users license to "whistle past the graveyard" with e-mail and Internet usage.

Before you jump on the new-policy bandwagon, make sure you aren't walking into a minefield. Here are a few tips:

✔ Who is responsible for the development and enforcement of the policy? Do you know this person or group well?

✔ Can you convince the policymaker(s) that new policy is required? If not, get some higher-ups who can help to make your case.

✔ Does policy even matter in your organization? If policy is dusty, out-dated, or disregarded, it might not be worth your time anyway.

Chapter 19 delves into policy a lot more, in case you're the company's policy wonk.

Re-Engineering Business Processes

Who would have thought that dealing with some annoying e-mail or rogue ActiveX control would lead to such large issues? Believe it: In all likelihood, one or more of your business processes will change as a result of having implemented an enterprise-wide spam or spyware solution. As with other changes that have an impact on the organization, your best bet is to begin addressing these issues *now*. If you wait until after you've implemented spam- and spyware-blocking solutions, you'll need a larger bottle of aspirin.

I discuss a few typical business processes here, but your organization's list could be longer, shorter, or just different (different order doesn't count).

Managing user accounts

User Account Management (UAM) is the set of processes and procedures governing user accounts on your organization's information system — creating, maintaining, and (eventually) retiring individual accounts and their user IDs.

In an organization with more than several dozen users, the UAM process usually encompasses various procedures — request, approval, fulfillment, and notification — and includes a recordkeeping system. You not only have to know who's who, but also keep track of (and record) everything that transpires for each addition, change, or deletion. The goal is to prevent hackers and spammers from using old user accounts to create IT mayhem. (But you knew that.)

When an anti-malware solution is implemented in an organization, it will probably affect UAM processes and procedures, possibly on a surprisingly wide scale. For example, the spam-blocking application may add one or more steps to the configuration of every user's identity within the system. That can add up to some serious time commitments, and additional complexity, for your IT department.

Managing user workstations

The configuration of end-user workstations may get a bit more complex to accommodate an enterprise spam- or spyware-blocking solution. This may be true even if the solution is entirely centralized. For instance, if Microsoft Outlook or Eudora uses a few new DLLs to support extra toolbar buttons for blocking or unblocking specific messages, every user's installation will need those DLLs. Also, the workstation-side e-mail storage may include an extra folder named "Spam" or "Junk." (Resist the urge to name it something more, ahem, colorful.) Internet Explorer may contain additional settings — visible or not — that are used in conjunction with a spyware-blocking solution.

Even if these additions are subtle, you may need to consider implementing them on your standard PC images or setup scripts. The idea is to ensure that end-users who are issued new/upgraded computers have all the same nuts and bolts that they need to make the solution work correctly the first time they use it (and every time thereafter).

Helpdesk

Every organization can be assured that any spam- or spyware-blocking solution will impact the helpdesk. For sure, you can count on a lot of extra support calls after a spam-blocking solution is implemented. The helpdesk people who provide phone support (or support in any form) need to be familiar with the blocking solution, be using it themselves, and be prepared for all the common questions that users will have and situations that end-users will find themselves in.

You can bet that anti-spyware will generate more helpdesk calls, particularly if you have implemented a solution that requires user intervention.

Helpdesks that have prepared scripts and troubleshooting diagrams will need new scripts for all new support scenarios. And whoever is responsible for these scripts also needs to modify existing scripts — especially those related to e-mail and the Web browser. For instance, a user complaining that she is not receiving e-mail will need to be guided through any additional steps such as checking a spam-message quarantine or modifying a whitelist.

End-user training and orientation

Without question, your end-users need the right information (in various forms) to prepare them for changes in policy and procedure that take effect when a spam- or spyware-blocking solution is implemented. Typical training and informative measures include these:

- Advance announcements
- Reminder announcements
- "Brown bag" sessions
- Formal training
- New-employee orientation

You will need to determine which departments are responsible for each type of user education — and equip and empower them appropriately. If the solution is going to work, all end-users need to understand how it works and how they interact with it. Training is the key to fulfilling this goal. See Chapter 7 for more on user training.

E-mail administration

Keeping e-mail fed and watered involves many routine tasks, as well as a number of troubleshooting and maintenance duties. Many such activities have to change when a spam-blocking solution is implemented. I list some of these processes here (your organization may have others):

- ✔ **E-mail account provisioning:** When a new employee joins the organization, the administrator of e-mail or user accounts must create and configure a new e-mail account. When a spam-blocking solution is present, it may add configuration steps or otherwise change the procedure for creating a user's e-mail account.

- ✔ **E-mail account maintenance:** You may not see much change in some routine account-maintenance tasks (such as group administration), but others (for example, employee name changes) could require separate changes in the spam-blocking system.

- ✔ **Data management:** Implementing a spam-blocking solution may affect tasks such as moving user accounts from one e-mail server to another, adding e-mail servers, and managing storage quotas for individual mailboxes. New tasks, such as managing the storage of quarantined messages, may be necessary from time to time.

Network management

In an enterprise that has already implemented capabilities for managing its systems (or network), spam- and spyware-blocking hardware or software should be "wired in" to the central management system. If individuals (or an entire team) are monitoring the health of other network elements and systems, then the spam- and spyware-blocking solutions should also be similarly monitored — especially a spam filter that is a critical part of the path in the organization's e-mail infrastructure.

Managing the data center

Procedures in the data center are likely to change with the introduction of a malware-blocking solution. Here are some typical examples of procedures that may be affected:

✔ **Backups:** Whether the solution is an appliance or software in a server, it may create additional file systems or volumes to back up.

✔ **Startup, shutdown, and recovery:** Procedures that describe system startup (how to start each one, and the order in which systems must be started), shutdown (ditto; usually, but not always, in reverse order), and recovery must take the new solution into account.

✔ **Planning for business continuity and disaster recovery:** These important processes cannot be overlooked when you're implementing a spam-blocking solution. Rain, sleet, or asteroid strike, the (real) e-mail must get through! Similarly, if a spyware-blocking solution is in a critical path, it will also impact Business Continuity Planning (BCP) and Disaster Recovery Planning (DRP).

Defining Roles and Responsibilities

The ramifications keep right on coming: With the addition of a spam-blocking solution, some jobs will certainly feel the impact: Someone has to feed, water, and ride herd on the new capability!

✔ **IT:** Certainly, IT bears the brunt of changes in who-does-what. No one gets off scot-free. The preceding section, "Re-Engineering Business Processes," explains how spam- and spyware-blocking solutions affect the many IT functions.

✔ **Human resources:** In some organizations, HR is the powerful policy-setting body for the entire organization. Its reach may include deciding which job functions have an e-mail quarantine and which don't, or how strong spam filtering should be (for reducing the risk of offensive materials landing in users' mailboxes), for instance.

✔ **Users:** Some spam-blocking solutions give the end-user some weapons for fighting spam — capabilities such as adjusting configuration settings (which can include whitelists, blacklists, and other mail-filtering rules). One concern that goes along with such capabilities is the possible impact on users' productivity: Tweaking spam filters can take up a surprising amount of time, which must be weighed against the benefit of enlisting all that additional vigilance.

Users with quarantines in place must check them periodically to ensure that no important mail has been caught in the spam net. That means changing work habits — which may mean some more training for your end-users, including the occasional refresher course.

Chapter 6

Evaluating Anti-Spam and Anti-Spyware Solutions

At some point, you'll need to choose what spam- or spyware-filtering product will work best for your organization; in this chapter, I provide some guidelines that should help you with that choice. Vendors can be a tricky lot. Be prepared when you head into negotiations with them, or you may come back from the market with nothing but a handful of magic beans.

Ensuring the Anti-Spam Cure Is Better Than the Original Spam

I have been involved in many enterprise-wide projects that required the evaluation and implementation of software. It's funny how some projects — despite an implementation that went perfectly — are branded as failures because the project team failed to foresee the full impact that the solution would have on the organization.

Anti-spam projects often get that particular bum rap, for two primary reasons:

- ✔ **The very definition of spam is subjective and slippery.** True, spam is unwanted e-mail, but that's a superficial understanding of the spam problem. Those who settle for such a simple definition are in for a disappointment, because . . .

- ✔ **Blocking spam is not an exact science.** It's far from 100 percent accurate — and spammers are highly motivated to find ways around the blocking. They keep trying new tricks, so even the best spam blockers let in *some* spam — and (alas) also block some legitimate e-mail messages. It seems that even the best machines aren't as smart as the "worst" people.

Spam blockers — even the best of them — are no silver bullets. This section explains why in a bit more detail.

You are evaluating not just the technical performance of the spam-blocking solution, but also how well the solution will work *in your specific organization.* Some points to keep in mind include these (I discuss these points in more detail in Chapter 12):

- ✔ **Some spam still gets through (false negatives).** Success of your project does not mean that *all* spam will be blocked, but rather that it will be *reduced* to a manageable level. Exactly what is a manageable level depends on your organization and, to some degree, individual preferences.

- ✔ **Some legitimate messages are marked as spam (false positives).** Like the preceding point, success does not require 100 percent perfection, but rather in the shifting of the tide.

- ✔ **Users must examine quarantines.** Spam blockers don't give employees *all* their wasted time back, but rather shift the burden of tasks and makes managing spam (hopefully) less of a nuisance.

- ✔ **Support may cost more.** Remember the organization's big picture and why you are choosing to implement a spam-blocking solution. Employees' efforts to sift through spam may transfer to the IT helpdesk, so make sure IT has the resources to handle the new tasks.

The point I'm making in these examples is that *your criteria for success should not be set at an unrealistic level.* No matter how good your eventual solution, you won't block 100 percent of the spam, you won't pass 100 percent of the nonspam, and employees won't get *all* their wasted time back. But it's still worth doing. Getting a spam solution is about restructuring how employees spend their time. The less they have to deal with spam, the better they can focus on being productive.

Choosing a Spam-Filtering Platform: Software, Appliance, or ASP?

Unless your organization has a clear and obvious need to implement a specific type of solution, your requirements should not "box you into" — nor arbitrarily eliminate — any specific type of solution. Step back for a minute and ask yourself: Does it *really* matter what form the solution takes, as long as it performs its primary functions properly? In most cases, you can simply do what works.

Before you make your choice, however, make sure you take the necessary step of developing a good set of business and technical requirements. If you're anxious to get your hands dirty and slap some spam filters in there, I can just about guarantee that your project will fail — unless you've already taken the time to put these two big ducks in a row:

- ✔ Understand and document your business objectives and requirements. (Chapter 5 describes this process in detail.)

- ✔ Make sure your requirements have the approval and backing of the people in your organization who sign the checks.

If you're not yet familiar enough with spam-blocking solutions to know for sure what type of solution is best for you, read this section to get an overview of the different ways spam can be blocked. (You don't have to disconnect the wires. Honest.)

Here's where business objectives and technology objectives intersect. Regardless of what type of spam solution you ultimately choose, *it must first satisfy business objectives*. (This of course is true of *all* technology projects, right?) Of course, you should choose the solution that also works well in your technical environment.

The irrational exuberance of the 1990s (I'm referring to the technology boom that went bust in 2001) turned a lot of principles about IT and business on their heads. The myth that many technologists embraced was that business existed for the sake of IT. With technology firmly in the driver's seat, many businesses failed because of this mistaken belief. The fact is this: *IT exists to support the business and to meet business objectives.*

Before walking through the primary characteristics of each type of solution, it's worth taking a quick look at a favorite target of spammers: a generic e-mail infrastructure without a spam filter in place. Figure 6-1 shows a tempting example.

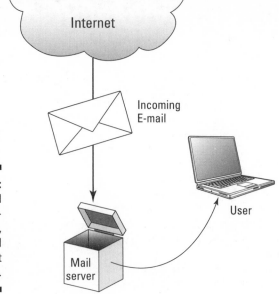

Figure 6-1:
A typical
e-mail infra-
structure,
unprotected
against
spam.

Can you say *sitting duck?* Better do something about this fast. The upcoming sections describe different types of anti-spam solutions.

Software solution

A software-based spam-blocking solution comes in the form of (you guessed it) software that you load onto one of your servers — either an existing server, or a new one.

Depending on the product — and on what e-mail system your enterprise uses — you might install the spam-blocking software right *on* your enterprise mail server, or on a different system that might be (from the point of view of incoming e-mail) "in front of" or "behind" your mail server(s).

An example of an architecture that uses software as a spam-blocking solution appears in Figure 6-2.

Some reasons why you might choose a software solution include these:

✔ You want a solution you can integrate so tightly that it appears to be an integral part of your existing e-mail infrastructure.

✔ You want complete control over the operating systems in your environment — which would make an appliance solution infeasible. (Normally you don't get to see, much less tweak, the OS that comes with an appliance.)

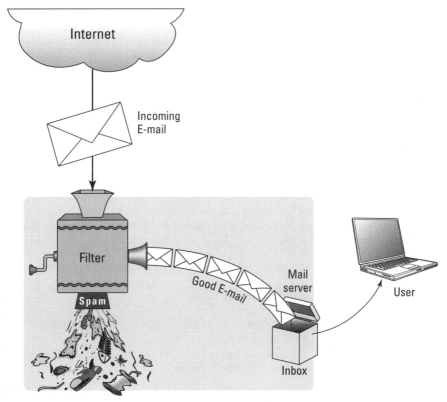

Figure 6-2:
The spam-
filter
software
model.

✔ You want to save costs by avoiding additional hardware purchases.

✔ You want to reduce complexity in the infrastructure by combining everything onto a single host. (You might be on a power-cord — er, host —
reduction program in order to achieve simplicity.)

✔ You want to simplify administration by just extending administration of
your mail host.

Such criteria make a software solution attractive — but there are always
some gotchas with any type of solution. A few of the problems that may be
looking for you include the following:

✔ You have to be careful what you do with the underlying operating
system (OS). If you make some configuration change in order to fulfill
some technical or business objective (say, change how you do authenti-
cation), you could inadvertently break your spam filter.

✔ You could end up in a no-win situation regarding operating system
patches and updates. For instance, if your spam-blocking solution runs
on a Windows server, the latest Microsoft patch that blocks the vulnera-
bility-du-jour may cause your spam blocker to behave in unexpected
ways (say, get a sudden urge to take out the garbage).

✔ More generally, you could end up between a rock and a hard place on almost any OS-level issue where you may need to make some change that the spam-blocking vendor tells you is unsupported, or just flat-out breaks your spam filter. The OS may be unstable or insecure without the change, but if you make the change, your spam filter may not work.

✔ Software solutions depend entirely on the viability and stability of the underlying operating system. Because of that dependency, they tend to be somewhat less reliable than special-purpose appliances or ASPs, which I explain in a moment.

I'd have to say that the software solution may be the gutsiest way to go, but it will give you more say-so over how you implement your solution. You'll take more risks (as discussed here) but you'll be in complete control — well, *almost* complete control. Like the Ghost of Christmas Yet to Come, the problem scenarios described above are not so much a portrayal of what *will* occur as what *may* occur: They are uncommon, but they do happen.

Appliance solution

Unless you're from (insert your favorite butt-of-the-joke region here), you're probably familiar with appliances as an aspect of computer networks. But please bear with me as I bring the clueless among us (no, don't raise your hands — it's our secret) up to speed.

Appliances, in the IT world, are no-maintenance or low-maintenance add-on devices with a power cord, a network connector, an "is-it-running" light (the editors made me take out the *real* term for those lights), and a knob for setting how dark you want the bread toasted. Seriously, though, an appliance is very much like a software solution, but without an underlying OS to worry about and maintain. (Well, okay, there *is* an OS lurking in there — but it's a special-purpose critter and not something you have to worry about.) Because software and appliance solutions are so similar, I'll cite differences and similarities between the two.

Differences between software and appliance solutions include these:

✔ The appliance solution is far simpler to maintain because it doesn't have an underlying OS — or at least one that you're permitted to see and do anything with. The software solution is more complicated because you (or someone you know) will be responsible for maintaining not only the spam-blocking software, but also the OS.

✔ An appliance model is more likely to be able to repel directory service attacks and protocol-level attacks, thereby relieving the e-mail server of the burden of dealing with these attacks directly.

✔ Appliance hardware is typically special-purpose as well. It's dedicated to its task; extraneous stuff like USB ports and high-end graphics cards are not needed — or included. Often this back-to-basics concept helps make the appliance simpler, more stable, and more secure.

Similarities between software and appliance solutions include:

✔ Both run in your data center, and you get to decide where in your architecture the spam blocker will be put.

✔ Both depend on frequent updates to ensure that filtering rules and software will remain up to date.

✔ Both insert into your e-mail infrastructure from the inside. You don't have to reroute your e-mail to an outside source to get rid of spam.

✔ Both add only one potential point of failure to your system. At any rate, that's usually the case, unless (say) you buy two and put them in different cities, each alongside an e-mail server. If someone accidentally knocks out the power cord, inbound e-mail stops — but that's about it. E-mail messages won't be lost, just *backed up* (queued) somewhere, and will eventually be delivered, as long as the outage is less than several hours. You actually have a lot of possible options — for example, local redundant pairs or clusters of appliances — but you get the idea.

Figure 6-3 illustrates a typical e-mail infrastructure with a spam-blocking appliance.

Application Service Provider solution

I think that the Application Service Provider (ASP) solution for blocking spam is the most interesting of the choices available today. It offers unprecedented levels of simplicity for the customer, but the customer also gives up a degree of control. Depending upon your needs, these differences can be beneficial, or not.

In an ASP solution, there are no additional computers, appliances, or software. Instead, all e-mail meant for your organization is sent *directly* to the ASP vendor (instead of directly to you), which filters out spam on its own computers. Then the vendor forwards your e-mail to you — minus most of the spam-laden messages.

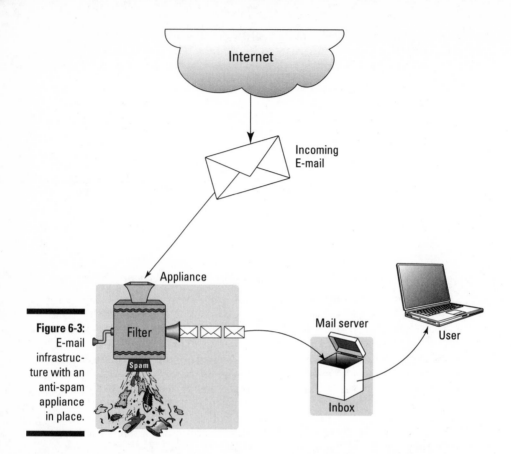

Figure 6-3:
E-mail
infrastruc-
ture with an
anti-spam
appliance
in place.

Another advantage of ASP-based solutions is that the vendors can afford to create redundant data centers and carrier-class server installations with nearly undreamt-of capabilities. Because the ASP offers aggregated services to many clients, you reap bonuses in actual fault tolerance and disaster recovery capabilities that are far beyond the reach of most companies. The benefit of multiple data centers in different cities is this: If a disaster was to occur in one of the cities (say, an earthquake, a fire, a tornado, a hurricane, or a flood — or a human-made disaster such as sabotage or arson) and cripple one of the ASP's data centers, the data center in the other city would be able to carry the entire load, with little or no interruption in service.

Having an ASP filter your e-mail for spam is — in some ways — the simplest solution that you can implement. Mostly this is because you do not need to change anything in your e-mail infrastructure, as shown in Figure 6-4.

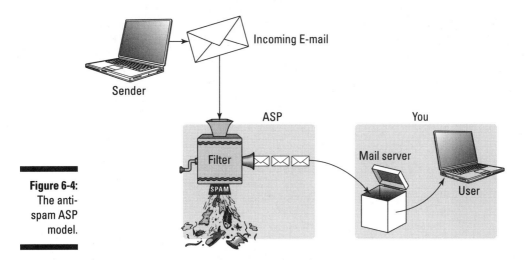

Figure 6-4:
The anti-spam ASP model.

One pitfall of an ASP solution, though, is the risk of complacency. It's too easy to let the *other* aspects of the anti-spam project slide. Organizations that yearn for simple solutions often underestimate the impact of spam filtering on their total operation. That's because the impact on IT is a task that's (ahem) asymptotic — math-speak for "always getting closer to just right, but never quite there." Believe me, the amount of preparation and training required to implement an ASP spam-blocking solution is no different from what's needed for a software- or hardware-based solution: A shipload.

Another consideration (when you're looking at ASP solutions) is whether it bugs you to have your confidential e-mail prodded and poked by an outside entity. ASPs are quick to mention that the Internet isn't a protected environment in the first place — and that other people might have access to your e-mail as it travels from the sender to you anyway — but in reality, a hacker would need to have direct access to networks or routers between you and the sender to read your e-mail. That's rare. In the case of an ASP, the e-mail is arriving at the ASP, getting read by automated processes, and then *most* is passed on to you. Any good mail that accidentally ends up in quarantine will actually sit around on the ASP's disks until you specifically identify it and then forward it or delete it. For that reason, you should look carefully at the contract the ASP is offering, and see what protections it offers your company from these pitfalls:

✔ The ASP's employees routinely reading your e-mail

✔ A rogue employee at the ASP reading your e-mail

✔ Someone who breaks into computers at the ASP reading your e-mail

With appropriate legal protections (specifically, contract provisions that protect your organization), the risk of your mail getting read at the ASP can be mitigated to a large degree. You can also help limit the risk if you assume each e-mail message you send to be about as private as a postcard. If you're sending or receiving e-mail that is so sensitive that you're concerned whether someone else may read it, you should encrypt such messages, whether or not you use an ASP-based spam-blocking solution.

Client-side solution

When you're blocking spam for enterprises, you can do so on either side of the client-server relationship. *Server-side* solutions reside on the server; *client-side* solutions are sold for individual use on users' workstations. It's an arrangement that empowers your users. But a client-side solution — when left to its own devices (so to speak) — has a couple of drawbacks:

- ✔ **Inconsistency of protection:** Users' ability to use anti-spam software can vary — and so can their tolerance for spam and their judgment of which messages are safe to open.

- ✔ **Little or no enterprise-level visibility of any kind:** You probably have no access to spam-tracking statistics, short of walking around to each user's workstation to see what each workstation's filter is doing.

Unless you have fewer than a few dozen end-user workstations, you probably don't want to even consider an unmanaged client-side spam filter. The only things worse that I can imagine are unmanaged antivirus and unmanaged personal firewall programs. Why? Same deal: There goes the control and visibility you need to protect the enterprise consistently.

Let me back up one sec — I mean no disrespect for client-side, single-user spam filters. They work well (I have them at home) and — for the most part — do what they are intended to do. However, if you have more than a couple dozen end-user workstations, you need a solution that has central management, reporting, and control.

Most e-mail client programs come with built-in spam control — and while you could argue that this provides additional defense, beware: All you may get out of it is one more cubbyhole to ransack when mail goes missing. Check with IT: If your company has chosen some other method of spam control, client-based filtering may be more trouble than it's worth. If that's the case, your helpdesk will thank you if you turn it off, or say "we told you so" if you leave it running.

Figure 6-5 illustrates a typical e-mail infrastructure with a client-side spam-blocking solution.

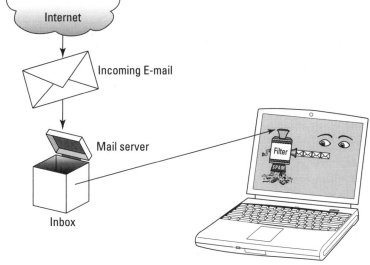

Figure 6-5:
Client-side
filtering as
an anti-
spam
model.

The solutions side-by-side

Personally, I love side-by-side comparisons, and so I offer one for you in
Table 6-1. It helps to see each type of anti-spam filtering solution go mano-a-
mano with the other types, under different conditions.

Table 6-1	Side-by-Side Comparison of Anti-Spam Solutions			
Comparison Point	**Software**	**Appliance**	**ASP**	**Client-Side**
User training required	Considerable	Considerable	Considerable	Considerable
Amount of extra helpdesk support required	Some	Some	Some	Lots — users must turn the knobs themselves
Administration of underlying operating system	Up to you	Little or none	None (after all, that's why you outsourced it)	Not fun, because you have dozens, hundreds, or even thousands

(continued)

Table 6-1 *(continued)*

Comparison Point	Software	Appliance	ASP	Client-Side
Enterprise policy administration	Centralized	Centralized	Centralized	Forget it!
Enterprise-wide whitelists and blacklists	Centralized	Centralized	Centralized	Who ya kiddin'?
Need for performance upgrades	Up to you	Work with your vendor	The ASP should take care of this so that it always runs fast, which is why you outsourced it	Variable
Signature and algorithm updates	You have to make sure they work	You have to make sure they work	Little, if anything, to worry about, which is why you outsourced it	Difficult and out of your control
Space in your data closet	Depends on whether it runs on your e-mail server or a stand-alone server	Very little (appliances are pretty small)	None	None
Reduction in inbound e-mail traffic that hits your e-mail servers	Some change, or no change, depending upon exactly how it is implemented	Most spam is blocked before it reaches your e-mail servers	Most spam is blocked before it reaches your e-mail servers	No reduction (spam still arrives and is stored in end-user's mailbox on the server before it is detected and deleted)
Directory-harvesting attacks	You may still be subject to this	With the right architecture this goes away	Nothing to worry about	Still a problem

Comparison Point	Software	Appliance	ASP	Client-Side
Your level of control	You have absolute control; you can turn it off or remove it any time you wish	You have a lot of control; you can turn it off, but you probably cannot tinker with its insides	You have no control	Little or none

Choosing Spyware Filtering: Workstation or Centralized?

The anti-spyware market is really still pretty immature, and not as many choices are available as for spam filtering. In the case of spam, it's all about e-mail — but spyware can worm its way in (literally, some spyware is delivered via Internet worms) via many different routes. These include Web browsing, e-mail, software installs, and removable media. For this reason, even centralized solutions (where the spyware-blocking capability resides on a single server or appliance in the data center) typically include a workstation component. It can be hard to protect the organization from spyware acquired by laptops on the road, unless you have something running on the laptop itself to detect and block it. This is a similarity to antivirus capabilities: The protection must be present at the point of potential infection or infiltration.

That said, some centralized solutions depend on scanning individual computers remotely, and having regular access to all computers on the network. If your organization already uses Microsoft's Systems Management Server or something similar, you're already halfway there. A centralized spyware-filtering platform can (in some cases) piggyback onto the existing management architecture, without requiring additional distribution, management, or reporting infrastructure.

To see whether a spyware-filting solution can leverage a management infrastructure (and vice versa), you need to have several conversations with both your potential spyware-blocking vendors as well as your management vendor, and perhaps three-way conversations, too.

Workstation solutions

Most anti-spyware programs on the market today are workstation-based solutions. Some of these have centralized management, reporting, and other enterprise-level features such as signature updating, but the product itself runs entirely on each individual workstation.

If your company is small enough that a noncentralized deployment is practical and manageable, a workstation-based solution might be the ticket. That way you don't have to pay for expensive management software you're not using. The bigger the company, however, the more vital central management becomes. Table 6-2 lists some pros and cons of workstation-based spyware-filtering solutions.

Table 6-2	Pros and Cons of Workstation-Based Spyware Filtering
Pros	**Cons**
It's the current standard, offering greater product selection.	In large enterprises, managing individual workstation software is not very efficient; it's hard to determine coverage without visiting each workstation; and the spyware filter can be locally disabled without administrative knowledge.
It has a better chance of identifying spyware (which has to unmask itself to install).	If it doesn't provide central logging or reporting, you don't have a good view of what's happening (if anything).
It places control of signature update in the workstation.	No central management of policies may mean that some spyware signature lists will be out of date and configurations inconsistent.

Centralizing the anti-spyware solution

Centralized solutions for spyware filtering are somewhat harder to find in the current market, but essential for the medium-to-large enterprise. A centralized spyware solution has its own challenges, due to the many ways that spyware propagates, but if you filter at least your company e-mail and Web traffic for spyware, you have most of your bases covered — and it's easy to put centralized hardware or software in place that monitors and controls each of these. In fact, it would be surprising if your organization doesn't already monitor e-mail or Web usage (for completely different reasons).

Centralized Web filtering for spyware

Monitoring and controlling live Web traffic to block spyware is the newest area in a relatively new technology. To accomplish this objective, the monitoring software has to interpret the incoming HTTP stream, compare what it's seeing to the list of known spyware, and then choose to block what's coming in — or not. In the meantime, a user is sitting at her desk, waiting for the link she just clicked to show up on-screen — as are several dozen other people who all clicked links in the last few seconds. As you might expect, hardware that can handle this demand while checking for spyware — all in real time — has to be seriously fast and (often) somewhat expensive.

Because the central filter has so much to do, and so very little time to do it all, it's prone to errors. Virus scanners typically have the luxury of receiving an entire file, decoding it, and then scanning it before sending it on. Live spyware filtering for the Web requires the program to decide whether to block in scant time with less information. Sometimes it has to work with partial files, or (in the case of compressed files) mere filenames — all in real time before users can notice the latency. Inevitably, some lag is inherent in centralized spyware/Web traffic filtering. That's because the best place to detect an incoming spyware program is where it unmasks as it gets ready to install itself — in its final form, it becomes recognizable to a filter. Where that happens is on the user's workstation.

So, why bother with centralized Web spyware filtering? It's another layer of protection against the folks who are trying to snoop around your network and rifle through your hard drives. The more layers you have defending you, the better off you are. Even if you only catch 50 percent of the incoming spyware at this level, that's 50 percent you won't have to deal with elsewhere.

Centralized mail filtering for spyware

Mail filters have it easier than Web filters, because mail filters have the opportunity to receive the entire e-mail, then decode it and see what's inside. Users generally find several seconds' latency time acceptable for the transmission of e-mail.

An interesting side effect of spam filtering is that it will remove the vast majority of incoming spyware in e-mail without knowing anything at all about spyware. Inbound e-mail with spyware in it will almost always be or at least look like spam, unless your friends or associates decide to send you some spyware for fun (keep in mind that if their computers are infected by spyware, and they're sending you mail, that will *still* look like spam).

Proactive filtering versus scanning

Many of the free spyware blockers on the market have only one way of dealing with spyware: They scan the computer's memory and hard drive for any signs of already-installed spyware every once in a while, and tell you about what turns up. The problem with this approach is that when a spyware program is detected in memory or on the hard drive, you have *already* been infected for some period of time — and the anti-spyware program is just trying to cure a disease that you have already contracted. In the best of all worlds, your anti-spyware program not only scans your memory and hard drive, but also has *proactive filtering* of some sort going on as well. The idea is to catch spyware *before* it can infect your computer. Many of the newer and more advanced spyware blockers have this capability, and it's definitely a feature to watch for.

If you've been in the computer business long enough to remember the dawn of viruses and antivirus software, you'll recall that antivirus software started out much like anti-spyware is going today: First there were scanners, then came the blockers, and then came enterprise control and management. Anti-spyware software is going in exactly the same direction, but there's more: Because antivirus and anti-spyware have such similar roles and missions (defending computers from malware and undesired programs), the two will meld into single product offerings that do both.

Many of the spam-filter vendors are already looking at what they can do on the spyware *filtering* side. Capturing those spyware e-mails that don't get flagged as spam puts a spyware filter in direct competition with e-mail virus scanners. Antivirus vendors tend to see e-mail scanning as their turf. Whatever, guys — here's the bottom line: You don't care who does it, just as long as *somebody* is filtering out this junk before it reaches your users.

Hybrid solutions

To do the best job possible of keeping spyware off your network, you will probably need to employ both centralized filtering and some software that runs on individual workstations. Many spyware-filtering solutions on the market have central reporting, central logging, and some degree of central management, but no central *filtering* capabilities. On the other hand, many of the antivirus, firewall, and spam filter manufacturers include at least some limited spyware-filtering functionality in their products.

For in-depth defense and the most effective spyware prevention, you should consider combining the best parts of each of these methods and products. Choose a best-of-breed workstation solution that provides central management and logging, and complement that with a gateway filter that provides as much protection as possible at the network level.

Defense in depth is an important strategy that you need to employ, if you haven't already. Chapter 13 is devoted to this topic.

Most organizations with a few hundred or more employees employ antivirus software on all user workstations, as well as on file servers and e-mail servers. The reason for this seemingly redundant protection is just that: to be very, very sure that viruses do not get inside the organization. This same principle easily applies to anti-spyware: Employ filters centrally *and* on user workstations to ensure that spyware never gets in.

Evaluating Information from Vendors

Mark Twain popularized the saying, "There are lies, damned lies, and statistics." Much information from vendors falls into these categories — some even qualifies as truth. The trouble is how to tell one from the other.

The bigger your organization, the more important it is that you get reliable, accurate data from the (hopefully short) list of vendors you're talking with. This is why *requirements* are so important. If your team developed good business- and technology-centric requirements, you have an easier row to hoe: Your prospective vendors fill out the requirement documents and spreadsheets and your project's team members can readily understand and discuss the vendor responses. Without good requirements and vendor responses, you're up a creek with a sitting duck and a mixed metaphor: All you have to go by is the vendor's word (and maybe their written or Web-based marketing) that its product is the right product for you.

Whatever you do, don't let vendors determine the requirements or the specification process for your anti-spam/anti-spyware solution. If you've had conversations with vendors early in the process, it's easy to allow their biases to slip into your thinking as you create your filtering requirements. After all (so goes the logic), any vendor you talk to probably knows more about spam filtering than you do, right? The vendor's whole business revolves around that market; for you, it's just another IT project. But hold the phone: What you know — and the vendor doesn't — is *your* business requirements. Allowing any vendor bias into your requirements puts a premature limit on your choices; you could miss out on a better product that would be a perfect fit.

Your mission, should you choose to accept it, is to discover what capabilities are out there without letting vendors influence your thinking. To complete this mission, you need to discipline yourself and objectively learn about many different solutions in order to understand which features you need.

Developing and analyzing vendor responses to your requirements are covered in Chapter 5. Now, you're a little past that, and you're sizing up a few of the finalists.

I want to make a point by showing you a table that may look humorous at first. Take a look at Table 6-3.

Table 6-3	What to Expect for What You Spend
Product Cost	*Information You Can Expect to Receive*
$1,000	Specifications
$10,000	Specifications, references
$100,000	Specifications, references, response to requirements
$1,000,000	Specifications, references, response to requirements, site visits
$10,000,000	Specifications, references, response to requirements, site visits, and almost anything else you want that's legal

What I'm trying to say in Table 6-3 is this: The more money you are spending on a spam- and spyware-blocking solution, the more information you are entitled to. At one extreme, for $1,000, you are likely to get little more than the time of day from a vendor. However, if your solution is going to cost millions, then the vendor will treat you like its long-lost and very rich relative.

Why is this? There are two sides to it. First, higher-cost solutions have more markup (profit), so the vendor can afford to make more time for you. And, correspondingly, if you're going to plunk down a pile of money for a solution, you're darned well *entitled* to receive additional information.

So, although you should not take Table 6-3 literally (but it's not far from the truth, either), you do need to understand the rules of the game.

Don't believe everything you hear

It might be hard to believe, but salespeople *occasionally* take liberties with the truth. Okay, some salespeople throw the truth out the window and use their own alternate versions of reality the first chance they get.

In a moment, I talk about verifying the facts by calling references (and other means of doing your homework), but I'd like to mention some things you should never take at face value when a salesperson says them, no matter how tempting it might be:

- ✔ "That required feature will be available in the *next* version."
- ✔ "The next version is coming out in three months."
- ✔ "Our product is so good, you don't really *need* a quarantine."

✔ "*If* you buy the product, we will fix that problem."

✔ (During a demo) "I've never seen it do *that* before."

If you feel the urge to say, "Yeah right — and the check's in the mail," that's just healthy skepticism.

Calling customer references

If you're spending more than a few thousand dollars, in my opinion you're entitled to the names and telephone numbers of some of the vendor's other customers. Done right, this part of your project is difficult and time-consuming, but will also yield a wealth of useful information.

Rather than just ask the vendor for a list of references, you need to qualify them so that you get references that are of value to you. Some possible criteria include

✔ Customers in the same industry as you

✔ Customers using the same e-mail client and/or server software as you

✔ Customers that are about the same overall size as you

✔ Customers in your geographic area (makes site visits easier)

Well before you start calling customer references, you need to develop good questions to ask each one. In order to be consistent and objective, you need to ask each customer reference the same questions. Sure, you're allowed to go off on some tangents, as long as they have business value, but you do need to develop your playbook and stick to it. Here are some topics worth talking about with customer references:

✔ Did the vendor do a decent job of supporting this customer before, during, and after installation?

✔ What difficulties were encountered during installation?

✔ What difficulties were encountered during the trial?

✔ What difficulties were encountered during the rollout to the enterprise?

✔ What end-user training issues were encountered?

✔ What other products were in the running?

✔ What surprises did you encounter along the way?

✔ What would the customer do differently if it could do the implementation all over again? Why?

Rescued references

It is always a good idea to ask vendors for a reference for one of their trouble customers — those who had difficulty implementing or supporting the product. Vendors may be reluctant to give you this information (they want you to think that 100 percent of their customers are 120 percent delighted with virtually every aspect of their products and/or services — yeah, right), but if you ask in a particular way, you may get what you are asking for. One approach I have used is to ask a vendor for a reference client who had a problem installation that was turned around and made successful. You want to hear an account of the heroism and valor displayed by the product-support or product-engineering people to see how the vendor performs when the going gets tough.

Every vendor has sunny-day customers — so what? If you can find them, the real gems are those who had some particular difficulty that they had to overcome. If the vendor can't seem to supply such customers, then Internet search engines are your friends: Look around for product names and keywords such as *problem* or *frustrated.*

As with requirements, charting out the responses can give you side-by-side comparisons that should prove helpful when you make a final vendor decision.

The customer-reference person you contact is probably no less busy than you are. Be sure to make the best possible use of his or her time, and do keep your time to a minimum. A good guideline is that the customer reference will have no more than 30 minutes to spend with you on the phone or on-site. For on-site visits, a good way to "buy" extra time is to buy the reference lunch if possible.

Visiting a vendor's customer on-site

You are fortunate if you have an opportunity to visit one or more customers who are using the malware-blocking software you're considering. As with telephone references, you want to make the best use of your time with each of those customers — and be sensitive to their time limitations. Resist the temptation to reminisce with the reference about the good (or bad) old days of punch cards and minicomputers with front panel toggle switches.

If it was up to me, there are three people I'd want to spend a few minutes with at a customer site:

 ✓ **A helpdesk person who supports users.** Find out what problems users are having, and what tools the helpdesk person has available to him or her to see what's going on and help the customer.

✔ **A system administrator who installed and is supporting the product.**
Discover what problems he or she experienced during and after installation. Find out what the system administrator likes and doesn't like about
the product.

✔ **One of the trial-period users.** Find a *non*technical user who has been
using the product for a long time, hopefully even from the trial period.
Ask the user what he or she likes and doesn't like about the malware-
blocking solution, and if it was easy to learn how to use the product.

Take good written notes to document your conversations. Get names and
numbers (and ask for permission to call if you have a *short* question) in case
you forget some *tiny* detail.

Visiting vendor sites

If you're putting a lot of money on the line for your solution, you need to plan
on visiting one or more vendors' premises. But (as with reference calls) this
process isn't *all* wine and caviar — okay, maybe just a little. . . .

Seriously, though, you need to cover many important details during your
visit. Don't let the prospective vendor take up all your time with an impressive multimedia slide show or drag you around to shake hands with the CEO
(or VP, or any manager if they can find one). Social niceties are fine, but
you're there to do some serious fact-finding.

Make sure that the vendor's people understand your agenda well before you
visit so they can accommodate you. Here's what you need to do when you're
on-site:

✔ **Visit the product-support department.** Be there physically during working hours. How many support people are on-staff? Make sure you can
speak with the product support manager; ask him or her questions
about how the folks in the department handles incoming calls, who
those calls are escalated to, how they keep track of each call, and how
soon they get upper management or engineering involved when there is
a serious issue.

✔ **Visit the product-development department.** Talk with one of the engi-
neers and with the department manager. Ask them about the development life cycle and methodology:

 • How do they decide what products, features, and fixes will be
introduced?

 • How do they test their product?

- Do they use secure programming techniques? If they answer yes, ask them which ones.

- How do they handle support calls that escalate into product development?

✔ **Visit someone who was present at the creation.** Talk with the most senior product architect or visionary who is available. Ask questions regarding the future direction of the product.

✔ **If you are visiting an ASP vendor, get a tour of its data center.** (Make sure that someone in your company who has expertise on enterprise-grade computing environments is with you.) Ask questions about the ASP's electric power — one or two entrances? (Two are better.) Check out the ASP's equipment — how is the ASP fixed for redundant Internet connections, Uninterruptible Power Sources, and generator capacity? Ask about the building's HVAC (Heating, Ventilation, and Air Conditioning); are there redundant or backup units? Is the ASP running its solution on adequately sized and operated enterprise-class servers? Is the place neat and clean? How many data centers does the ASP have? Where is the ASP located? Ask about maintenance windows in the schedule and what the drill is during system outages (everyone has them).

And here you thought you were going to get a fun trip out of this. Sorry, but you have your work cut out for you.

Other ways to obtain vendor information

There are many good reasons for networking among your peers in other companies (besides looking to change jobs someday). One really good reason is to have acquaintances you can ask regarding some specific vendor's performance. In Seattle, where I work, I have contacts in a few dozen companies — and access to people in many more local companies. From time to time, I ask around — especially if I am considering a particular vendor for some solution.

Sometimes I ask the vendor's salesperson if there are local clients. "Not that I would want to call them," I hastily add. (Well, *maybe* not.) If you know people in a lot of different companies in your area, then you can drop names (cite your acquaintances) if the salesperson names some customers. The salesperson knows that you and your acquaintances will be discussing not only the product, but local sales and support personnel as well. In and of itself, this is an excellent tool for extracting truthful information from salespersons. If they know you're going to talk to clients not necessarily on the "approved references" list, they may be a bit more forthcoming.

Evaluating Anti-Spam and Anti-Spyware Vendors

You may be fortunate enough to have an opportunity to actually try out one or more solutions prior to purchasing one. This is a time-consuming learning opportunity that will help you to determine which — if any — solution you will choose.

If you'll actually be taking some vendor's spam- or spyware-blocking solution home to try out for a few weeks, you'll need to arm yourself with all of the preparation required for a "real" rollout, even though your evaluation is probably going to be covering only a small set of real users. Chapter 8 discusses how to set up a successful trial — keeping in mind that logistically a trial and an evaluation are nearly identical (in some lexicons even the words are identical). What I get into here is a closer look at some of the more detailed characteristics of vendors — including how they plan for their products' futures.

In past projects I have participated in, there have been vendors who I got along with right from the start, and others who had (ahem) people problems — flaky salespeople, quirky support people, or something else that really bothered me at the relationship level. Whichever vendor you choose, you are choosing to establish not just a long-term business relationship, but also several long-term person-to-person working relationships between people in your organization and people who work for the vendor. There has to be a "spark" there from the very beginning. When discussing each vendor's merits, include the impressions you're getting from the individuals with whom you expect to be working over the long haul.

Understanding vendors' long-term product strategies

A great deal of your investment in any new software product is its acquisition and deployment cost — which often figures out to far more than its long-term operating cost. More money up front means it makes sense to exercise care when choosing a product from among the offerings of several vendors. You want to make the right choice the first time. You don't want to have to do the project all over again just because you chose the wrong product (in which case, you're likelier to be employed elsewhere — and *someone else* will inherit your mistake). But you also want to make sure the product and vendor you choose will be around for the long haul.

When does the timer start?

For most trial software and appliance demos, there's a timer that starts when you receive the appliance or install the software. In some cases, the timer starts when it leaves the vendor's door. In any case, you have a limited window in which to install and evaluate your trial, so it's best to have your resources ready when you ask for the trial. I've been on both the customer and vendor sides of this, and it's frustrating for everyone when for some reason the trial timer is about to expire by the time you get around to putting it all in place. If you're spending on the low side, you'll get a lot more respect (and attention) from a vendor if they see that you're organized and can pull off a trial with some finesse.

In the absence of a crystal ball (mine is frequently in the shop), your requirements should include some of the fuzzier topics — such as the future direction for the vendor's products — and the vendor's answers had better be actually useful. If there's a lot of money on the table (many hundreds of thousands of dollars, or more), then you have earned (that is, *bought*) the right to quiz all your prospective vendors on their long-term technology and business goals. Don't get me wrong. You can always ask these questions, no matter how much money is on the table. Just expect somewhat lackluster responses in cases where the total investment is small.

I've spent many a vendor visit (when I visit them, or they visit me) making time to discuss the vendor's long-term product strategy. Let me explain in some detail:

- Is the vendor going to stick with its current model (hardware, software, ASP)? Why or why not?

- Is the vendor's market position strong enough to lead the evolution of all anti-spam or anti-spyware products?

- What new features will future versions of the product have?

- What hardware or software platforms will be supported in the future? Will support be discontinued for any currently supported platforms?

- Does the vendor have plans to integrate its spam/spyware-eating product with its antivirus solution? Why or why not?

 The primary reasons for asking these questions is that you want to know what your vendor finalists will be doing over the next several years. You need to know this because a long-term business relationship needs to be established with whichever vendor you choose; you might as well choose a vendor that will actually be in existence a year or two from now, *and* whose product(s) in the future will meet your needs over the long-term. It's also just interesting to listen to the responses to understand how your vendor thinks about the market and its role in it. Sometimes it's not the answers them-selves, but the *way* the vendor answers. Sometimes it's not what the vendor says, but what it *doesn't* say that matters.

Twisting vendors' arms to get the deal

While the negotiation of terms and conditions is an art form best left to the experts, a few points worth knowing can make a difference in your project planning.

You want to select a vendor that has enough resources to do what it takes to make your anti-spam/anti-spyware project successful. If you need your vendor to send an engineer on-site for a few weeks for free — in exchange for (say) a joint press release — then that vendor had better be able to make good on this item without breaking its bank account, and disrupting its devel-opment or support groups.

You may, on the other hand, need your vendor to toss in a part of its product that it normally charges good money for, in return for something else (for instance, a second management console for your disaster recovery site). Can your vendor do this and still have the funds required to support you?

In these examples, I have a couple of points that I am trying to get across to you:

- ✔ Is the vendor big enough that it has the resources required to go the dis-tance with you?
- ✔ Is the vendor small enough to sit up and take notice, and do what's needed to make your installation successful?

Notice how these two points seem to be mutually exclusive. Well, okay, in your particular case, they may *be* mutually exclusive — or not. Either way, stay focused on the brass tacks: Your business objectives must be met in a way that satisfies you as a customer. The likelihood of making this work has a whole lot to do with how important a customer they consider you to be.

Know the vendor's sales cycles

One way of getting more attention than usual (and possibly better discounts than usual) is to know the vendor's sales cycles. For publicly traded compa-nies, quarterly earnings reports are very important to their perceived health, and sales are usually the big driver in keeping these numbers up. It's also good to know when a vendor's fiscal year rolls over — vendors are generally eager to book business prior to the end of the year, and may offer more dis-counts to achieve it.

Negotiating prices and asking for freebies is almost always more effective if your purchasing decision will happen about two weeks before the end of the vendor's fiscal quarter (or year) — the sales team will be looking for quick-closing sales to meet quotas. On the other hand, near the beginning of a sales cycle, you can expect very little attention from the sales team unless you represent a significant (big) sale. Timing is everything here. This scenario is most pronounced in public companies — and the larger privately held companies behave in much the same way. Bottom line: Almost all salespeople work from quotas: They gotta "make the numbers" (sell enough to stay employed).

Know your marquee qualities

In some special cases, your company might have special value on a vendor's client list. For instance, if your shop is a well-known ISP, listing you as a customer for most vendors would be a great boost for their marketing. Knowing this can help you in your negotiations. Without *saying* you know this in so many words, you can drop hints about the fact that for some consideration on the sale, your company might consider participating in a case study, joint press release, client showcase, or at least allow the vendor to list you (neon optional) as a customer.

It never hurts to ask

Say you have, well, none of the advantages I talk about here. You're making a smallish purchase, it's the beginning of a quarter, and the vendor could care less about having you on its customer list till after you've topped the Fortune 500. When it boils down to the residue, two rules of negotiation really apply here:

1. Always ask for what you want.

2. Always be ready to walk away if you don't get what you've asked for.

If you don't ask for what you want, you'll never get it. If you do ask, you might be surprised by the response. Also — and I can't stress this enough — your willingness to walk away from any deal is directly related to how seriously your requests are received. If the salesperson senses that you're already committed to purchasing their product (trust me, they *can* sense that), you will receive few or no concessions.

Part III
Deploying Your Chosen Solution

The 5th Wave By Rich Tennant

How To Block Spam and Spyware

"Can't I just give you riches or something?"

In this part . . .

In a movie, this part would be the action sequence with exploding mopeds and lots of screaming monkeys. Instead, this is the part where you get to explore all the actions required to go from zero (the point where you've chosen a product), to fully trained users, a fully installed tested filter, and a fully prepared support staff.

In keeping with the action sequence theme, this part describes all the actual steps for successfully implementing a filter and keeping your users happy. Hey, it's not as fun as exploding mopeds, but then, what is?

Chapter 7

Training Users and Support Staff

● ●

In This Chapter

▶ Setting user expectations

▶ Training sessions for users, helpdesk folk, and administrators

▶ Understanding user manuals and online documentation

● ●

Sometimes, talking to technologists (or even worse — talking to technology vendors) can leave you with the impression that installing XYZ-Extreme hardware/software will solve all your spam and spyware woes, prevent tooth decay, wash and fold the laundry, and leave a minty-fresh smell around the office. In nearly every case, technology is about 10 percent of the solution. The rest is about people and the way people interact with the technology.

You need to provide the users and support staff with some vital information so that they'll be comfortable with the new spam-filtering solution. Training is a pretty broad topic, and in this chapter, I offer ideas for making that training effective and targeting training for users versus IT folks.

The Many Methods of Training

At most companies, user training is also complicated by myriad other issues competing for users' attention, and training isn't ever at or near the top of their lists. Thus you need to offer information to users in various forms, and the success of each method lies in the delivery.

By offering training in several different forms, your users can participate in the way that makes the most sense for them.

In the following sections, I offer general guidelines for the three main types of training and information that businesses provide: seminars, user guides, and online guides.

Offering effective seminars

Seminars are a traditional approach to user training and are a good way to provide the users with something beyond the "click this button to delete" information. If you think you can get a group of users to sit down for half an hour to an hour for a seminar on effectively dealing with spam and the new spam filter, take the time to create a seminar that won't put them to sleep. The following tips can help you make your seminar more effective:

✔ **Focus only on the objectives you have for your audience and the information your audience needs to know in order to meet those objectives.** Face it. Most general users aren't interested in the cool Bayesian-filtering technique that the filter uses or any of the fun technical stuff, and they don't need that information anyway. You may even make them feel like you're wasting their time (or, worse, talking down to them) if you start a seminar in this way. That's not to say such information isn't relevant — your IT staff might like this information and find it gives them insight into troubleshooting problems with the filter.

Avoiding unnecessary information has the added benefit of helping the audience focus on what you need them to know. Even if a user *does* care about Bayesian filtering, you don't want a user to walk away from the seminar with a detailed knowledge of this filtering and no idea how to check their quarantine, because the user was so absorbed in understanding the technical details of filtering that he or she tuned out the rest of the seminar.

✔ **Inject some variety into the program.** Tell a joke, include a cartoon at key points in a slide presentation to draw people's attention, or do whatever you think might generally liven things up a bit. Although a snazzy seminar title like "E-mail prophylactics and how to use them" may or may not go over well in your organization (or suit your personality), try to find something to break up the seminar, put the audience at ease, and keep their attention.

✔ **Involve the audience.** You can do this by asking questions, getting different audience members to help demonstrate techniques during a review, or even having users follow along during the demonstration on their own computers, if that resource is available to you.

✔ **Try to meet as many different learning styles as possible.** Visual learners (and most folks are visual learners, to some extent) will benefit from live demonstrations with the real tools, showing the people what they'll be doing. You may include examples of actual spam. Auditory learners want to listen to someone explain something. Some people like to work in pairs whereas others prefer to learn alone at their own pace.

Although it might sound a little cheesy, music or rhyming, such as the slogan "Checking your quarantine twice a day keeps false negatives at bay" can also help convey your message. (Feel free to use that one; I can just about guarantee people will mock it, so it will achieve the purpose.)

✔ **Be redundant without being obviously redundant.** Repetition helps people learn and retain information, but you still need to keep the presentation varied. Your mission then, is to find new, fascinating ways of saying the same things in different ways. Here's a basic outline for thoroughly covering your topics:

1. Introduce the topics that you are going to cover.

2. Discuss the topics in the same order that you introduced them, fully fleshing them out with details.

3. Close with a wrap-up that describes the topics from a different perspective.

   For the purposes of repeating your message, remember that you have other ways to reach these users. Posters, e-mail, and other forms of company communication can help you reinforce the important points.

✔ **Include time for review.** How many times have you walked away from a seminar and realized 20 minutes later that none of what you heard actually stuck around in your brain for any length of time? One of the important tools for learning is recall. If you lets folks walk away without trying to recall and apply any of the knowledge you just imparted, they won't retain it.

Because you aren't trying to grade people, one nice way to help with recall is a short quiz at the end. Keep the questions focused on the key things you want the audience to understand how to do. Have the users write their answers down, and then provide the answers. Try to make the recall quiz fun and nonthreatening (nobody has fond memories of grade school pop quizzes). A short quiz can provide an important feedback mechanism for the learning process.

✔ **Keep the presentation short (less than 40 minutes) and leave time for the audience to absorb the information afterwards.** All work and no play makes Jack a dull boy. All work and no pl . . . ahem. What I mean to say is that learning is best done in small doses, followed by a rest period (for the brain), which actually allows new information to stake out some pathways and get comfortable in your head.

Actually, in an ideal world, shortly after a training session you could tell the class to go to sleep, but most companies frown on kindergarten-style nap time, so you have to settle for scheduling your seminars just before a natural break time in the work schedule some time when your class won't immediately go back to work and mess up all those new neural pathways. If you offer a coffee and small snack after the presentation as a thank-you for attending, that provides the mental break and makes a nice incentive to come to the training.

Creating paper user guides

One way of disseminating information is the printed word. Unlike a training session, a user can refer to a printed guide over and over again, at the user's convenience.

User guides can take a lot of different forms. A document that is easy to use will be used, and users will learn from it. Conversely, a document that is difficult to use will probably be ignored after a short while, if not discarded altogether. By including the following features, you can create guides that people are more likely to use:

- ✔ **Table of contents, index, and headings:** Because your users don't want to read everything in the guide, you need to give them ways to find the information that they need quickly and easily, and these elements help people do that. Even if you have a large amount of information to convey, break it up into small, digestible, *actionable* chunks. If your guide is just a couple pages, these aren't necessary, but anything larger should include ways to quickly find the right page.

  This book includes each of these elements, so if you're looking for examples, just flip around these pages.

- ✔ **Glossaries:** Glossaries define the words or phrases that a typical reader might not understand in the context of the guide. Almost every user guide should have a glossary of terms. Remember when you were assembling the orbital laser cannon and didn't know what "Raman effect" meant? No, it's not about noodles.

- ✔ **A logical, predictable organization:** One way to prepare an organized guide is a chronological presentation starting with the first steps and leading the user through each required step to accomplish a task. Another way is to cover related topics as a unit. For instance, you might want to talk about everything related to spam quarantine in one place, even though monthly maintenance isn't chronologically anywhere near searching for *false positives* (normal mail that gets identified as spam).

  Do what makes the most sense for the material you're presenting, but plan the document before writing it and have someone else take a look at the plan. Then create the document and have someone take a look at that as well before you unleash it on the masses. Even the best writing can be improved by skillful editing (or so my editors tell me — repeatedly, and with *much* red ink).

- ✔ **Illustrations:** A few simple illustrations in your user guide will greatly aid the visual people in your audience. A picture tells a thousand words, and frankly, I'd rather spend a few minutes creating a high-level, conceptual line drawing than try to explain the same concept in several paragraphs.

The folly of jargon

A major problem exists in technical manuals, user guides, and in general most technical writing. Technical writers seem to think that if they don't make tasks sound complicated and hard:

✔ Folks will lose respect for the technical genius of the writer.

✔ The information will be diluted in reams of explanation.

✔ Ordinary people will learn the secrets of IT and technology, leaving technologists without a job.

The truth of the matter is that just the opposite is true in nearly every case. People respect technologists who can explain things in language that they can understand. The skill of actually explaining even complex technology is the mark of someone who really knows what he or she is doing. Complicated jargon-laden smoke screens are a sure sign that the writer isn't familiar enough with the material to lay it out in any better way than what he or she has already heard.

If you write clearly in plain language and don't ever make the mistake of assuming your users are stupid just because they don't know technology, you can attract a lot more readers.

I know from long experience that technologists who are able to explain difficult concepts in terms easy for nontechnologists to understand are actually *more* valuable on the job market than their less-eloquent peers. Being able to explain what you do to others makes you look smart; it doesn't make your job look easy.

✔ **Approachable language:** Use as little jargon as possible when explaining things. Remember that your target audience is primarily nontechnical, and their eyes glaze over when you start in on the geek talk. Although you may have to introduce them to some new jargon, do so specifically and define your terms as needed. Although it may be cool for geeks to talk computerese while ordinary citizens are listening, your user guide — or any other learning setting, for that matter — isn't the place for it. Save your *double-ROT13 zero-bit parity error Bayesian learning curve* for another time, away from your users.

✔ **Correct grammar, spelling, and punctuation:** *Don't get you user guide tossed with out being red fist.* If your user guide has typographical errors, misspelled words, lousy grammar, and/or poor word choice, your users will at best have trouble reading it, and at worst just ignore the content. A lot of people rely on computers to correct anything that might *bee* wrong with *they're righting,* and some pretty obvious mistakes *our* made. Don't fall into this technology trap. Re-read your writing, and then be sure to have someone else proofread it. Like a spam filter, a word processor just isn't as smart as a human being.

Posting user guides online

Many companies have an *intranet* for hosting network resources available only to people inside the company. In most cases, this takes the form of an internal Web portal with links to any number of important internal resources. For instance, your human resources department may have a Web page where an employee can log in and get information about the benefits package or make selections regarding tax withholdings.

If you don't have space on the intranet already, you may want to carve out some server real estate for documenting IT projects and providing easy access to user documentation. Your spam filter's user guide would be a great addition to this area, and adding it would give you a nice place to point people when they ask for instructions. Creating spam-filtering information for your end-users would be good justification for building that intranet site in the first place; spam filtering would be a handsome passenger for your intranet's maiden voyage.

For years, people made the mistake of thinking that online reading was exactly the same as reading a paper and that the writing and structure of online text was no different from putting the same subject matter together for a printed page. So many things are wrong with that assumption that I can't even begin to correct them all in this book, but in the following sections I take a look at a few of the important differences and how to best take advantage of them.

Save the extra words; nobody reads them

Online reading habits have been studied ad-nauseum; people don't just start reading at the top of a Web page and continue reading through to the end. Build your Web pages for scanning, allowing readers to pull out the critical parts quickly without having to read through all the text. To facilitate this

- ✔ **Break up paragraphs of text** with elements that the user can visually scan, such as bullet lists, images, and diagrams.

- ✔ **Use text formatting to bring out important points in the text.** Colored text is something that might be rarely used on a printed page for cost reasons, but can be used for great effect to attract the readers' eyes to something specific in an online document.

- ✔ **Make the individual chunks short.** If you have a ten-page user manual, don't present ten pages in a long, scrollable document. Present one page at a time with frequent section headings so that the reader can digest it in chunks. Small chunks also make for easy scanning.

Help people navigate

Because nobody wants to read the whole user guide, you need to help guide them to the parts that they *do* want to read and leave a trail of breadcrumbs for them to get back. Start off the document with a short table of contents with hyperlinks for the section titles so that if someone just wants to read about retrieving lost e-mail he can click that and go to the section. On subsequent pages, present links that go forward and backward in the document with an annotation like "forward to learn about deleting old spam from quarantine." Also, include a link on each page that goes back to the table of contents in case the user wants to look at a new area entirely. Links to the glossary could also be handy in the event that the reader needs to understand what Bayesian filtering really means.

Include a feature that lets the user search the full text of the user guide, if possible. Users can't always remember where they read something, but they might be able to find it by searching for related phrases or words. Not all internal portals or intranets have this capability, but if it's there, use it to your full advantage.

Use the third dimension

Printed pages have width and length, but that's about it. In an online document, you have the ability to present additional information at the user's request by adding links. In the discussion of paper documentation earlier in this chapter, I talk about how important it is to provide indexes and glossaries to help users navigate the terminology and find their place. It's just as important online, but you can do things like make a word a link to its definition, rather than have the user flip manually to a glossary.

Although not strictly needed in an online user guide, people sometimes also appreciate links to outside sources that reference the topic at hand. You never know when someone reading about phishing might get interested in the criminal aspects of that spam and want to read more about it on some external site that can talk about the gruesome details. (For a list of such sites, check out the Web resources in Chapter 18.)

Training Users

Inertia is the tendency for a body at rest to stay at rest or of a body in motion in a straight line to keep going on that straight line unless acted upon by some outside force. You can modify that definition to describe the behavior of almost all users. *User inertia* is the tendency of users to insist that the way they have always done things is the *only* way to do things, unless acted upon by management — and even *then* they will resist. This law has a corollary, which is that *all change is bad.*

Training is one of the ways to start to overcome user inertia. Through training, you can present all the advantages of using the new technology in new ways that can improve users' experiences with e-mail and cut down on the spam.

Looking at the technology from a user's point of view

Although computers are good at calculating and performing repetitive tasks, no one has managed to get any computer to reason or intuit, yet. For that reason, you hear comments like, "Stupid computer. It should have known that this e-mail from my farmer friend talking about his bumper crop of watermelons wasn't spam." Never mind that the subject line was *exactly* the same as 5 million porn spam messages received by the filter that day — a human would have known the difference.

Although you *know* you're smarter than computers, you often might feel that the computers are in charge. If the technology takes actions regarding your incoming e-mail, and you don't know exactly how to change or reverse those actions, you may feel like the computer has the upper hand. If, on the other hand, the technology blunders, and through training users know how to deal with it, users can go about their business. Make sure you point out that user training will help them feel this empowerment to handle e-mail problems quickly and effectively.

The corollary to the corollary that "all change is bad" is "unexpected changes are the worst." People like to feel that they have some control over their lives, or at least have some idea of what's going to happen next, and although you may not be able to do anything about that for most of your life, you can help when it comes to new technology in the workplace.

If you're careful to include people in educational activities and workshops as you prepare to roll out a new spam or spyware filter, they'll start to feel some ownership of the eventual solution and move away from the "users versus IT" mentality. Generally, people who are included will help, and people who feel excluded will hinder.

When it's practical, include users in the decision-making process regarding how your new filter will work. Solicit user suggestions regarding training, schedules, and implementation. The more your users are involved in the process, the better they will feel about the results.

Explaining the filter to users

Used properly, cellular phones are a boon to politeness and manners. When I know that I'm expected for an event and will be late, I can call and let folks know when they can expect me to be there. Being late in the first place isn't very polite, but leaving people hanging is much worse. As a matter of fact, the earlier that I know I'll be late, the earlier I can tell people, and we may just end up moving the expected start time with no waiting around at all. You have the same opportunity with setting user expectations for spam-filtering technology.

You know how the spam filter is going to behave and at least *some* of the ways that it might misbehave well before you roll it out to your users. If you can frame the new environment in such a way that you don't surprise users by the occasional false positive or false negative and they know how to deal with these and other events, then you can at least direct their annoyance with such problems at the product (or better yet, at the spammers) rather than yourself. For example, if a user receives a spam after the filter is in place (a false negative), knowing that this was likely to happen and what to do about it will be much better than just being frustrated with the new filter not working properly. Training isn't just about teaching people how to use new technology. It should also include preparing them for the *experience* of using the technology.

Overall, you need to overcome the expectation that spam filtering has any hope of being perfect. People have become accustomed to computers doing tasks such as calculating payroll, storing files, and calculating the 115th digit of *pi* and doing it perfectly. In fact, when an operation like this doesn't happen correctly, people look for some correctable human error or bug in the program that they can fix so that the error never happens again.

Spam filtering will never be like calculating *pi* because the filter is trying to simulate something very slippery — human judgment. Your users will still be required to do several tasks in a spam-filtered world to maintain their e-mail health and spam-free status. The following sections discuss the tasks that you need to explain to them in your user training.

Fortunately, users will have to do few, if any, tasks to keep the spyware filter running smoothly — unless you choose a program where scanning and updates are manual.

Examining quarantine for important messages

Your filter can deal with incoming mail that's classified as spam in just three ways:

- ✔ **Delete:** This is dangerous, so almost nobody does it. You can lose legitimate — and even important — mail this way.

- ✔ **Mark:** This just marks the mail in some way as spam, and leaves it up to other systems, or users, to deal with. This requires more steps and is not used that much.

- ✔ **Quarantine:** Messages identified as spam are moved to a special repository, which can be viewed by system admins and users if needed.

Deleted isn't worth talking about training-wise because the spam is gone and there's not much you can do except ask the sender to resend it, 40 percent less spammy this time.

Your users can treat marked and quarantined methods as the same because they both set the alleged spam apart from the rest. Users can then deal with the spam at their leisure.

Even experienced users tend to ignore their quarantine folders until they realize that something is missing. Senders often don't check in until an expected reply is well overdue. Unless the user occasionally looks at her quarantine, she won't know about potentially important mail that she's missing until it may be too late to do anything about it because some quarantines delete anything that's older than a maximum age.

Deleting spam from quarantine

When your users are thumbing through their quarantines, delete the real spam so that next time they take a look, the pile isn't quite so large. If their quarantine doesn't include aging and auto-deletion of old spam, it's important to delete old spam so that it doesn't accumulate into some sort of spam singularity, sucking the rest of the company data into itself.

Maintaining whitelists

One of the ways of avoiding ever having to deal with picking through a quarantine for lost mail is to maintain perfect whitelists. For any company-wide whitelist to be complete, everyone needs to play. Although this is the single most effective way of avoiding important mail being marked as spam, submitting a good list for the whitelist is one of the most difficult tasks to get users to perform. For more detail on managing whitelists, take a look at Chapter 11.

Reporting false negatives

Spam that gets through the filter is annoying, but in many cases, users can do their part by reporting it and helping to improve the filter. Many of the filters on the market can "learn" by being shown e-mail that you *know* is spam and thus get better at identifying that kind of spam. In some cases, the filter remembers that particular spam and will never allow it through the filter again, possibly saving your co-workers from having to deal with it at all.

Training Administrators

Training the people who will be administrating your filtering solution is easily as important as training the users themselves. Administrators will be in charge of the care and feeding of the filtering solution, and how well it functions operationally will be largely in their hands.

In general, the advice in the section, "The Many Methods of Training," earlier in this chapter, applies to training administrators, but you need to cover some specific areas for admins that users don't care about (and in some cases, should not know about). For a far more captive audience, look to the people whose jobs include maintaining the spam or spyware filters; working with the new filter is their responsibility. Don't take that as license to make the training dry and boring, though. E-mail administrators are people too.

Put yourself in administrators' shoes

Think administrative thoughts. If you've been involved in selecting the spam- or spyware-blocking solution, checking out the technical merits of the solution you've chosen over all the available ones on the market, and understanding the solution's impact on the organization, you might assume that other IT folks will have much of the same knowledge and understanding of the product or service that you do. Dream on.

Almost all IT administrators have some protective instinct that prevents them from learning anything about new technology until the instant before they need that knowledge. They've watched too many projects get derailed before it was actually time for them to pick up the reins, and don't want to waste precious brain cells on anything that they might never use. Respect this instinct: It's saving you from screaming hordes of torch-bearing administrators pounding on your door the next time a project is scrapped in the late stages of deployment.

System administrators are a bright lot of folks and have the ability to learn new systems quickly and retain what they learn (or at least read the manual from time to time). The good news is that you don't have to spend time writing up special user manuals for the admins because they will have access to

- ✔ The user manuals you've provided to regular users
- ✔ The user manuals provided by the manufacturer or service provider
- ✔ The administrative manuals provided by the service provider or manufacturer

The slightly less good news is that you need to spend a lot more time with them in training because you have to cover the entire product, including the technical details. You must familiarize the system administrators (as well as any administrators who may have to intervene) with your company's policies for ways that spam and spyware are handled by the filters; if you don't, they may make decisions (rogue and otherwise) on their own, resulting in outcomes that were never intended.

Including practice in the training

One of the best ways to cement the learning pathways is to have students recall the information themselves. With administrators, you want to take the next logical step and have them actually *practice* the things that they're learning regarding administration of the system. Have the admins practice on test installations, rather than where your users are really using the technology. Do this before the system is in production and it's too late for that sort of practice.

Although you might be tempted to have your admins pair up or practice in groups, you end up with the more advanced students doing the practicing and everyone else doing the watching (and not really learning much). I know that helping them practice individually takes more time, but better that than letting a half-trained, unpracticed admin wreak havoc on your baby. I've been that half-trained admin before, and it's *not* a comfortable feeling for anyone.

Give slightly more than needed

System administrators are typically the first people that users call when something goes wrong. Because of that, they need some good diagnostic skills and tools to help them understand what might be wrong and fix the problem. One of the best ways to cultivate those diagnostic skills is for the admins to learn systems that are directly linked to what they're expected to operate. For example, they don't need to understand internal combustion engines to drive a car, but if they have some basic understanding of the engine and how it works, they can talk to their mechanics more intelligently and maybe even fix some minor problems themselves from time to time. The same is true for computer systems. If their task as administrators is to keep the spam filter up and running smoothly, a good basic understanding of the underlying operating system and mail system will help them considerably in understanding what might be going on when things go wrong.

Training the Helpdesk Staff

The helpdesk workers are the front lines in the battle to keep users happy. If the helpdesk workers have the training and the skills to do their job, the user population will be happier and more productive.

One of the natural next steps for helpdesk staff is system administration, and training is one of the places where they can anticipate such a career move. So, although few training items (such as how to walk users through the interface via telephone) are specific to helpdesk staff, have some of them sit in on the system administrator training. It will also give the helpdesk staff some insight into how escalated problems are handled.

One of the most striking differences between training the helpdesk staff and everyone else is that the knowledge and information they need for the first week of live operations of the filter are different from the second week, and things may continue to change as people get more used to the new technology. Some end-users learn quickly and progress to more advanced issues, but others get stuck at the starting line, wondering what this spam thing is all about.

Anticipating user questions and issues

It's important to anticipate what kinds of questions people will be calling the helpdesk with so that you can prepare the helpdesk personnel to field those calls quickly and effectively. Because you are familiar with your users, you will best know what kinds of questions your users might ask, but these are some tried-and-true favorites that users will ask about spam:

- ✔ I was expecting some e-mail and didn't get it. How do I know whether it was blocked?
- ✔ Where does spam go when it dies?
- ✔ How do I get to my quarantine again?
- ✔ I found what I was looking for in quarantine. How do I get it out?
- ✔ How do I add senders to our/my whitelist/blacklist?
- ✔ I just received a spam. What should I do?
- ✔ I sent someone an e-mail, but she hasn't received it. Did our spam blocker block this?
- ✔ Someone sent me something. I didn't receive it, and it isn't in quarantine. What happened to my e-mail?

Standing firm

Some of what makes spam filtering and quarantine work on a large scale is that IT is able to unload some of the work of dealing with quarantine to each individual user. However, the first time some users take a peek at their quarantine folder to find a missing e-mail and discover that they have 3,000 spams to sift through to find the missing missive, they will call the helpdesk and ask them to find it for them. If the user is an executive who literally doesn't have time to go looking for it, the helpdesk worker needs to exercise some judgment. However, generally the helpdesk worker should gently persuade users to do the task themselves and delete the extra spam in the quarantine while they're at it.

Revisit the training after the trial implementation

One sure way to anticipate user questions is to make careful notes of what questions your sample group asks during a trial implementation. With that list of questions in hand, you should do two things:

- ✔ Make changes to the implementation, eliminating as many of the difficulties as possible before the rollout to everyone.
- ✔ Brief the helpdesk personnel on what came up during the trial and how best to answer the known questions.

Make the escalation path clear

Helpdesk workers should know when to cut bait on a user program that they do not understand and exactly who to escalate the problem to. There's nothing more frustrating to users than having the feeling that their problem is stuck in first level support when it should be handed up the chain to someone that can make more progress with it.

Building a knowledge base

The most effective training tool you have at your disposal is experience. The collective experience of everyone who has been working with the malware-blocking solution can be a lot of useful information if it's well organized and available. Instead of having many different persons solving the same problem over and over, have the first person who solves it tell the others how.

Plan to capture good solutions from the start by not only collecting all your training and reference material into a handy online database, but by tracking and collecting all the resolutions to helpdesk tickets during both the trial and eventual production rollout.

Several software packages are available for organizing a knowledge base, but not all of them can handle diverse information types and sources. When you're building a collection of information regarding a complete system, use knowledge base software that can accept text, images, hyperlinks, and entire documents in several formats, and that ultimately interfaces with your helpdesk trouble-ticket software to use the information collected there.

Although you do want to collect information from as many authors and sources as possible, the information in the knowledge base must be accurate. To provide accuracy, you need an approval process that allows trusted administrators to mark information collected as correct before the information is visible to other users of the knowledge base. This can be a somewhat tedious process, but without it, automated collection of information from some sources can lead to inaccuracies in your data, which can cause a lot of wasted time for people using the knowledge base.

Chapter 8

Planning the Rollout

· ·

In This Chapter

▶ Project planning

▶ Allocating resources

▶ Planning a spam filter trial

▶ Planning a spyware filter trial

· ·

I've been witness to some of the most spectacular IT rollout failures imaginable, mostly as an outside observer, and occasionally as the one selected to mitigate the disaster. I've seen companies roll out new Web services without any load testing, just to discover that the new Web pages require six times more bandwidth than they currently have. I've seen a firewall installation for one of the world's largest oil companies fail because the firewall manufacturer failed to provide adequate hardware specifications. Among my favorite rollout flubs is a cereal company that started a Saturday morning commercial inviting millions of children to come play its online games, but its game servers could handle only thousands of players at a time, not hundreds of thousands — oops.

The point to bear in mind is, with almost no exceptions, the pain and agony of a failed rollout could have been entirely avoided through proper planning, testing, and more planning, followed by some additional planning.

This chapter lays out the planning process to get your chosen malware-filtering solution in front of your users. In many cases, I present a list of tasks, followed by a detailed explanation of those tasks. The explanations are to help you understand the processes and also help you estimate how long each will take. Take special note that although I cover both trial installation and rollout to your company, many of the tasks associated with these two tasks are identical, so I note only in the production rollout where trial rollout and production rollout are different.

Sketching Out a Plan

My high school wood shop teacher used to tell the class to "measure twice, cut once." I proceeded to ignore this advice for the next 15 years or so, only to finally realize that he (and every other shop teacher on Earth) was really onto something. In IT, the same principles of planning apply, because only two kinds of projects exist: projects that cause no disruption of any kind and couldn't possibly result in an awkward meeting with the CTO about lost productivity and IT getting a bad reputation; and real projects.

And a spam filter is definitely disruptive. As I explain in Chapter 6, no matter what type you choose (client-based, gateway-based, or ASP-based), the filter must be placed directly into the mail path for your company so that the filter can process all inbound mail and sort some out as spam. In the worst case, your implementation could disrupt e-mail delivery for hours or days and (horrors) actually lose or destroy all incoming e-mail.

A spyware filter is only slightly less disruptive: It's blocking downloads of undesirable scripts and cookies, and preventing scripts from altering IE settings. Gone wrong, spyware could make IE unstable, stop important internal Web sites from working properly, or just continue to let the bad stuff in.

To sidestep such disasters, I recommend an iterative approach to planning. A quick comparison illustrates what I mean:

- **A linear approach** assumes that the variables, resources, and timing are well known and that planning can proceed from these known starting points. In the real world, this approach is almost never possible.

- **An iterative approach** requires scoping elements of the project (creating a quantitative understanding of the project parameters), inserting them into the timeline, and revisiting them as new facts and resource limitations come to light — well before an implementation ever begins.

The truth of the matter is that every planning process uses the iterative method; some people just come to that realization during the implementation phase when it's too late to actually do anything about it. It's not unlike the regret that a skydiver feels when he realizes that he should have paid better attention in parachute-packing class. In the sections that follow, I offer some how-to advice for identifying and defining project elements, using the iterative approach, of course.

Involving the right people

Projects affect different parts of a company in different ways. Installing a new projector in the conference room might primarily affect sales and management because they're the ones giving presentations. Installing a new spam filter certainly has some effect on everyone in the company who receives e-mail, but it will likely have special interest for at least the Human Resources department and the Legal department.

> ✔ **Human resources** is in charge of helping users understand company policies regarding spam and spyware and integrating new procedures into new employee training.
>
> ✔ **Legal** is involved in setting company policies and helping the management team formulate responses to spam and spyware incidents.

Planning a spam-filtering solution should include discussions with each of the stakeholders (people with a vested interest in the success of the project) so that they have a chance to help steer the implementation and influence its outcome, prior to the outcome.

The stakeholders themselves may not be aware that a new malware filter is something they should be interested in. In those cases, the task falls to you to educate them and bring them into the planning process in such a way that they feel some ownership of the eventual outcome. Helping them understand the larger perspective (regarding how filtered e-mail is handled, what e-mail gets filtered, and what to do about the growing quarantine piles) is essential to acceptance of the new filtering solution by the rest of the company. Fortunately, it's somewhat easier to plan for the visible effects of a spyware filter, because there are practically no visible effects.

As odd as it might sound, getting stakeholders involved in the testing and validation processes can be very helpful. In most cases, they know better than you what constitutes a successful test, because they get to define the parameters of success. The more you get stakeholders involved, the more powerful advocates you'll have at the table later when explaining why some executive's Curling Sports News newsletter is accidentally getting blocked.

Planning for disaster

I like to start planning a change to infrastructure by trying to think of all the things that can go wrong. Then I figure out what I can do about each scenario. Depending on whether you're using an ASP solution or local solution (for examples of each, see Chapter 6), things can go wrong in an anti-spam project in different ways.

In my experience, it's helpful to plan for the following things to go wrong in an ASP implementation for a spam filter:

✓ ASP (Application Service Provider) isn't ready: For whatever reasons, when you direct your inbound mail to the ASP service, the service isn't ready for your mail and rejects it, throws it away, or claims that it must be something *you* are doing wrong.

✓ ASP is forwarding good mail to the wrong address (yikes!).

✓ You've already stopped allowing mail from anywhere but the ASP, but the new MX records for your mail haven't propagated to the rest of the world yet (people are still sending mail directly to your mail server).

For local implementations, the worst-case scenarios that a spam filter might cause are a little bit different:

✓ The product worked fine when you were testing it with two or three e-mails per minute, but fails at the rate at which you actually receive mail.

✓ The spam sensitivity is way too high, and half of your legitimate e-mail is being quarantined or deleted.

✓ You've underestimated the volume of spam that you need to keep in quarantine, and the quarantine disk fills up.

✓ In a highly available environment (one with built-in redundancy), your anti-spam solution is a single host, and it fails.

For spyware-blocking implementations, I recommend planning for the following problems:

✓ The third-party automation tool for your large-scale installation fails to install in a large percentage of the workstations.

✓ Installation works across all workstation platforms, but an untested configuration on some workstations makes the spyware blocker fail silently.

✓ The scheduled automatic update of signatures from several hundred internal machines at once overwhelms your Internet connection every day, causing service disruption or failed updates.

In most cases, when the problems outlined in the preceding lists occur, you need to be able to revert to using your mail system as it was before the spam changes. That can mean just cutting the filter out of the mail path or just repointing the MX records from the ASP back to your mail host. In some instances, it may mean restoring the mail server from backups, but that's why you made backups just before you made the changes, right? Right? Fortunately, the impact and effort required to revert to a prespyware-filter state are probably less drastic. Probably.

While I plan for the worst, I always hope for the best. Rather than just rely on hope though — careful planning and attention to detail greatly influence the success of a project.

Keeping your objectives in mind

Approximately 50 percent of all IT projects fail to meet their business objectives. Although this number seems staggering, you have to carefully read the crafty language I used here. I didn't just say "fail." I specifically said "fail to meet their business objectives." But then, it would be difficult to consider some new enterprise application that installed perfectly but doesn't work right as a success. There are many flavors of failure — none of them are sweet.

IT professionals many times get too caught up in the technology of a project and lose themselves in the joy of its creation. Take, for example, a firewall installation. The business goal of any firewall installation is to protect company assets while allowing business communications to flow. As often as not, I've seen the first objective met (protecting company assets) while the second part is ignored, or nodded at with a polite but disinterested smile. One person's success is another person's failure.

In many ways, failing to meet objectives furthers the notion that IT is an expensive drain on company resources with little to show in return. However, when you pay close attention to the business objectives, your budget increases, work generally goes better, and you get to keep your job for a while longer.

Scheduling

You need a schedule to stay on track. A good schedule names all the major milestones, such as the end of product and system testing, approval for the changes, installation, and post-installation testing. It also names each of the smaller steps, such as hardware preparation and testing, equipment rack preparation, space allocation, and internal and external notifications for system outages and installation. And most important, it specifies who will do the work, and how much work is required of each person.

As you begin scheduling when tasks for your rollout will take place, keep the following points in mind:

- ✔ **Check when other IT maintenance is already scheduled so that you can work around those times.** Because service-interrupting events are usually scheduled weeks or months in advance and usually occur on evenings or weekends when most people won't be impacted by the interruption, you need to know when your resources (usually personnel) will be available and ready to put the new filtering solution in place.

- ✔ **Note any scheduling constraints you need to work with.** Although life is easier when you can start with resources and processes and work forward, oftentimes the reality is that you start with a deadline and work backward from there.

✔ **For ASP-based implementations, remember that you're coordinating with the ASP as well as inside folks.** Most ASP-based solutions require changes to your company's DNS information, which may be outsourced. Without getting into the technical details here, a change to DNS can take several days to propagate throughout the Internet, so leave your old mail infrastructure in place while the new one is coming online. And keep it there, at the ready, until you totally trust your ASP to continue to do the right thing.

✔ **Take into account the worst case in scheduling too.** In the case of an installation disaster, how long will it take to recover? Will all the required resources be available until everything is back to normal?

With your schedule planned out, you need to communicate that schedule to management, who can decide when to share the pertinent parts, such as outages, and when new features will be in effect with everyone in the company. All parties should get to know and love the project schedule. Here are some tips for delivering the news:

✔ Although you may be used to working evenings or weekends, other people involved may not. If you need non-IT people for testing or validating the implementation, they need lots of warning and usually bribes.

✔ Alert everyone about changes to the schedule as early as possible. Don't wait until the last minute, hoping that the original schedule is still possible. Early notice is happy notice.

Allocating Resources

The resources for a rollout project boil down to (in decreasing order of scarcity)

✔ **People time:** Most companies try to keep track of what people are spending their time on. Even if you're the only person involved in the project, the time you spend on this will take time away from other duties and projects and will need to be accounted for in advance. If other people are involved, their time will need to be spoken for as well.

✔ **Money:** Money spent on software and hardware needs to be budgeted and assigned to this project. In the case of using an ASP, a continuing expense to pay for the services of the ASP must be allocated.

✔ **Facilities:** If you aren't using an ASP, you need space on equipment racks, network access to the place where the filtering hardware will be, power to the new equipment, and possibly even additional air conditioning and uninterruptible power. I hope that you have enough rack and floor space for this one latest addition.

> ✔ **Product:** For many products, there can be a significant lead time for purchase, meaning that if you place the order today, you will not see the product for several weeks. If your product comes with vendor assistance for installation, you'll need to consider the installers' schedules as well.

In the following sections, I offer some assistance in identifying each of these kinds of resources more specifically.

Whose time do you need?

People time is always the hardest resource to obtain. When you ask most co-workers what they're doing, you almost never hear "nothing much, just killing time." People who are good at their jobs tend to be very busy, and those are precisely the people you want involved in your project. Most non-IT people assume that the human resources needed to accomplish an IT task are either equivalent to zero or readily available. Because that's not true, you need to break the project down into tasks, assign the tasks to the various individuals best suited to accomplishing them, and make sure that they have that time reserved for the spam project on the schedule you've outlined. In the following sections, you find out which people you need to involve from IT and other areas of your business. You also find tips for finding tasks that various groups are ideally suited for.

Information Technology

IT personnel resources will be hardest hit because they will be actually performing the rollout. Everyone involved in the delivery chain for e-mail (which includes the Internet connection, DNS, firewall, internal mail server, and internal virus filter) should be a part of the planning process. At the least, have them on-call when cutting over the filter into production. A spyware-blocking project impacts IT a lot less than a spam-blocking project, but it would be unrealistic to say that there is no impact on IT during a spyware filter's rollout.

Here's the rundown of IT people you may need to involve in your project and the tasks you'll want to allocate their time for:

> ✔ **Helpdesk:** For both spam and spyware projects, the helpdesk should be involved from the design phase onward. Because these folks talk to people about their IT problems daily, including spam (and, to a lesser extent, spyware), they have a lot of knowledge about what is causing the most pain, and who is most impacted. If they understand the installed system because they helped design that installation (right?), they support it as owners of the solution instead of as observers who had no choice in the matter.

Also, be sure to involve helpdesk people in the composition of any instructions for end-users, as well as documents for fellow helpdesk people. If these documents are well crafted, they can be very helpful because they will guide users through procedures that they can perform themselves. This saves helpdesk resources for more important problems for which no self-help tools exist. I cover training materials more fully in Chapter 7.

✔ **Security team or expert:** Your security team needs to be involved from design onward on your spam project. Security will have things to say about the underlying platform and the position of the filter in the infrastructure, as well as being involved with hardening the base operating system in the case of a software solution. In some cases, spam and spyware filtering are considered to be primarily security projects, in which case the security folks are actually running the whole show. In a smaller company that doesn't have a security team or even a security expert, hopefully someone in the company has a job description that includes data security. If not, now is a good time to bring that up with management. Whoever in the company is interested in the security role should be involved as I describe here.

✔ **IT Architecture:** Larger IT departments have an IT architect, or perhaps an IT Architecture department. IT architects generally establish protocol and product standards, as well as reference architectures, to ensure consistency in the IT infrastructure throughout a larger organization. By all means, you need to include IT Architecture if you want your project to succeed. Because they are involved in setting standards, you need them involved early in the process, or you may find that your solution doesn't conform to established standards and you have to start over. Smaller companies without an IT architect may want to seek the help of an IT consultant instead to get an external view of the project and its implications.

✔ **Change Control:** A mature IT department often has a process that requires any proposed changes to any part of the IT infrastructure or services to first be approved by a group of people taken from representative areas of the company. Although this group operates as an approval process, this group is usually also good at rooting out whoever else needs to make changes to their respective infrastructure components to accommodate the new service. Change Control should be involved in scheduling the actual installation of hardware/software and anything that might affect IT services in the company.

People outside information technology

In addition to people in IT who work directly with the spam filter, you need help from several other departments, too. In the following list, I explain how you might involve the following departments in your spam filter's or spyware blocker's rollout:

✔ **Power users:** Remember that you need support services, too. For instance, in addition to actually working with the hardware and software, you may need people to help with the following tasks:

- If you do a trial implementation, the users involved in the trial require training, handholding, and time to report about their experience in the trial.

- When you test key applications, you need people to help verify that the various services in the company work as expected after installation.

The folks who offer these types of support services are usually *not* IT and require lots of notice to show up for a midnight cutover on a Saturday. (*Note:* For some users, the amount of lead time necessary for Saturday work approaches infinity.)

✔ **Legal:** If your company is large enough to have in-house legal counsel, the legal counsel should be involved in helping to establish new policies regarding the spam-filtering product and changes in e-mail handling.

One interesting area for lawyers to examine is in the area of data retention, especially with respect to spam quarantines. I've heard a lot of opinions about how spam should be treated with respect to data retention policies, but your own lawyers are the only people that should be deciding this policy for you.

You probably don't need to involve the legal department for spyware policy — just block it all!

If you don't have in-house counsel, you should ask whomever you do work with to take a look at data retention, privacy issues, and company policy regarding who has access to employee e-mail and files. If you live in a place where employees have expectations of privacy for company e-mail, the act of blocking spam could actually be a violation of that privacy.

✔ **Human Resources:** With any large change to the way business information is handled, there should be changes to policies that help everyone understand the changes and how they affect everyone. Because no spam or spyware filter is perfect, you face several issues that you must directly address. The fact that you're trying to block the bulk of it by no means implies that you're responsible for blocking all of it.

Basically, Human Resources (HR) will want to create a disclaimer that tells folks that offensive, reprehensible, dangerous material will still get through and they might occasionally still need to press Delete. And, depending on a person's role in the company (for instance, one who regularly receives e-mail from customers), she might frequently need to sift through her quarantine — enduring all the filthy and offensive subject lines — in order to harvest legitimate messages from customers.

With a spyware filter project, you probably don't need to involve HR. The effect of a spyware filter project is akin to antivirus: benign and practically invisible, I hope.

✔ **General population:** Most of this category won't be involved at all unless you want to count "unwilling guinea pig" as involvement. You might make an exception, though, if you have some especially cooperative, helpful staff in roles where they can report unexpected behavior before it turns into a flood of helpdesk calls. The general population is involved in the final rollout, because the solution is aimed at helping them. But you'll want to tap them for advice regarding special needs of their departments and users' perceptions of the spam and spyware problems early in design as well.

Estimating time for key tasks

How do you estimate how long it will take to accomplish a task that you have never done before? Time estimation for projects and subprojects is a skill that comes with experience. Even without experience, though, you can compare the new task to similar ones that you've done before, and then add 50 percent more time to be safe. Star Trek fans know that the starship's engineer, Scotty, did that all the time with Captain Kirk, then pulled off the "miracle" of saving time at the end of his task, always within 45 minutes. Be like Scotty: Underpromise and over-deliver (although it will sometimes take longer).

The first task in time estimation is simple enough: Make a list of all of the tasks that must be accomplished. After you identify the tasks, you can make a reasonable stab at allocating the time for each task, deciding who should be responsible for it, and determining which tasks depend upon the completion of other tasks. For just about any IT rollout project, these tasks boil down to these categories:

✔ Developing the architecture

✔ Assembling the pieces

✔ Putting the pieces together

✔ Testing the pieces

✔ Testing the whole thing

✔ Training the helpdesk

✔ Fixing what your testing shows is broken

✔ Testing the stuff again (this can happen many times)

✔ Documenting the production environment

✔ Training and informing users

When to leave it to the lawyers

You want to leave some decisions in filtering entirely to Human Resources. Working in a university environment in the 1980s, I was presented with the problem that the several hundred Usenet news groups that composed a full Usenet feed were starting to fill up the allocated disk space too quickly. (Note that there are currently in excess of 85,000 Usenet news groups. Times change.) The suggested solution was to eliminate the various `alt.sex` news groups as they were potentially offensive and were taking up a large amount of the space.

In discussions with the university's lawyers and librarians, I discovered an interesting thing. After you decide to be the arbiter of what is good, you can in some cases be held accountable for your good/bad filter. In other words, you've said you're keeping bad stuff out, and folks might feel that they have a right to believe that everything getting in is now good. (*Remember:* This was a conversation with a lawyer.) The same principal has at least in one case been applied to spam. Let the HR and Legal departments take the heat on what gets blocked and what doesn't. You'll sleep better.

✔ Putting the stuff into production

✔ Blaming the manufacturer or VAR for annoying defects

I take a look at each of these tasks in detail later in this chapter in the section, "Planning a Spyware Filter Trial," and also in Chapter 9. I also provide a sample project plan in Appendix A.

Money, money, money

Because you're planning your rollout, your budget has been decided for a while now, but you need to take another look at it now to make sure that your plan won't break the bank. Take a look at the resources you have identified in your plan and make sure that hardware, software, and human resources stay within the budget parameters that you set.

The type of solution you're planning for determines the kinds of budget items that you should be checking on in the planning phase. For spam, you need to consider the cost of the software, appliance, or ASP. For spyware, you're primarily interested in the software pricing. For all solutions, you need to budget for annual maintenance, including signature updates and software upgrades as well as any direct expenses for overtime on your project.

If your planning appears to put the project over budget, be sure to take a look at Chapter 4, where I talk about calculating return on investment. The bean counters are always pleased when you can show that parts of the IT budget are going to create a reasonable return, and the better you do this part, the more money you have for the project.

Rounding up the hardware and software

The hardware and software resources that your rollout requires are entirely dependent on the product selected. In the case of an ASP solution, no additional internal hardware or software should be required at all. Typically, with software solutions, you have to make four hardware choices:

- ✔ If it's a standalone product, you can usually either run it on an existing server or its own dedicated box. I don't recommend using an existing server usually, because the disk space requirements for archive and quarantine can be extensive if those functions are local.

- ✔ If it's an appliance, it comes with its own hardware, and you don't have to make any choices.

- ✔ In some cases, spam filtering is an add-on to existing filtering products, usually virus filtering. In this case, the product would run on top of the existing filtering hardware.

- ✔ In the case of spyware filtering, this is often performed on users' workstations. Aside from a management console (if you selected a product with central management and control), you may not have hardware issues to deal with.

Remember too that in a highly available environment (multiple servers in a load-balancing and/or failover configuration) and/or distributed environment, you multiply all hardware requirements by at least two, sometimes more.

Working with outside resources

Outside resources come in three basic flavors: vendors/manufacturers, consultants, and service providers. The success of the rollout might depend on the timely assistance or performance of one or more of these outside resources. The following sections explain how to work with outside resources in the planning stages so that your rollout will go more smoothly.

Manufacturers

Whether you're talking about hardware or software, the *manufacturer* of the product that you're rolling out is a critical resource to know and love. The manufacturer is the go-to resource for anything closely related to the behavior or misbehavior of the system after eliminating user error as an issue.

It is increasingly rare for product manufacturers to offer free installation support other than their overburdened telephone support lines. However, at the high end of the market (and possibly for large installations), you can generally get the attention of a local sales engineer who can help. In cases where the manufacturer is selling mostly direct rather than through resellers, the manufacturer could most likely arrange to put a qualified engineer or two on-site for your installation and testing. If you will be using the manufacturer's engineering help in this way, be sure to communicate your schedule and implementation plan with the manufacturer as soon as possible so that it can provide the engineering resources when you need them.

Vendors and consultants

Vendors or consultants are usually at least *somewhat* involved in the planning and installation of an enterprise spam-filtering product. Sometimes installation assistance is provided as a part of the purchase price, and sometimes it will incur additional costs, but it's almost always available.

Initial configuration of some of the products in this market can be pretty tricky, and having an expert on hand for the rollout can make a huge difference. A good value-added reseller has done the kind of project that you're working on dozens of times and can provide insight to the planning process after you select a product.

The level of assistance available from consultants varies from planning and management advice to complete management of the project with pricing to match. Most companies settle for somewhere in the middle to keep a rein on costs, but still have in-depth expertise available for the project.

Keep in mind that good consultants are busy consultants, and scheduling their time well in advance is always a good idea.

Service providers

If you've chosen an ASP (Application Service Provider) spam-filtering solution, the product and the outside service provider are the same thing. The good news here is that an experienced ASP has done the kind of rollout that you are planning many times, and knows its end of things very well. Because the ASP does know it well, I always like to get the process documented in writing from the ASP, along with schedules and timing, so there are no surprises. For more details about what an ASP solution is, please see Chapter 6.

Other service providers might be involved with the delivery of your e-mail — your Internet service provider (ISP) for one. Chances are good that your ISP is providing only a data pipe through which the mail (and spam) flows, but it may also be responsible for your DNS, which tells the world exactly what Internet host to send your mail to. For an ASP-based solution, you almost certainly must change the IP address or host name where your mail is delivered, so that your ASP can filter it for you. Whoever is operating your DNS needs to be in the loop and ready to make the change when required.

Changes made to DNS are rarely instantaneous because hundreds or even thousands of DNS servers throughout the world will have cached the current (old) server name and IP address where your e-mail is to be delivered. It could be hours or even days before all those DNS servers decide that their cached entries for your server should be refreshed — only then will each respective server know the new server where your mail needs to be delivered. Because there may be long delays (perhaps as long as 10 to 14 days), you need to plan when these changes happen in order for the full effect of the DNS change to occur on schedule.

Tracking Tasks

When you plan for a rollout, it's essential to develop project-management tools and skills for tracking how each task or phase of the project is progressing. You need to keep track of two kinds of time:

- ✔ **Calendar time:** How much time a task is expected to take. This will be a far larger number than project time.
- ✔ **Project time:** The actual hours spent on the task.

Be realistic about estimating both of these. For instance, if you calculate that a particular task will take about 16 hours of Billy's time, it's probably not going to get done in two uninterrupted 8-hour days, back to back. If Billy has other things that he must be doing, you need to take that into account when figuring out when that task will be complete.

Make sure that everyone — including their managers — whose time is a part of your plan knows how much of their time has been spoken for and when they will be needed. If you're creating a detailed project plan with each person's tasks listed, provide them with copies of the detailed plan so that they know what to expect and when.

By having everyone involved in the project give status reports, you can more easily see where you are in the process and to know whether you're on track for a timely completion. I like to use PERT charts to help me understand what changes to task completion do to the overall project, but other methods are available, including Gantt charts. The goal is to have some representation that shows you what effect changing completion dates for milestones has on the project.

PERT and Gantt charts are graphical representations of all the project tasks that allow you to get a handle on relationships between tasks (PERT charts are best for this) and between tasks and schedule (Gantt charts show schedules best). Figure 8-1 shows a simple Gantt chart.

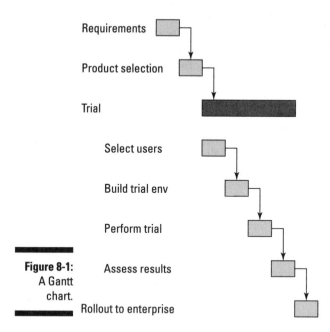

Requirements

Product selection

Trial

Select users

Build trial env

Perform trial

Figure 8-1: Assess results
A Gantt
chart. Rollout to enterprise

Although in team projects, you need to make sure everyone stays on task to accomplish their parts on time, you can make this happens without becoming known as The Taskmaster — or, worse yet, The Project Manager. The best method I've seen so far is to keep project reporting and discussions very open and group oriented. Although an individual may easily explain away a lack of progress to you, he'll find it harder to share that with a group of peers when they *know* he's been spending his time installing that new projector in the conference room and "testing" DVD playback with the four-hour extended version of *The Lord of the Rings: Return of the King.*

Putting Together a Spam Filter Trial

E-mail is a particularly difficult environment to test because making small changes is darn hard. For instance, you can easily say, "All mail for `example.com` goes to `mailhost.example.com`." It's somewhat more difficult technically to say, "All mail for `example.com` goes to `mailhost.example.com`, except for `bill@example.com`, `mary@example.com`, and `ed@example.com`, whose mail should instead go to `filtertrial.example.com`."

By doing a trial, you better understand what bugs exist in the system you've so carefully planned and can resolve at least *some* of those issues before the full rollout.

In the case of gateway- or ASP-based spam filtering, you may not have an option of doing a trial — it may be all or nothing. In that case, plan carefully and rely on the experience of your ASP or reseller to help you test prior to launch. You can test SMTP by using telnet or fake DNS entries, but this book doesn't have enough room for me to cover that. If you are familiar with these methods, you probably already know that you can force an e-mail to your company to be delivered to the ASP by using telnet (which I cover in Chapter 12) or create a DNS subdomain so that you can test the ASP by using mail to billy@spamtest.yourcompany.com. If you aren't familiar with using these methods, you have to just cut over and hope for the best.

Some host-based filters may allow you to install the filter on the inside mail host (typically Microsoft Exchange) but only activate the filter for certain users. If you're using client-based filters, it's even simpler: Just load the filter onto the clients you selected for the trial. In these situations, test the solution on a limited number of users in controlled circumstances in order to better understand what you'll be facing when you roll out the solution to the enterprise. Similarly, you'll probably have greater control with hardware (appliance based) filters by selectively filtering mail for just certain trial users. Whatever form your spam filter takes, you would do well to make sure the filter you choose gives you the flexibility to test it with just a few users.

Developing measurable success criteria

Often, people are tempted to think that success or failure is some sort of absolute measure that will be obvious to anyone observing the process. Although that's true for simple systems or tasks, it becomes less true the more complex the task or system becomes.

Because you're working on filtering malware and not doing something really complicated like predicting the weather, you can settle on some pretty useful criteria that will tell you a lot about how well you're doing. Malware filtering success is (mostly) all about the numbers. Table 8-1 is a sample table for scoring a spam filter trial.

Table 8-1	Scoring Success for the Trial	
Test Trial #	*Expected*	*Actual*
Percentage False Negatives	3%	
Percentage False Positives	1%	
% Loss	0.05%	
Whitelist failures	0	
Blacklist failures	0	

Test Trial #	Expected	Actual
Average Delay	2 seconds	
Helpdesk calls (per 100 user days)		

You will almost certainly have criteria of your own to add to this table, but this is a good starting point. The idea here is that in the testing phase of your trial, you're testing and fixing things until you consistently see the results in the Actual column turning up the same or better than the numbers in the Expected column.

The Expected column is derived from what you understand about the capabilities of your solution. If the manufacturer makes claims about what its product can do, those claims will be represented here. The actuals should come from reports that the product itself generates or from analyses of helpdesk calls.

Performing tests

Testing is all about measuring and breaking stuff. I was once asked to test a Web site to 80 percent of its capacity, rather than all the way to failure at 100 percent. The person asking was in charge of a large IT department and paying me to help, so I didn't ask the obvious question — how do I know what 80 percent is if I don't know what 100 percent is?

In a trial, you're looking for all the bad behavior that your chosen malware solution can dish out, and you fail only if you can't make the solution itself fail.

Load testing ASP solutions to failure is not polite, and will likely violate your agreement with the ASP. Consider asking the ASP whether it has done load testing. If it has, get a look at the results. You can also ask whether the ASP has a separate test platform just for load testing.

Use the descriptions of the tasks in the following sections to help with your planning and resource allocation for your test.

Step 1: Collect the pieces

Usually, you need hardware, software, and people. I like to fill my computer rooms with lots of systems that do only one task each (Microsoft seems to like that, too), so for me, the hardware part is all about getting a new computer or computers to install the filter software onto. In some cases, the hardware and the software combine into a magical oneness that's called an *appliance,* which comes from one manufacturer and is supported as a unit. In any case, there will be lead times for ordering the various items required, and you can divine those lead times from the folks taking the orders.

Step 2: Put the pieces together

Whee! This is the fun part. You get to plug all of the stuff in, sniff to check for smoke, and start loading software. You've done this before with other software — you know *exactly* how long this part should take. Write that number down, and then multiply it by three to come up with your time estimate (which gives you time to read the manual if you run into problems). You forgot how many times you would have to reboot the whole mess to get it installed. You forgot that the version of Windows you're using doesn't come with drivers for the network cards, and those drivers have to be carted in on a hay wagon from Timbuktu. Oh yeah, because this system will be dealing with the e-mail equivalent of toxic waste, you need to make sure the OS is encased in kryptonite, or hardened to NSA standards, or both. Just take my word for it, use your best guess times three.

Step 3: Test the pieces

Depending on the solution you're looking at, you need to do the following types of testing:

- ✔ **Unit testing:** This is the testing of all the individual testable pieces, such as the new firewall rules that redirect the mail from the original mail server to the new filter.

- ✔ **Systems testing:** This comes after unit testing. In systems testing, you look at how the whole system performs together.

- ✔ **Redundancy testing:** If you have a redundant architecture (multiple identical systems with automatic fail over), you need to make systems fail to know and understand how this part is working.

- ✔ **Content efficacy testing:** The core of the filtering product is to filter. How well is it doing that?

- ✔ **Unit failure:** If individual parts of the system fail, what effect does that have on the rest of the system? For instance, if your quarantine server fails, does mail just stop getting delivered?

- ✔ **Load testing:** This is one of my favorites because I just like pushing things until they break. It turns out that this is also useful in that it tells you something about your *actual* capacity, compared to your *design* capacity, or your best guess.

When performing system tests, things may happen that are unrelated to the testing, but important to the project, which should be noted. One example of this would be that the new hardware sounds like a jet engine during takeoff, and will thereby earn you the wrath of all the pasty white denizens of the computer room. Things like noise, power load, heat load, onerous maintenance, and poor color choice may or may not affect your installation, but should all be a part of what you observe while testing.

Marketing speak: Appliance

Before 1998, the generally accepted definition of an *appliance* in information technology was a device with an embedded operating system that performed a single task — like routing packets. The old-style appliance was generally considered to be more reliable than a computer running an off-the-shelf operating system with proprietary software and a hard drive spinning away 24/7, with its usual systems administration life cycle of break, fix, change, break, fix, change, and so on.

Then marketing discovered that everything in IT would be 32 percent more buyable if it was an appliance, rather than just an ordinary combination of hardware and software. Thus the term *appliance* was applied to whatever they wanted to sell. And it's especially lucrative selling something called an "appliance" to an IT executive, who will think — sometimes correctly — that the appliance is as easy to use and as inexpensive to maintain as an RFC2325-compliant drip coffee maker (for an explanation, go to www. faqs.org/rfcs/rfc2325.html).

Nowadays, the appliance moniker doesn't really mean much. If you're lucky, it means that the product comes as a single package with a power cord, Ethernet connector, power switch, and powered-on light — all supported directly by the manufacturer. Always read the fine print though, because sometimes *appliance* just means that you buy it all from the manufacturer, paying huge margins on hardware that you could have bought yourself, and the support for the hardware comes from the original hardware manufacturer.

For a spam filter, you're interested in two things from a content testing perspective: Does it filter spam and does it allow nonspam? Sounds simple, right? In practice, you want to combine spam-filtering content tests with load testing in case there's a mix of spam and nonspam that breaks everything. For instance, if you do load testing with all nonspam, you might not discover that the spam-filtering process uses much more CPU than just processing normal mail, and get a false reading on capacity. Based on current mix of spam to nonspam on the Internet, one good test is 25 percent nonspam to 75 percent spam. That's pretty close to reality these days.

 When testing your spam solution, sample e-mails that are guaranteed to trigger the filter every time are really handy. Because you and I both know that none of the filters are perfect, a guaranteed spam e-mail isn't such a simple thing to devise unless someone has already covered this ground and come up with something clever. As it turns out, folks have agreed upon a simple string of characters that should always set off any spam detector. This simple string is called the Generic Test for Unsolicited Bulk Email (GTUBE), without actually including any spam. The GTUBE will be rejected as spam because spam-filter manufacturers have all agreed that if their product detects the GTUBE string (shown in the following code) in mail, the product will treat it as spam, even though it's not really spam. Your spam-filter manufacturer may not support this handy spam-testing tool, but if it doesn't, please call it and tell it that it needs to. Being able to simulate spam without actually sending spam is important to those of us in the spam trenches. For your enjoyment, here is a fully formatted spam e-mail in RFC822 format, ready to use:

```
Subject: GTUBE Test
Message-ID: <GTUBEID.baddie@domain.com>
Date: Tue, 5 Oct 2004 12:32:00 +0900
From: baddie <baddie@domain.com>
To: Victim <victim@domain.com>
Precedence: junk
MIME-Version: 1.0
Content-Type: text/plain; charset=us-ascii
Content-Transfer-Encoding: 7bit

The line below is the Generic Test for Unsolicited Bulk Email
        (GTUBE)

XJS*C4JDBQADN1.NSBN3*2IDNEN*GTUBE-STANDARD-ANTI-UBE-TEST-
        EMAIL*C.34X

This should never make it past a spam filter.
```

When you schedule testing, allow enough time to run through all the scenarios you can think of that might break the spam filter in interesting ways. Because I have a deviant destructive streak, my testing can take a long time. And then, of course, you need to allocate time for fixing what you just broke in a way that makes it not happen again, which is the subject of the next section.

Here are some examples of tests that you will want to perform, but you will no doubt have more that these based on your unique environment and user needs:

✔ Load test using typical e-mail sizes and a mix of 70 percent spam.

✔ Load test using 100 percent spam.

✔ Load test using 100 percent spam, each message 200 characters long (tests exhaustion of file handles).

✔ Load test using 100 percent spam, each message 2MB long until the quarantine is full.

✔ Test using 70,000 accumulated known spam e-mails, looking for false negatives.

✔ Test using 30,000 normal e-mails, looking for false positives.

✔ Test sending known spam from a sender on the whitelist (it should not get marked as spam!).

✔ Test sending spam with a spoofed From: address claiming to be a whitelisted entry.

✔ For appliance solutions, turn off the inside mail host and perform all load tests in this list.

✔ Test using image-based spam without text.

Step 4: Fix what your testing shows is broken

If your testing is successful, you've broken your spam-filtering solution a bit. This is really one of the most difficult time estimates facing you at the beginning of the project. You have to assume that your testing will show flaws in the design, the product, and so on, but you have no idea to what degree.

Here are some handy tips for fixing some of the more common kinds of problems you may have discovered in testing:

- ✔ **Capacity problems:** If any of the tests show that your new filter just doesn't have the capacity to handle the kind of loads required, your only choice is to beef up the hardware that's not keeping up. If it's an appliance, consider load balancing (splitting the load evenly across more than one appliance).

- ✔ **Filtering problems:** If the filter is quarantining too much e-mail, you need to relax the spam filter's rules somewhat. Alternatively, consider improving your whitelists by including the source addresses that are getting quarantined.

- ✔ **Storage capacity problems:** If any of the testing is filling up your hard drives with spam, log files, or normal e-mail, increase the disk capacities of your quarantine, mail server, or filtering appliance to compensate for the additional space requirements.

My advice about time estimates in this area is to pull together the best people you know in the field, go over the numbers very carefully, possibly creating spreadsheets for "what-if" scenarios. After that, do some sophisticated mathematical modeling (based on chaos theory and NASA's heat distribution graphs for the space shuttle bottom tiles during re-entry), and then use whatever number seems right at the time. I call this method "guessing." Archimedes perfected guessing when he, uh, guessed his own specific gravity. Had he been around in the 21st century, no doubt he would have been a computer scientist or a project manager, and he'd still be guessing.

Typically, this testing takes from about a day for small companies with a few dozen employees to a couple of months for larger companies with thousands of users and dozens of internal mail servers.

The problem as you plan is that you don't know what the problem is. The information you gather during testing may tell you that the whole solution is unworkable, and furthermore, it can't be fixed using your chosen product. At that point, you pretty much have to go back to product evaluation (see Chapter 6), and your timeline goes out the window. Pick some numbers for time estimates here that make sense given a limited number of problems from testing, and see how well you did when all is said and done. Moreover, make sure management understands that you may need to reject a chosen spam- or spyware-blocking solution based on your testing and evaluation.

Step 5: Test the stuff again

After you fix the problems you identified from the first test, you need to test again. For this round of retesting, you can just concentrate on what you had problems with, but you will eventually have to go back and test everything again, which I describe the following section, "Step 6: Regression testing."

After the second round of testing, you can probably stop.

You might have to run through this process a few times, but eventually, your testing won't show any problems that rise to the exalted level of "show stopper." Your testing isn't complete until no more serious problems are found.

The bad news here is that a second stage of testing isn't usually any shorter than the first stage. How can that be, if all you need to test is the stuff that broke in the first round of testing? After all, it should be a shorter list the second time around. That's only true if you leave out regression testing.

Step 6: Regression testing

In any large system, changing some variable to fix a problem almost certainly affects other parts of the system that you didn't intend to change. You can imagine, for example, that fixing the filtering characteristics so that it goes from catching 20 percent of your spam to 98 percent of your spam might cause the quarantine area to fill up five times faster than in previous tests.

When you make any changes to the system, go back and check all the things that were working perfectly before, to make sure that they are *still* working perfectly. This is known as regression testing, and it makes the second stage of testing actually longer than the first stage, because you spend extra time looking at what you fixed, and at least the same amount of time looking at the stuff that was working well the first time.

Spam is almost "analog" in its methods for evaluating messages: Yes, what spam filters do is deterministic, but oftentimes their complexity is beyond normal understanding. This is why regression testing is so important.

Selecting users for a trial

Suitable users for a trial are a precious resource, and in most organizations, the best ones have been used for this purpose often enough that they may be in hiding at this point. Put some cheese out in a darkened room and sit quietly for a while, and eventually those users will be curious enough to come around and see what's up. (I'm only half kidding here.)

Curiosity is one of the traits that you should be looking for in your trial users. In addition, you need to select users from the population at your company who

- ✔ Reflect all of the major use cases for e-mail that you have: power users, executives, administrative assistants, infrequent users, road warriors, and people whose addresses are named on your Web page.

- ✔ Are willing to put up with a bit of disruption in their e-mail for the greater good of the company.

- ✔ Are willing to spend the time to report their experiences back to you.

In exchange for these users' good will and extra effort, make the disruption as minor as possible and the reporting process as simple and uniform as possible. Wherever you can, provide feedback forms for these folks to fill out, e-mail addresses for sending feedback and asking questions, and phone numbers for them to call. That makes it simple and quick for them and it gives you a uniform format for all of the data you are getting back from your trial guinea pigs.

You should also feed your selected users. No, I really mean that. Provide snacks at meetings and bring coffee when you stop by their offices to check on things. These folks are spending time and effort to help your project go as smoothly as possible when you roll out to the whole company, and I doubt that it will show up as a plus on their next evaluation. If anything, any loss of productivity from the disruption will reflect poorly on them. Plus, it's a way to put doughnuts on the project expenses (but please send me the extras).

Evaluating trial results

If your trial has gone well, you have lots and lots of information about end-user experiences, how effective the spam filter is (or is not), and how helpful and useful the helpdesk at the ASP or vendor is.

Take another look at the success criteria that you developed for testing earlier in this chapter. In a real live test, using real users:

- ✔ Did the filter yield the same results as in your earlier testing?

- ✔ Were your expected results reasonable/okay with real users?

- ✔ Was product support — both internal and external — up to your expectations?

- ✔ Were there any surprises?

To find answers to these questions, you need to interview your users, and as much as possible, make sure you get standardized results, as I explain in the following sections.

Interview your trial users

Plan to interview your trial users at the beginning and again near the end of the trial. If you have any users who had a particularly bad time during the trial, plan to talk to each of them separately so they feel comfortable telling you everything they experienced and what impact the trial had on their work. Some people aren't comfortable bringing up issues in front of a larger group, especially if nobody else is "complaining." Some people don't like to be a spoiler.

Also, get all the trial users together for a group discussion regarding their experiences with the trial. If an issue hasn't yet come to light in the numbers or the feedback forms, group discussion can bring out the fact that several people noticed the same thing, but nobody reported it, thinking it was only his or her problem.

You might also entertain the idea of having the users do their own focus group, where they can discuss the trial away from you and other project people. Give them an agenda, issues to discuss, and direct them to produce some written deliverables. Be sure to pick a group leader from the user group who will keep the rest of the group focused. Away from the presence of project people (like you), they may be even more forthcoming.

Standardize your results

To the degree that you can, use feedback forms, questionnaires, and automated information gathering to summarize the results of your trial. It may seem tedious to wade through all the stacks of feedback forms and other paper generated by the process, but this kind of information gathering helps point out the differences between someone just having a bad day with e-mail and a serious flaw in your product or implementation.

Incorporating lessons learned into your deployment plan

Albert Einstein said, "Insanity is doing the same thing over and over again and expecting different results." (I presume that he didn't know about chaos theory.) Now that you have the results from testing and a trial installation, you should correct the mistakes in the trial that caused problems and perform a perfect rollout to our users, right?

Would that it were so simple. The problem is that you don't have specific cause-and-effect data staring you in the face. What you have at the end of testing and trials is a listing of effects, and it's your job to root out the various causes so you can avoid them. In the testing phase, you do unit testing, trying to isolate all the individual pieces of the new solution and test them independently. It may be time to try that again, with some specific problems to solve.

You can easily zero in on technical problems that you know how to solve and ignore or discount some of the human problems, which are often far more important to the success of your project. For instance, if almost everyone in the trial didn't understand how to maintain the spam quarantine, it's not because your trial users were stupid, but rather a problem with the documentation, training, or the product itself. You must solve these kinds of problems before rolling out the solution to the whole company, or risk dealing with a revolt of your helpdesk staff.

Sometimes, you need to repeat the whole testing and trial phase of a project, if sufficient problems (the software just doesn't perform as described by the manufacturer, for example) are encountered in the trial. It doesn't do wonders for your deployment schedule, but it can mean the difference between your users embracing a new technology or grumbling about the latest broken thing IT is forcing down everyone's throats.

Planning a Spyware Filter Trial

Compared to the complexity of a spam filter trial, a spyware filter trial doesn't require a lot of preparation, primarily because a spyware filter is less disruptive. Whereas you insert a spam filter between incoming e-mail and your users, a spyware filter works behind the scenes.

A spyware filter that only scans and removes spyware is the least intrusive of all. While a user is using his or her workstation, no spyware-filter software is running — the PC is operating virtually unchanged from before. However, because there's a remote chance that installing the spyware filter may have an adverse effect on a user's workstation, regression testing the important functions on the workstation is still a good idea. That way, you're sure that everything is operating normally before you have installed the program on dozens, hundreds, or thousands of workstations!

In the case where the spyware filter is running in the background all the time, watching for spyware trying to install itself, the installation can be considerably more intrusive because it's trying to hook itself into the same places as antivirus software. This sort of blocker is more effective, but also requires more testing for this reason.

Needed: Measurable tests and results

Before you embark on your spyware blocker trial, you need to develop objective, testable criteria so that you will know whether your testing was successful or not. Rather than a casual "does it install okay and work okay" approach, you need something more formal such as checklists and spaces to write down specific findings and values while testing. A few such tests might be:

- ✔ Does the product install correctly?
- ✔ Can the product be removed correctly and completely?
- ✔ Does each important function on the user's workstation still function properly (you need a checklist for each item)?
- ✔ Does the filter properly identify and handle known spyware components?
- ✔ If there are automated components, such as spyware signature downloading, do those components operate as expected?
- ✔ Are there useful activity logs being generated that the IT staff can examine regularly?
- ✔ Do any manual tasks users do operate properly, and are instructions accurate?

Your checklist needs to be much longer than this and detailed enough so that no problem will go unnoticed. The more thorough you are during testing, the less likely you are to have problems later on when you deploy to the enterprise.

Identifying false positives

You need to make sure that the spyware filter does not exhibit any false positives — that is, you don't want the spyware filter to finger something business related as spyware. Although this is unlikely in signature-based spyware programs, spyware filters that begin to rely more on heuristics (like antivirus programs) might flag something you use as spyware. Testing is the time to identify and manage these kinds of issues.

Users' chores

Spyware filters that rely upon users to perform regular chores, such as signature updates and scans, require more careful testing. If you plan to send reminders to users that it's time again to update signatures and rescan for spyware, make sure that they understand the instructions and will actually carry them out.

It works fine from home!

Diagnosing what is wrong when browsing to specific Web sites can be a real challenge. Between Apache, IIS, Firefox, and Internet Explorer, many combinations don't work together as well as one would hope, and that is ignoring the fact that some of the more intelligent firewalls out there are now enforcing RFC-compliant HTTP and HTML to prevent some Web-based exploits from working. On the other hand, Internet Explorer is generally pretty lax about the protocols and HTML and will do its best to display even the most poorly constructed Web pages. So, when you are working with business users inside the firewall, the common complaint is that when they go to this site at home, it works fine. There must me something wrong with the systems at work. In fact, the opposite is true. The work systems are filtering out bogus HTML, JavaScript, dangerous ActiveX, and other things that may well be causing the Web page to render poorly, but that's by design!

When you rely on users to help with updates, I recommend auditing from time to time to make sure that the user tasks are being performed. Usually, you can accomplish auditing by asking your helpdesk workers to take a look at any machine they touch for some other maintenance task, see whether the signatures have been updated, and run a scan. But you may need something more scheduled and formal to be sure that everything is being taken care of.

Nondisruptive browser use

Active spyware filters — those that detect and block spyware in real time — require more testing than scan-and-remove filters. Make sure that known and often-visited Intranet (internal) sites all work properly. Oftentimes an organization uses active scripting in order to enrich functionality; you've got to make sure that these all work as before.

Even if you carefully test all the Web sites that people tell you they need to use, expect some to crop up after testing due to the fact that users forget about sites that they use only infrequently and new sites appear all the time, which might be of business interest to your users. The fact that the spyware filter is in place is another thing to put in your diagnostic toolbox when someone is asking why a particular Web site isn't working properly for them.

Chapter 9

Rolling Out to the Enterprise

In This Chapter

▶ Implementing spam and spyware filtering

▶ Installing software and hardware solutions

▶ Measuring early results

▶ Creating backout plans

*A*fter you have a plan, actually getting a spam or spyware filter implemented should be a walk in the park, right? Although I feel that a good plan is essential, *experience* is usually the thing that makes or breaks the installation phase. When cables and wires and install CDs start flying around, it's nice to have someone involved who's done this stuff a few times.

If you or your co-workers don't have that experience, never fear, because I'm going to give you the next best thing in this chapter: Advice from an experienced person. I've participated in hundreds of installations like the one you are contemplating, and in this chapter, I share what I know about getting it all rolled out.

Implementing Spam Filtering

Putting a spam filter in place in a business that has never had such a filter before can be a little tricky. The biggest problem that you will have is that you're taking something that everyone in the company uses every day, making drastic changes to it, and forcing them to change the way that they use it. Because of this, small mistakes can be easily blown out of proportion, and large mistakes can cause serious harm to productivity, or worse.

Furthermore, your current e-mail infrastructure might have been built in a hurry by a contractor a few years ago, and it might also be poorly documented, or not documented at all. If you are in a larger organization and have multiple mail servers and/or mail servers running sendmail, you may be proceeding down a somewhat risky path. If no one in the organization really knows how e-mail flows today, the introduction of a spam filter in the path is going to be interesting.

Because proper e-mail delivery is so important to your company, you should exercise care when putting a new e-mail infrastructure like spam filtering into place, and you should choose the best possible solution within your resource constraints. Remember a few things to help smooth the way:

- ✔ A service interruption is unavoidable, and you will only be able to *guess* at the duration.
- ✔ Although unlikely with proper planning, it is possible that some mail will get permanently lost in the transition.
- ✔ Even a perfect installation will still confuse some users.
- ✔ There's no such thing as a perfect installation.

I cover the basic hurdles of implementation here for all the major anti-spam models that you might choose, but each installation is unique, so what I'm really trying to provide is come clear guidelines for success.

All spam-filtering solutions have a few things in common when it comes to implementation, such as the fact that careful planning is required, and user training is critical to success. The following sections get a little more detailed about implementing the most common forms of spam filters. Then I offer some advice for notifying users.

Installing a software solution

A software solution is technically simple, but it also carries some of the greatest risk in terms of impact to your mail system. Because the software solution will be running on the mail server itself, any problems in the installation of the spam-filtering software are magnified by the fact that they may also impact the mail system directly.

Because of the potential harm to the mail system due to a problem installation of the spam software, I recommend that you do some test installations on a mail host other than the production mail host (meaning that the mail host isn't a part of your current mail system and is temporarily devoted to just testing) to get the feel for how it works and how you want to respond to installation prompts. If you don't have sufficient hardware and software licenses to do this, I recommend following these steps before installing a software solution on your production mail server:

1. **Perform a full image backup of the mail server, making sure that it is possible to restore it to the original state quickly.**

   This process is sometimes just called *imaging,* and the restoration process is called *reimaging,* as in, "I really messed that system up. I need to reimage it."

2. **When you are ready to install the software on the mail server, turn off mail at the perimeter.**

   This is simple at a firewall or router — just stop letting mail in at that point. This will prevent legitimate mail from getting chopped up or deleted while the new, untested system is coming online. E-mail messages that other organizations want to deliver to your e-mail server will wait in their queues until your mail server is running again.

   Plan the installation for after work hours, and estimate downtime as however long it would take you to restore the system to its original state if the installation fails plus the time it will take to know whether the new system will be okay.

3. **Install the software per the manufacturer's instructions. Use defaults wherever possible and make sure that the defaults fit your environment.**

   I suggest that you have a sales engineer from the manufacturer or a VAR (value-added reseller) in attendance for this step, because they will have done it before many times.

4. **If you can, test the installation manually by spoofing an incoming e-mail to the system (the real incoming mail is still turned off at this point). See what the filter does with your spoofed mail.**

   I explain how to spoof an e-mail in Chapter 12.

5. **Also test internal mail by just sending some mail to someone else in your company to make sure that nothing has been affected by the filter installation.**

6. **Turn e-mail back on at the network perimeter briefly.**

   Give it ten minutes or so of delivering e-mail in and out and then turn it back off. Check the disposition of all the e-mail that came in and out while things were back on and fix whatever might have caused e-mail to go astray.

7. **Depending on how well your system responded to the tests outlined in these steps, you need to either back out or proceed with the installation.**

   If the installation is not working and you see no way to make it work, start backing out of this installation however you can to get things back to normal. If the new software will uninstall cleanly, do that. If the new software is dug into the bowels of your mail server, it's time to reinstall and recover from backups.

   If everything seems to be working well, you can turn mail back on at the perimeter for good, and then start debugging the smaller issues. Watch things very carefully for a while on the mail server and the network to make sure that everything is working as expected. Keep that image backup of the mail server handy for the first few days of operation, but as time goes on and new mail accumulates, your ability to restore the mail server with the image backup diminishes. Make sure that the mail data backups that capture only e-mail are being done regularly during this time.

Plugging in a hardware solution

Putting a hardware solution into place is far less hazardous than installing a software solution because, with a hardware solution, you are introducing something new in the infrastructure that can be removed if necessary without a serious amount of work. There is also almost no impact on your existing mail server(s), so getting back to your preimplementation state is much easier.

Putting a new hardware-based spam filter into place happens one of two ways, depending on where your mail is being delivered now:

✔ **Incoming mail currently is delivered to something other than the mail server, such as a proxy-based firewall or virus scanner.**

In this case, all you need to do is tell the host that currently receives mail first to deliver to the new spam filter, and tell the spam filter to deliver mail to the mail host (or quarantine, depending on spam status).

If you are having serious problems with the new hardware solution, getting back to where you were before the spam filter is just a matter of telling the virus/firewall box to send mail to the mail server instead of the new spam box and everything is back to working like it did before. Note that you can and should leave the new spam filter pointing to the mail server for delivering mail because this will cause no harm, and if e-mails in the filter still haven't been delivered when you cut back to the original configuration, those will get a chance to work their way through and get delivered.

✔ **Incoming mail delivers straight to the mail server.**

In this case, you have two choices. You can give the new hardware solution the IP address of the mail server, and then tell the new hardware to deliver to the mail servers' new IP address, but this means a change to the mail server itself and possibly all the mail clients in the company.

By far the easier method would be to change the address to which mail is initially delivered. Typically, you do that by changing either the DNS Mail eXchanger (MX) records for your domain, or making a change to the perimeter firewall that redirects the inbound e-mail. In either of these cases, you can recover the system to its original state by just redirecting incoming mail to the original mail server.

Putting a new hardware solution in place is not free from worries, but you do have simple options open to you if all goes wrong. The fact that it doesn't interfere with normal mail delivery until you start sending mail also means that it's somewhat easier to test than the software solution. Just set up the new hardware, tell it where the mail server is, and start sending it test mail.

Cutting over an ASP solution

ASPs (Application Service Providers) are wonderful from the aspect of what must be done, and abysmal from the aspect of understanding what is going on if something goes wrong. While some ASPs have the ability to turn off filtering for all but a test group in order to test the service, you still have to send *all* of your mail through the ASP in order to even test.

If things aren't working after you've cut over, about all you can do is call the ASP and ask what's up. You won't have much diagnostic visibility into the ASP's operation, so be prepared to get the information you need from someone at the ASP, just in case.

So, get your agreements in place with the ASP, write down all the phone numbers of people you want to be able to find there if things aren't working well, cross your fingers, and change your DNS MX records to point to the ASP's incoming mail servers. Believe it or not, that's all you have to do to make the cutover work. The good news here is that if all is not well, you can cut back the same way: Just move the MX records to point back to your own mail server, and all will be well in a few minutes.

Why a few minutes? Because of the way DNS works, anyone that's been sending you e-mail and has the old MX record will continue to send mail to the ASP until a timer associated with your MX record expires (called the Time To Live or TTL) and that sender looks to see if there is new data. If you are in control of your own DNS, you can set the TTL for these records to a low number to minimize this problem, but keep in mind that really low numbers mean that servers on the Internet will be querying your DNS server a lot more than they need to.

The bottom line here is that cutting over and cutting back with an ASP solution is really simple, but you need to keep in mind the time lag because of DNS propagation when cutting over or cutting back.

Taking care of the administrative details

Along with the filter installation comes a long list of administrative details you need to take care of just before or just after that installation. Those administrative details are the focus of this section. So, think of installation as a simple single task — like flipping a switch — and use this section to help you focus on the human and administrative details that accompany this part of the project.

Notify users

Any change in the enterprise is viewed with a fair amount of skepticism by almost everyone. It doesn't matter that you are trying to make users' lives better; it's change and it's bad. Even worse is *unexpected* change, because that implies that it all just happened on the spur of the moment, perhaps because of poor planning or a mistake.

The way to keep users calm and happy with their fate — okay, resigned to their fate — is to make sure that they understand every step of the way what is about to happen and how it will affect them.

However, don't expect users to read everything they receive from IT carefully and with great attention. If you send daily progress reports on how the roll-out is proceeding, chances are they will soon tune them out when they realize that the progress reports don't seem to mean much to them. Many users may assume that because the message went to everyone in the company, either it doesn't apply to them specifically or someone else will read it and give them the abridged version.

Making announcements during staff meetings is a good way to broadcast the message about what is coming down the pipe. It's also a good way to hype the solution. Although you want to stick to the important points and keep the information short and sweet, you do need to offer a bit more than a spam message in a circle with a line through it. The following list outlines the important points you should make in your announcements to users before, during, and after the installation of a new spam filter:

- ✓ **Tell them where their filtered mail is going.** If mail identified as spam is to be deleted without quarantine, let users know. If there is a quarantine, tell them how to look at it, how frequently to look at it, and what to do with false positives (mail identified as spam that isn't) and false negatives (spam the filter didn't catch). Give them the tools they need to handle the filtered mail or understand what may have happened to it.

- ✓ **Let users know what changes to expect in their e-mail, if any.** For example, make users aware of any tagging mechanism that identifies spam by editing the subject line.

- ✓ **Tell users how to follow up if a specific sender or sending company needs to be whitelisted.** Help them understand that if a specific sender is chronically getting shuffled off to the spam pile, they need to get that sender on a whitelist.

- ✓ **Tell users who to call when they have questions.** They *will* have questions. If your company has a helpdesk, make sure that the helpdesk is prepared to handle users' questions or point them in the right direction.

Make the gory details available (abridged)

IT has a tendency to treat users like slow children, just giving them the information they need for basic survival and assuming they are too ignorant of the mysteries of computerdom to grasp the wonders of the newest masterpiece.

The truth is, a lot of smart users are out there, and some of them would *really* like to know what's happening. If you can present the technology that's being put in place in a way that some of those smart people can understand, a wonderful thing happens: They tell others. They tell others in their peer groups with whom you would never have been able to relate to as well, and soon many people have a clue about what's going on in IT and are interested in the success of the rollout.

Migrate trial users to the spam filter

When you know exactly how the filter works, and you've dealt with potential problems in deployment by looking carefully at the trial results, it's time to put it all in place. Cross your fingers and hit the big "on" button. Keep in mind that a group of people (the trial group) are already used to the filter and have been using it for a while. Moving them over to the production filter should be a snap, and you can do it without any real change in their experience. Make sure you get their whitelists and other configuration pieces transferred to the production filter, as needed.

Put the filter into production

Before you can move the trial users over, you need to build and test the production environment. The process is *exactly* like building and testing the environment for your trial, which I cover in Chapter 8, except that you know more now, and you won't make any of the mistakes you made the first time (well, you can hope). Instead, you want to focus on making all new mistakes. After the production environment is up and stable, you can migrate the trial users over, verify that it's working as well or better than the trial, and then move the rest of the company.

Get serious about time allocation

Time estimates need to be as accurate as possible. Everything prior to production installation can be wrong, and at worst, some schedules slip. If the production implementation schedule is inaccurate, it can have a company-wide impact.

The actual time estimates for production implementation should pretty closely match what you used for creating the test environment, only shorter for a couple of reasons:

> ✔ **You don't have to create a test environment.** You should already have the systems and software assembled and tested — and test environments are notoriously harder to create than the production environment that it's mimicking, because the test environment has to be realistic, but fake.

✔ **There should be no surprises at this point.** Thus you can include specific make-it-or-break-it time limitations on phases of the production installation.

Another aspect of time allocation is avoiding the key temptations that arise in a major implementation such as this one:

✔ **Avoid last-minute troubleshooting; revisit the schedule instead.** Some of the worst experiences in my career have been when a project is not coming together as expected, and the team decides to give it just a few more minutes of troubleshooting. Somewhere around 3:00 a.m. (when the team isn't in top mental form), you discover that it's not going to work, and you don't have time to cut everything back to normal before the workday starts. If there's something wrong with the plan and your testing, pull back and try another day.

✔ **Fight the temptation to sleep in the day after a successful installation.** Late to bed and early to rise keeps an IT person tired but employed (apologies to Benjamin Franklin). On the following day, users will do far more extensive testing than you were able to, but this time without the training wheels. Hard as it is, you have to be in *before* everyone else the next day, *not sleeping in,* but bleary-eyed and ready to take on any gotchas from the night before that don't surface until everyone in the company starts reading their mail in the morning.

For more about responding to serious problems effectively, see the section, "Creating backout plans in case something goes awry," later in this chapter.

I prefer Thursday nights for this sort of rollout, because that means I can catch up on my sleep on Friday night or spend the day fixing things on Saturday morning before the users return on Monday.

Validate the production environment

As I explain in Chapter 8, anything in a complex system requires regression testing. Well, you just changed almost everything in the system by moving it from the test environment into production. It's time to regression test again. This is the last time, I promise, until you decide to make another change. (Which will be a long time from now, right? Heh.)

Validation has very specific meanings in some government or government-regulated organizations, but I'm just talking about the process of proving that everything works as expected, so that if something odd crops up later, you know that something has actually changed. Maybe you don't know *where* the change is, but you know there *is* one.

Document the production environment

So, you've just spent hours and hours becoming really familiar with the new spam solution, and you know it so well that you could teach it as a college-level course, complete with slides and lab exercises. You have no need for additional documentation, and never will. What's more, you have other pressing matters that you have been neglecting to get this project finished so that you and the rest of the company can use your time more productively than deleting spam. There are 78 reasons for *not* sitting down to write documents describing the spam filter production environment. You know, because you just sat down and listed all 78, annotated the list, and added illustrations. It took a while to draw an emu, but it was an effective addition to page 30.

Nobody likes to document IT infrastructure, and most of us, myself included, will go to great lengths to avoid it or justify why it's not needed. The hard truth is that by *not* documenting your work in this way, you are throwing away a large percentage of the investment the company just made in this project.

What happens when your emu illustration is discovered by the wildlife illustration art underground and you're whisked off to Jackson, Wyoming, to join the movement and live the life of your dreams as an artiste? The day after you leave, the whole spam-filtering solution will catch fire. Computer, software, wires, sticky notes with support authorization codes and phone numbers, and even the cute little plush Sammy, the spam weasel from the vendor booth at SpamCon, are all consumed by a fire that miraculously doesn't seem to harm anything else.

While your former co-workers are sifting through the ashes of what was once a mighty warrior in the fight against spam, they are wondering how to rebuild it, and where you documented the whole process. If you're lucky, they will believe that whatever documentation that once existed perished with Sammy. If you're not so lucky, they will call you and ask where you put the documentation.

In a perfect world, all IT projects and infrastructure are documented fully and correctly, to the point where a competent technologist could re-create any part of the system with only the documentation as a guide. While I usually have to settle for somewhat less, I like to spread the word of peace, love, and IT documentation when I have the chance. How long it takes to perform this step is highly variable, based on writing speed and proficiency with documentation tools. It gets faster when you do a lot of it, so practice, practice, practice.

Failure to properly document projects is nothing short of pathological, self-destructive denial. You shouldn't simply walk away from a job half-done, without consideration for the consequences you inflict upon your successors.

A reasonable documentation project includes the following items. Many of them you may have already created in the planning and design stages of your filtering project.

- A drawing of the physical network supporting the spam solution
- A diagram showing the information flows
- The requirements document (see Appendix B for a sample)
- The project plan (see Appendix A for an example plan)
- A description of the working system including changes made to accommodate conditions unique to your company
- Complete instructions for rebuilding the filter from scratch, if required
- All user and management documentation produced both for training and production (which I cover in Chapter 7)

Blame the manufacturer or reseller for annoying defects

This is the last critical step in nearly all IT deployment efforts. If something is not quite right, make sure that interested parties, such as the reseller or manufacturer, step up to help. If you bought the product from a value-added reseller, this is one of the places where they can add some value. This might sound tongue-in-cheek, but I'm quite serious about post-installation support, and how much time it can save you. If you're having a specific problem, it may be one that the manufacturer has seen many times and knows exactly how to solve.

Measuring early results

As the company's employees are coming to work the next day, returning to their new, less spammy inboxes, keep an eye on the helpdesk, or whomever users call when they have problems. Once again, you have a perfect excuse to create another form for folks to fill out, and this time you give it to the helpdesk. There's a good chance that they'll be flooded with calls, even if everything is working perfectly, because 20 percent of the users ignored every e-mail, every memo, and notice of any kind that a change was coming. These users will be completely surprised that there's a new spam filter in town, and they'll call the helpdesk to find out why they weren't told.

The forms you give the helpdesk should be short, but include all the questions you want answered when someone is reporting a spam problem:

- False positives (a message that was tagged as spam, but is legitimate)
  - Who sent the mail?
  - Are they on the whitelist?

- Are they on the blacklist by mistake?

- Can you retrieve the original e-mail for study?

✔ False negatives (spam that got through)

- Same questions as for false positives, except who it faked.

- If your spam filter has training capability, was this one sent on to the training alias, or marked for processing?

✔ Missing e-mail

- Same questions as false positives

- How does the user know it was sent?

- How does the user know it reached your e-mail infrastructure (and didn't "die along the way")?

- Was the mail rejected? Can you get a copy of the rejection from the original sender?

Just like in the trial, you need to keep track of how things are behaving and make sure that the filter's behavior matches your expected results. If your trial group was a good representation of the overall user community, and your production environment closely matches the trial, the numbers should not be very different, but it's impossible to predict all possible scenarios, and you may have some hiccups.

Implementing Spyware Filtering

Spyware filtering in most cases boils down to a program that runs on each workstation in the company. If you are using one of the few centrally *managed* spyware filters, you may be able to automate the process of installing the program on each desktop. For the vast majority of spyware-filtering programs on the market right now, vendors have provided no real enterprise friendly way of doing mass installation. However, you might have Microsoft SMS (System Management Server) or a third-party tool that you use for installing patches, programs, and updates that you'll want to consider using for installing spam filters on desktops.

Starting with a trial installation

First, you should install your chosen spyware filter on a small number of machines that represent all the various workstation configurations you have in the company. If the software can only be installed locally, you'll need to visit each of these machines and install them one at a time.

After the software is installed on the trial computers, you can commence testing, which in this case means scanning the computer for spyware, deleting spyware, and regression testing everything that the workstation is supposed to be able to do that *isn't* spyware related. This testing is mostly just to establish that the spyware filter does in fact work, and that installing it on company machines doesn't make other stuff stop working properly. Chapter 8 covers regression testing in more detail.

Installing throughout your business

When you are satisfied that the trial machines are working properly, and the software is doing what you expect it to do, you can begin to consider the production installation. Because most of these programs don't come with enterprise friendly installation methods, you may have to create your own installation plan. I list three different ways to accomplish this in the following list, but be aware that there are certainly more than three ways to approach installing the spyware filter, and your company may have its own way of deploying standalone software to multiple desktops.

- ✔ **Shared directory:** One simple way to accomplish your installation is to locate the installation program and other needed files in a shared directory that everyone on the network can see, and send everyone a link to it with instructions for installation. Although this method works fine technically, you have to depend on each user to install the filter him or herself. If some users ignore the e-mail with the link, the product isn't installed on their workstations.

- ✔ **Login script:** Most network operating systems enable you to execute a login script when each user logs into the system. With some good scripting skills, you can create a script that checks to see if this user has already installed the spyware-blocking software, and that launches the installation if not.

Using a login script works better than relying on the user to initiate the install, but this method will probably still pop some windows up while it's installing and ask for confirmation (unless your filter has a silent installation mode).

- ✔ **Microsoft SMS or similar administration tool:** If you have access to SMS or an administration tool similar to it, you should be able to remotely install the software on each workstation without relying on user intervention or user interaction in any way. These tools are made to handle this sort of thing, but this method is also the most expensive of the three, so I only suggest using it if you already have such a tool in place.

Creating backout plans in case something goes awry

For *any* IT project, there is some risk that things will not go as planned. Sometimes, you can recover from the problem and continue on with the project and call it a success. Other times, you realize partway through implementation that without major changes and/or rethinking, the new solution will never work. At that point, you've already broken the old solution, so you might start feeling somewhat stuck.

Always walk into an IT project with a way to put everything back the way it was before you started. Anything else is like walking the high wire without a net. In the implementation scenarios I propose earlier in this chapter for spam-filter installation, I provide some ideas about how to back out if needed, but you'll need to include specific instructions based on your unique environment in your backout plan.

One last thing about being able to back out changes is that you should *never* rely on the ability to just uninstall a program the normal way. Everyone has seen programs that just don't uninstall all the way, and if you are talking about your mail server, you don't want to just ignore the fact that you may have problems uninstalling and hope it doesn't cause a problem later on. Be ready to reimage important servers in these cases.

Keeping Everything under Control

For the first few days after a large IT change such as installing a new malware filter, you'll need to keep a close eye on things. The new system isn't yet part of your routine maintenance, and you may not even know what form that maintenance will take yet. For instance, if your filter creates a spam quarantine, and the items in the quarantine aren't automatically purged after a few days or weeks, you may end up with users that never look at their quarantine and have gigabytes of spam laying around taking up valuable space. Although you can write policies to deal with this, policies (and laws) are only as good as their enforcement. If your quarantine control is based on policy alone, be prepared to confront some users about their huge piles of spam.

You need to monitor systems and try to have your finger on the pulse of the company, so that you see problems brewing and you're able to head them off before they turn into career-changing events.

Early warning signs of trouble

It's best to deal with issues before the villagers are at the gate, torches and pitchforks in hand. The following sections cover a number of places you can look for early signs of trouble, so that you can deal with issues in the early stages and prevent them from blowing up and taking you with them.

Incomplete whitelists

For a spam filter, if folks are reporting lots of false positives, you know that two things are going on:

- ✔ People are sending an awful lot of legitimate mail your way that looks a lot like spam.

- ✔ When you asked everyone for their business contacts to add to the whitelist, some users ignored you. Now is a good time to make another round of asking people for their business contacts, explaining that it will help solve the false positives problem.

Unrealistic user expectations

In Chapter 12, I talk about setting user expectations, so I won't cover that ground here. If users were expecting a perfect filter and zero spam after the install, you'll be getting a call every single time a spam slimes its way past the filter. It's best to handle this *before* the install, but it's never too late.

Scaling the solution

Scaling is about making sure that your solution will work at the loads required of it today, as well as the loads you expect in the foreseeable future. You can't always take a solution that works for 100 people and just plug in 1,000 or 10,000 people and have everything work. What's interesting with scaling is that it's also not a matter of looking at the 100-user system and increasing its capacity by a factor of 10 for 1,000 users. You have to look at all the resources in a system that you are scaling, and adjust things as needed. A 1,000-user company with a single T1 to the Internet can scale its spam solution to any capacity it likes, but the incoming mail will be trickling in at 1.54 Mbps, no matter what. That's the speed limit. Keep track of how much of each resource you are consuming, and watch out for resources that are near capacity. If you're near capacity when you roll the solution out to your users, almost any growth in the company will mean that the solution is underpowered, so make sure that you have excess capacity by purchasing more than you need at rollout.

With spyware, users should know that the spyware filter is far from perfect, and the fact that it's installed doesn't mean that users can be lax in their browsing habits and click links they get in e-mail. They should expect that some spyware is still going to get past the filter, unless they are careful (and lucky).

Hallway grumbling

It pays to listen to what folks are chatting about in the hallways and around the coffee machine. Many users would never consider directly complaining to IT when they are annoyed with something, but they are more than happy to share with their friends, their boss, and the package delivery service person. Of course, I'm not suggesting you *eavesdrop* — people often grumble loudly and publicly enough that you can't help but hear their complaints. One or two people complaining is natural — just be ready to identify trends.

Unsolved mysteries

Unraveling what happens when e-mail doesn't work perfectly can be a bit of a chore and is somewhat specialized when it comes to reading all the headers in a bounced e-mail, *especially* when the sender (spammer) is going to a lot of trouble to try to confuse things. It is important in a post-installation environment to track down the root causes for anything unexplained in e-mail delivery, even if that requires outside assistance. If things aren't behaving the way you expect, even at a small scale, it's a problem you must solve because unexpected behavior can be a sign of much larger problems in the system. You really don't know until you figure out what's actually causing the problem.

Changing the plan in mid-sentence

When you discover that the filter just will not work the way you planned, which you could discover during installation or even after the solution has been in place for a while, you have a difficult decision to make. Do you revert to your premalware filter state (you do have a plan for that, right?) and regroup, or do you make changes on the fly and hope that the changes don't make things worse?

If the hardware chosen for the job just isn't up to the task, you probably don't have more powerful spares lying around that you can install, test, and have online at a moment's notice. You'll need to back off and do an abbreviated version of your rollout plan again.

Sometimes though, the problem is not so drastic. Say that you started out not using whitelisting, because in the trial, you were seeing no false positives at all. But in the production install, lots of people are missing e-mail from business associates, because the division that works with "low low low rate home loans" refused to participate in the trial. It's certainly plausible that you might *carefully* activate the whitelisting feature to solve this problem on the fly.

Testy testers

The good news about making changes to a production environment is that you have lots of people out there testing the system for you. No need to worry about unit tests and regression testing — everything will get put to the test, very quickly and fairly thoroughly. The bad news is that they don't think of themselves as testers — they think of themselves as users, and they expect things to just work.

It's very important when making changes to production environments to notify all interested parties before making the changes and to carefully document the changes made. In medium-to-large companies, there is usually a change control process that completely describes the life cycle of a change to production systems. In smaller companies, you may be responsible for notifying everyone directly. Don't surprise people in any of these situations. Keep them informed, and they will be more forgiving of the disruptions.

Chapter 10

Supporting Users

*A*fter you finish all the fun parts (design, selection, and installation), it's time to get back to business with whatever it is your company does to pay the enormous salaries that IT employees always demand. After all, in business school, the professors teach that the only purpose a company really has is to create a support environment for cool IT projects — right? Some companies create a by-product or two, which several people in the company call the "product," but IT people know the truth.

Try to remember the last time you called for tech support on a product and weren't satisfied with what you received. (That memory probably takes you back a day or two.) Now, how do you feel about that product? You probably feel like after finalizing the sale, the manufacturer abandoned you as a customer. In this chapter, I talk about how to create a support environment that doesn't make your users feel that way and that keeps things working.

Some universal truths regarding user support are worth mentioning before I go over the specifics:

✔ **Communicate:** Let users know what's going on even if you don't yet have an answer to their questions or problems. Nothing is worse than silence.

✔ **Track progress:** Don't let any users' issues spiral out of control by ignoring them. If you have a trouble-ticketing system, make use of it. Age is good for cheese and wine, not for user-support issues.

✔ **Escalate:** If the first level of assistance doesn't resolve the problem, send it up the ladder immediately. Users become frustrated when they know that the person they're explaining the problem to can't help them and won't escalate the problem to someone who can.

  ✔ **Talk plainly:** I always know if support people don't know what they are talking about because they start getting confusing. If you don't know the answer to a user problem or question, admit it and go find the answer. I've never lost respect for people for telling me they don't know something, but I have when they tried to hide that fact.

Understanding Common Support Scenarios

There's nothing quite like the little surge of adrenaline you get when you take a support call and realize you've never heard this problem before and have no idea how to fix it. However, the best way to provide timely, well-considered support is to anticipate the problems that a user might have and be prepared with answers. To be properly prepared, you need to anticipate what kind of problems your users might have and be prepared to handle them. You also need a thorough understanding of the system you're supporting so that you can troubleshoot the problems that you couldn't anticipate.

If you don't personally have experience with supporting users, go looking for someone with a reputation as a go-to person for getting your IT problems solved. Let her know what you're doing, which is trying to anticipate user problems and be well prepared to handle the aftermath of a new spyware- or spam-filter installation. Chances are good that she'll be more than happy to share her experience with you and help in the process because helping you will probably cut down the calls she gets from struggling users. Note that the person you're looking for here might not have any formal connection to operations support or even IT, but would be well known for being helpful in this way.

If you have some experience with supporting users, use this section as a guide for the kinds of knowledge that you want to put together for your support scenarios and successful support in general. I include concrete examples of some of the support issues I've seen when helping people with their spam and spyware filters, but you know your users best and you'll most likely add your own unique knowledge to what I've written here to complete your support tools.

Gathering information for support scenarios

Take a good look at the filtering solution that you're providing:

  ✔ Does any part of it make you feel a little bit uneasy from a support perspective?

  ✔ Does any part of using it seem unclear?

✔ Did people have lots of questions about certain areas during a trial installation?

✔ Are there any user tasks that aren't often performed and that the user might forget about?

Each question is fodder for support preparation. Document the questionable areas more clearly and prepare helpdesk staff to field the questions you might expect. A good example is quarantine maintenance. If your solution leaves this job to end-users, you can bet that it's not something that they'll do every day, and even if you carefully train them, they'll forget the training by the time they need to perform the task. Some users might even delay long enough between quarantine cleanings that they forget the training more than once.

If you think about your users and try to put yourself in their shoes, you very likely can foresee some of the problems that they'll have with the new malware filter. Be ready to provide timely assistance. About now you might be saying, "Hold it. If I know what their problems will be, shouldn't I make changes that make the problem go away?" To some degree, that's exactly what you should do, but some support issues you just can't fix. For instance, you can't force people to read the on-screen instructions no matter how well written and clear they may be. A large number of your users will ignore the on-screen messages and call for help if things aren't exactly like what they expect.

In the following sections, I outline other helpful resources for determining what scenarios you need to be prepared for.

Pushme-pullyou

Human nature being what it is, you can't count on people following instructions just because you provide them. If you have any doubts about that, go find a public door that opens only one way with a sign that clearly says whether to push or pull it. A large percentage of people do the wrong thing, and then correctly open the door without ever reading the sign. I used to think this was just because people are lazy and can't be bothered to read, but now I realize it's because people are just presented with *too* *much* information to read every second of the day, and they have to filter some of it out or be overwhelmed. The same thing happens in computer interfaces: Installing a program might include reading seven or eight popup messages and agreeing to various licenses and policies that range from 1 page to 50 pages or more. Users get used to clicking the button that will most likely get rid of the message without reading or caring about what the message says.

Helpdesk

The helpdesk staff knows your users better than anyone else in terms of how the users think and what sorts of issues are likely to throw them for a loop. If you had some helpdesk people involved in planning and testing, they will have all sorts of ideas about how things are going to break and what kind of calls they're going to receive. Pay close attention to what they have to say. Although the helpdesk's viewpoint is usually pretty focused on dealing with immediate problems, the helpdesk workers can be pretty helpful in predicting what is to come. Note too that helpdesk people for some reason are usually pretty pessimistic about supporting new software, but that's not a bad thing when you're assessing support scenarios.

Reference clients

You asked your vendor for reference clients, right? If the references are willing and have time to talk to you, they're a great place to look for user-support tips. Just the fact that the vendor was willing to share these customers' name with you means a couple things:

- ✔ The reference clients had a successful implementation.
- ✔ The reference clients aren't struggling too much with support.

Because that's exactly where you want to be experience-wise, the more tips you can get from the reference clients about how they accomplished everything, the better tech support will go for you and your users.

Because the reference clients are doing you a favor, be sure to efficiently use their time. Send them your questions in advance so that they can gather answers and deal with everything in one call or visit. If you combine your prepurchase reference check with the support questions, you bother the reference client only once.

If the reference clients are willing to share, any user documentation that they generated could be helpful to you, as well. The documentation itself may not apply to your situation because all installations are different, but just seeing what the clients have addressed can help provide some direction to your own support efforts.

Vendor

Getting support information from your vendor can be a bit tricky because providing it is like admitting that the solution doesn't install itself and then magically heal all your IT problems while you're having lunch. Because the salespeople said it would do that, they probably don't have a lot of written documentation to the contrary. You need to convince them that you aren't out to return the product, and you aren't working for their competitor and weaseling damaging information out of them for publication.

Instead, let them know that making the product a success in your company is in everyone's best interest and you're looking for every bit of information that they have to help make that happen.

If you purchased the product through a value added reseller (VAR), you should have an easier time getting information because the reseller isn't as closely tied to the product and should have plenty of experience supporting your solution in several different situations.

If you've purchased the solution from a reseller, consider having the reseller on hand for a few days after your rollout to help field user support questions and issues. Not only does this give you some ready-made expertise on the most difficult support days, it gives the reseller some real incentive to make sure everything is properly executed in the rollout and training because she knows she'll be there for the real test on the first days of use.

A sneaky way to get information on how to support your malware-filter solution is to talk to a vendor's competition about support issues with your chosen platform. Unlike your manufacturer, the competitor *will* have printed information on every single support problem your product has and how it will ultimately lead to the downfall of civilization. They're usually pretty happy to share that information with you, too. Take the information you get in this way with a grain of salt, but keep in mind that it's usually based on something factual. If you gather this information during the product-evaluation stage, you'll have it ready when you need it.

Documenting support scenarios

After you establish what the likely support scenarios are, such as "User doesn't understand how to retrieve items from quarantine," you should document them in a way that your helpdesk can use in preparing themselves to help users in the situations you have identified.

The documentation for support scenarios can be

- ✔ Helpdesk training materials
- ✔ Helpdesk support scripts
- ✔ Knowledge base entries

Equipping Support Staff with Tools and Knowledge

Support staffers want to be able to do their jobs. In fact, they insist on doing their jobs, sometimes with very little preparation, knowledge, or tools.

Imagine their relief, gratitude, and general happiness if some kind person was to prepare them to meet the challenges that they face.

In Chapter 7, I talk about training support staff, and here I take the next step and talk about the tools that the support staff needs to provide assistance to the general user population. You're sending these people into a battle with software bugs, network glitches, and Internet weirdness. If you want to emerge victorious, you must supply your support troops with tools and knowledge.

However, you can easily spend too much time training the support staff and run into a problem with diminishing returns. You can spend only so much time training folks: If the next ten minutes of training can save the company only two minutes of support time, the training just isn't worthwhile. You can see a graphic explanation of this in Figure 10-1, which shows that you want all of your training efforts to be spent in the area where you receive large gains for your efforts, but never to the right of the dotted line, where large training efforts bring little reward.

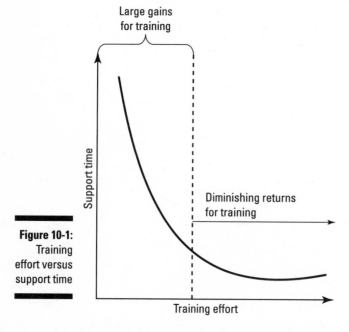

Figure 10-1:
Training effort versus support time

Seeing what the user sees

In some support situations, the helpdesk may need to see the actual screens that the user is seeing and watch them click the wrong button or type the wrong command. There are a number of tools on the market that provide this facility, and Remote Desktop Connection comes preinstalled in Windows XP and Windows Server 2003, but can be manually installed on Windows 95, 98, 98 Second Edition, Me, NT 4.0, and 2000 from a download page at Microsoft: `www.microsoft.com/windowsxp/downloads/tools/rdclientdl.mspx`. For most spam-filtering situations, you don't really need to watch the user click or see what's on his screen. You just need to see the e-mail or take a look at the quarantine. For spyware, you may need to see what the user is seeing on-screen as a result of the spyware itself or the anti-spyware software.

In the case where you're analyzing an e-mail, things can get a little tricky with Windows if Outlook is the e-mail client. To figure out what's happening with an e-mail, you typically need to get a look at all the mail headers associated with that e-mail. Microsoft Outlook, in order to protect your eyes from the awful complexities, does its best to hide these headers from you and make retrieving them difficult, even when you do want to see them. To make life just a little harder, Microsoft seems to have changed how you retrieve the header information several times. For the last few updates to Outlook, you can find it by opening the e-mail in question, and then choosing View➪Options to get what you see in Figure 10-2.

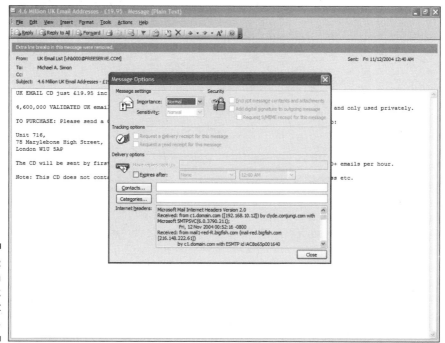

Figure 10-2:
Spam with Outlook Internet headers.

Look at that little window in the bottom of the Message Options box. Notice the scrollable text with the headers you're interested in. Your only recourse for viewing this in a useful way is to copy from this screen into Notepad, and then look at it there. After you do that, you see something like Listing 10-1.

Listing 10-1: Headers Pasted from Outlook

```
Microsoft Mail Internet Headers Version 2.0
Received: from c1.domain.com ([192.168.10.12]) by
          clyde.conjungi.com with Microsoft
          SMTPSVC(6.0.3790.211);
           Fri, 12 Nov 2004 00:52:16 -0800
Received: from mail1-red-R.bigfish.com (mail-red.bigfish.com
          [216.148.222.61])
          by c1.domain.com with ESMTP id iAC8o65p001640
          for <simon@conjungi.com>; Fri, 12 Nov 2004
          00:50:07 -0800 (PST)
Received: from mail1-red.bigfish.com (localhost.localdomain
          [127.0.0.1])
          by mail1-red-R.bigfish.com (Postfix) with ESMTP id
          C5CDD1F1AE4
          for <simon@conjungi.com>; Fri, 12 Nov 2004
          08:50:06 +0000 (UCT)
X-BigFish: vcs-
          16(z60eh519iz1922h14c3Pc8h7efIL122eh77ch15feh14b7r
          19c2izzzzz17h)
Received: by mail1-red.bigfish.com (MessageSwitch) id
          1100249406358630_31741; Fri, 12 Nov 2004 08:50:06
          +0000 (UCT)
Received: from 203.115.156.163 (unknown [203.115.156.163])
          by mail1-red.bigfish.com (Postfix) with SMTP id
          130FA1F15D4
          for <simon@conjungi.com>; Fri, 12 Nov 2004
          08:50:01 +0000 (UCT)
Received: from mail2.nowonline.net (mail2.nowonline.net
          [208.51.8.50]) by mx.mail.rcn.net with ESMTP; Nov,
          12 2004 07:34:57 -0700
From: UK Email List <vhb000@FREESERVE.COM>
To: simon@conjungi.com
Subject: 4.6 Million UK Email Addresses - £19.95
Sender: UK Email List <vhb000@FREESERVE.COM>
Mime-Version: 1.0
Content-Type: text/plain; charset="iso-8859-1"
Date: Fri, 12 Nov 2004 08:40:21 -0000
X-Mailer: MIME-tools 5.503 (Entity 5.501)
Message-Id: <20041112085001.130FA1F15D4@mail1-
          red.bigfish.com>
Return-Path: vhb000@FREESERVE.COM
X-OriginalArrivalTime: 12 Nov 2004 08:52:16.0203 (UTC)
          FILETIME=[E8F0D9B0:01C4C894]
```

Note that Microsoft wasn't willing to just make it hard to find the mail headers, it also put its own tag line at the top. The "Microsoft Mail Internet

Headers Version 2.0" line isn't actually a part of the mail headers. It's a line to tell you where you just cut and pasted from in case you were wondering. In Chapter 12, I cover the details of what you see in these headers. For now, just keep in mind that getting access to this information is an important support tool, and you need to help your support staff find this information.

Most other e-mail programs (such as Mozilla, Thunderbird, and Eudora) have a simple menu item called View Headers that allows you to see both the headers and the e-mail in its original form.

Knowledge

After you collect information on your support issues, you have the somewhat slippery task of turning that information into knowledge. You can find a lot of philosophical arguments about the differences between information and knowledge, but the one I use is simple. *Information* is raw data. *Knowledge* is usable data. So, the task here is to take a lot of raw data, collected from various sources, and turn it into something usable that your support staff can rely on when they need it.

The two key ways to do that are knowledge bases and scripts, which I discuss in the following sections.

Knowledge bases

Years ago, the process of turning information into knowledge was a painstaking process of classification, database design, and careful indexing of keywords. Fortunately, things have progressed to the point where full-text searching of large quantities of information is possible, and classification is required only for convenience.

You might choose to have several separate knowledge bases (knowledge organized into a searchable form) so that support staff workers can choose which pile of information they want to search through, but you might also pile it all together, and then teach them good search techniques. An example of separate knowledge bases is the Microsoft support knowledge base, which is devoted to knowledge about Microsoft products and allows you to focus on individual versions of specific products. The best example of a full-text searchable knowledge base is the use of any Internet search engine, which allows for searching on any topic and returns results based on what most closely matches your search terms.

Information sources for your knowledge base should include

- ✔ Known support scenarios (I explain how to gather and create these earlier in this chapter)
- ✔ User and administrator documentation and training materials (see Chapter 7 for details)

✔ Training materials

✔ Trouble tickets, both solved and unsolved

Full-text-searchable knowledge bases have the effect of amplifying information and presenting it just when it's needed. Because of that, bad information can propagate quickly and often becomes very hard to eliminate.

Make it easy to cull bad data from the knowledge base so that incorrect information doesn't pollute it and make the whole system unusable. Bad hits in the knowledge base should be reported by the worker who discovers the bad hit, and then reviewed and resolved as quickly as possible by someone with the ability to sort out good knowledge from incorrect data. An example of this kind of problem is a trouble ticket that was "resolved" by rebooting the spam gateway. If everyone using the knowledge base sees that as the correct resolution, the real problem may never get fixed, and you'll be doing a lot of rebooting.

Scripts

One way to help the helpdesk workers is to do a good job of figuring out what common support scenarios they might see. When you have the common support scenarios figured out, you can write up scripts for them to help them with their responses to these situations.

Scripts take the format of a tree of questions, and based on the answers, a branch could lead to either a solution or more questions to help narrow down the problem. For example, a script for a user who hasn't seen mail that was expected might look like this:

1. Have you verified that the sender actually sent the mail you're expecting?

   Yes: Go to Step 2.

   No: Could you please verify that it was sent and find out the exact day and time that it was sent? If verified, Go to Step 2.

2. Have you looked in your spam quarantine for this e-mail?

   Yes: Go to Step 3.

   No: May I help you get into your spam quarantine and see if it's in there? (Go to quarantine assistance script.)

3. When did you check your quarantine? (It might be beneficial to double-check because the mail could have been backlogged.)

   If the user checked prior to calling and it's been at least four hours since the mail was sent, go to Step 4.

   If it's been under four hours since the user checked, ask the user to check again at the four-hour mark.

4. Because this mail was sent and it's not in your quarantine, I'll need to escalate this to our systems people to look at the server logs. Your trouble ticket number is blah blah blah. . . .

You could certainly get carried away with these scripts and try to cover all possible scenarios, but what you really need to do is try for basic coverage of scenarios that you expect to see often and have a good escalation path for the dead ends, much like Step 4 in the example script. Remember to replace the "blah blah blah" part in this script with a real trouble ticket number so your users get the impression that you really are trying to help them!

Measuring the Support Effort

You need to measure how things are going for a number of reasons:

- ✔ **You may need to justify all the work that you've put into preparation for the malware filter's rollout.**

- ✔ **It helps you adjust your support efforts to focus your energies on the right problems.**

  For example, if 90 percent of your support calls are about how to retrieve a false positive (good mail treated as spam) from the spam quarantine, you really have two problems to deal with:

  - Your filter is too sensitive, and it's marking too much legitmate mail as spam.

  - The instructions for how to get into the spam quarantine aren't working.

The measurement effort should taper off after a few weeks of supporting a new filter, but during the early days, look at the statistics several times per day in order to head off any serious problems in specific areas. The way I look at this is that you can watch the stats and know how the support effort is going, or you can wait until a problem is bad enough that your boss calls and asks. I like to know ahead of time. This section focuses on the measurements, and Chapter 9 has more details on identifying problems early.

Tracking numbers of calls

The easiest measurement of how things are going is the total number of spam-filter-related and spyware-filter-related calls coming in to the helpdesk. You should expect a fairly large volume of calls coming in the first day after you install your filter just because the operational bugs aren't worked out, and because of a large number of people who pretty much ignored any efforts that you made to train them. These early calls should almost all be from people who aren't familiar with the new way of doing things and who need help with various normal tasks in the new environment. If the call volume *stays* at a high level, you might want to update the helpdesk messages to reflect the longer wait times.

After the first day or so, you should see a rapid drop in call volume regarding the new spyware or spam filter, and the remaining calls will be about potential serious problems with the solution, training, instructions, or all of the above. As a part of normal helpdesk operations, you should be tracking calls by volume (number of calls coming in), type (what is the call about), and duration (how long did it take to resolve the problem). You can easily enter these items into a spreadsheet to track trends in the first few days after installation. If call volume doesn't slow down considerably after the first few days, you may have a serious problem in one of these areas. Address the problem before it gets out of hand. If you have a fallback plan, it may be time to consider using it.

Tracking types of calls

If you know what kind of support calls the users are placing, you know what's potentially wrong. If you have a number of calls about mail getting delayed on its way in, look at the load on the spam-filtering hardware. If most of your calls are about spam that's still making it through, check the configuration of the filter and maybe turn it up a notch or two. If one of the company intranet applications has suddenly stopped working, perhaps the spyware filter is being a little too aggressive.

Beware of unrelated problems disguising themselves as spam-filter problems. If you happen to be unlucky enough to roll out spyware filtering for the company on the same day that a major new virus breaks out, you could potentially have many calls coming in to the helpdesk about slow Internet response, browser timeouts, and general odd behavior that has nothing at all to do with the new spyware filter. You'll never be able to convince users there's no correlation, so don't bother. Track those virus-related calls separately from spam-filter or spyware-filter calls.

Speaking of correlation, be sure to take a broader view of the types of calls coming in than just what category has the biggest numbers. If your high-volume calls are all about quarantine management, adding users to personal whitelists, and reporting spam that makes it through, you have a problem with the spam software itself — either a training issue or user interface problems with the software. If, on the other hand, your large-volume calls are about mail delays and missing e-mail, something is wrong with the guts of the whole solution — it may be a hardware, software, or basic configuration problem.

If you have chosen an ASP (Application Service Provider) spam-filtering solution, bring your support statistics to the provider's attention. Its support staff may have some suggestions on how to improve the situation. At the very least, it will be good feedback on how users perceive the product.

Tracking the effort required to solve problems

One of the most valuable management tools is the knowledge of how much time workers are spending on each task. To efficiently operate a support team, you need to know how long it takes to solve specific kinds of problems.

To track this information, you need to make the data easy to collect. If you impose a lot of laborious procedures for taking down the information and specifics about each trouble call, the volume of tracked calls drops dramatically, but not because things suddenly got better! Talk to the helpdesk workers about what kinds of calls they're getting, and have them help you categorize the calls so that they can just select a check box and fill in some details for your statistics.

For the helpdesk staff, extra minutes on the phone are minutes that could have been spent helping someone else. In the worst case, when the helpdesk staffers are spending too much time per call, you end up requiring more workers just to keep the waiting time down to some reasonable level. In many cases, you can avoid the extra expense by examining where the support time is being spent and finding a way to improve the delivery of that specific support. The following sections focus on a few specific issues that may consume too much helpdesk time and offer tips on how to successfully resolve those issues.

Reducing repeat helpdesk calls

If the helpdesk workers are spending much time laboriously walking caller after caller through some aspect of using e-mail with the spam filter, this may be the time to create a new document that addresses that specific issue with pictures and step-by-step instructions that the user can refer to instead of staying on the phone the whole time.

Dealing with lost mail

Everyone's pretty used to e-mail being close to a perfect communication medium in terms of reliability. Sure, everyone has stories about e-mail that disappeared into the Bermuda Triangle, but if you consider the millions of e-mails sent each day and how many actually don't make it for some reason or another, the percentage of lost e-mail is pretty low.

Even lower is the percentage of e-mails that are lost without a trace. In nearly every case, when an e-mail delivery fails, someone gets a bounced message with a fair amount of detail on why it didn't happen.

Even with such good odds, stuff happens. If your helpdesk staffers are spending too much time trying to trace lost e-mail, you have a problem that the helpdesk can't solve. Your spam solution isn't working properly, and it needs debugging. The only way you'll know this is by tracking how much time folks are spending on this problem.

Reiterating filtering basics

Spending lots of time helping users with the basics of the new spam or spyware filter can mean only a few things:

- ✔ The training didn't go so well.
- ✔ The provided user documentation isn't very helpful.
- ✔ The installation doesn't match the training, the documentation, or both.
- ✔ Your users are lonely, and the helpdesk people are just really nice to talk to.

In this case, you have a retraining and/or redocumentation task ahead of you. Don't leave the helpdesk workers stuck spending their time on basic user training; some people out there have real problems to solve.

Part IV
Maintaining Your Defenses

The 5th Wave — By Rich Tennant

@RICHTENNANT

"Someone want to look at this manuscript
I received on email called, 'The Embedded
Virus That Destroyed the Publisher's Servers
When the Manuscript was Rejected.'?"

In this part . . .

*E*veryone wants to live happily ever after, right? This part is all about living happily every after — or at least not ruing the day you decided to deal with that pesky spam and spyware problem.

In this case, living happily ever after requires regular system maintenance at both user and system levels. It also requires that you understand and be prepared to deal with the many (and some unexpected) user issues that spam and spyware filters cause, so I take a look at these issues and describe some methods for coping with them.

Finally, I show you a good general principal of all well-designed security: defense in depth. It's the spam filtering equivalent of wearing both a belt *and* suspenders.

Chapter 11

Everyday Maintenance

. . . .

. . . .

*M*aintenance isn't everyone's favorite topic. On the list of most neglected IT disciplines today, maintenance ranks near the top, along with security and documentation. In fact, a lot of the security problems that occur each day are the direct result of poor maintenance, so the two are pretty closely linked.

For example, a spam filter that was installed two years ago used Bayesian filtering, which back then was going to save everyone and was actually able to capture 97 to 99 percent of all spam. But spammers quickly figured out ways to trick these first-generation Bayesian filters, and over a short period of time, the filters were capturing only 60 percent of the incoming spam. Most manufacturers provided updates for the filter products to keep up with or stay ahead of the spammers, but if the user didn't update the installed product, its effectiveness gradually eroded. Keeping products up to date isn't the only reason for maintenance — not by a long shot. Poor maintenance of your spam filter can result in a number of problems with various degrees of pain, as I explain in the following sections.

You can easily add "angry natives come knocking at your door" to your problems, too, because none of these problems are likely to escape the notice of your users or your boss. No spam-blocking product is maintenance-free. If a spam-blocking vendor tells you his product *is* maintenance-free, offer him a box of free puppies and then run as fast as you can in the opposite direction.

If maintenance is so important, why does it get such little respect, you might ask. The problem with doing a perfect job of maintaining systems is that, when everything is working smoothly, nobody notices. In the following sections, I discuss the maintenance you need to perform on your spam filter and related systems so that nobody notices you doing a great job.

Managing Quarantines

A *quarantine* is a place where spam filters divert and store any e-mail that appears to be spam according to the filter rules and analysis. Quarantines have the nasty habit of growing larger and larger without bounds until you run out of hard drive space or someone suddenly pays attention. Huge quarantine collections of suspected spam have several undesirable effects:

- ✔ Filling up hard drive space by the terabyte, which costs money and contributes to global warming
- ✔ Slowing the filter as it accesses an overloaded file store and possibly stopping it altogether if the file store completely fills up
- ✔ Making it hard to find good mail that the filter sent to the quarantine

Different spam-blocking products handle quarantines in different ways. Most products do allow end-users and administrators access to quarantines so that they can retrieve good mail placed there in error. Most products also include manual or automated processes for trimming quarantines down to size.

Involving end-users

The very best way to keep spam quarantines clean and maintained is for users to examine and delete the piles of spam for themselves. This way distributes the task among many people, and they decide what mail to delete and what mail to retrieve.

Okay, stop laughing. I know that users generally check the quarantine *if and only if* they're missing some important e-mail, and never look at it any other time. The whole reason that the filter exists is so that they don't have to deal with spam, right?

 A more realistic view of what a spam filter does is that it permits users to deal with spam in batches at their convenience. With a spam filter, users can choose when to deal with spam and act on that choice by going to the quarantine to slay the hordes of spam.

Without a spam filter, users have to deal with spam one and two at a time as it arrives in their inbox. This interrupts a user's workflow and might make him forget what he was doing before the spam arrived. However, a good filter with a quarantine allows users to go in and delete whole swaths of hundreds or thousands of spams at once, which is more efficient than letting spam interrupt the workflow all day long.

Good luck getting your users to see it this way, but I thought I should share a realistic viewpoint that spam filters' vendors will *not* be sharing with you. However, in cases where you lack administrative access to users' quarantines, share this viewpoint with your users to aid their understanding of the process. (If you don't, the users might assume that someone else is dealing with their quarantine for them.)

Administrative maintenance

If you're the administrator for the spam filter, you handle two key maintenance tasks:

✔ **Helping users find e-mail they expected to receive but didn't:** People will ask you to retrieve messages from quarantine. Some of these people simply can't be bothered to do it for themselves, never mind the social or political issues. You'll almost certainly be asked to do this, and usually by someone that you can't ignore or politely ask to do it him or herself.

This is a good time to do the maintenance that the user should be doing. Delete all the obvious spam while you're in there. Not only that, but make sure the user pays attention: Show her how easily she can muck out her overflowing quarantines, encouraging her to do it for herself and whistling all the while ("see how much fun it is to jettison all of those nasty messages?!").

✔ **Keeping an eye on the size of the quarantine:** Be sure to frequently monitor the size of the quarantine just to have an idea of how things are going.

- A sudden *increase* in the growth rate for your spam quarantine could mean either that your filtering rules are misfiring and suddenly catching a bunch of good mail, or that you are the target of one of the many kinds of spam attacks. Either way, it's something you want to know about, and deal with before it has a significant impact on your users.

- A sudden *decrease* in the amount of spam being filtered to the quarantine is certainly not caused by a lack of new spam. (If that condition *was* to actually occur, you would know it by the dancing in the streets.) Such a decrease usually indicates that filtering rules are messed up, and you need to figure out what has changed or whether something is wrong with your mail system.

If you use a spam filter with automated outpaging capability, you can set the outpaging to automatically page the administrator when the quarantine size climbs too high or dips abnormally low. You likely already use this feature with other applications. It's particularly useful for making sure you don't run low on hard drive space and other resources.

Automating quarantine management

By far, the most likely way that your spam quarantine will be trimmed from time to time is via an automated process that deletes spam from the quarantine based on size, age, number of items in the quarantine, or any combination thereof. Based on what I know about user (and even administrator) behavior, the automated trimming of your overflowing spam quarantine is the only way to be sure it happens on a regular basis.

Yeah, yeah, detractors may wonder whether automatically trimming all users' quarantines enables their bad habits. However, the idea is to help users be more productive. And I can assure you that, after a user has had an important message purged from his quarantine, he'll be more attentive and check it eight times a year instead of four.

When you trim the quarantine automatically, you need to carefully consider the pros and cons of each parameter that's available to you:

- **Trimming based on size:** The benefit of this method is that absolute limits on the size of the quarantine guarantee that the quarantine won't completely fill whatever space is allocated to it. Size limits are typically enforced for both individual user quarantines and for the entire quarantine so that individual users can't use up all the space, and the whole quarantine can't consume the entire system.

  But of course, a downside does exist: Trimming the quarantine this way is unpredictable. You can't know when the automated process will eliminate any specific e-mail message.

  For example, say your spam quarantine is 500GB in size, and *usually* two months' worth of spam fills it up. But then either a goof in the spam ruleset (resulting in most legitimate e-mail being diverted to the quarantine) or a sudden increase in the volume of spam shrinks the two months down to ten days.

  In this case, the quarantine trimming continues working, provided the automated trimming is launched frequently enough to catch a quickly growing quarantine before it consumes all allocated space. However, user expectations will be skewed: Many users who are accustomed to viewing their quarantines infrequently (say, once a month) will suddenly find that they have only a few *days'* worth of spam instead of the usual two months' worth.

  This phenomenon reminds me of the label on dry cereal boxes that reads, "This package is sold by weight, not by volume." Spam can come in large volumes (many e-mails) or by weight (large spam e-mails). In the case of automatically deleting from quarantine by size of the quarantine, high volume will fill the quarantine quickly, but so will a small number of very large spams (with pictures or spyware included). What this all means is that you need to be very careful when you set user expectations regarding the size and time span of the quarantine. One phrase you might use is to say something like "The quarantine holds *up to* thirty days' worth, but sometimes only a few days' worth, of spam messages." It's not a minimum guarantee, but a maximum.

✔ **Trimming based on age:** The advantage of age-based trimming is that it's more predictable for end-users because they know exactly how long something will be in the quarantine. For example, if the quarantine period is 14 days, any e-mail in the quarantine that is 15 days old will be deleted.

However, age-based trimming is less predictable for administrators because it's more difficult to predict how much hard drive space the quarantine might consume. For example, your spam quarantine may be set to delete anything more than 30 days old, and the quarantine easily fits in the 50GB of space allocated to it. But if the volume of spam increases and you receive twice as much spam in a 30 day period as before, the 50GB of space allocated for the quarantine might not be enough.

✔ **Trimming based on number of items:** Trimming based on the number of items in individual quarantines is possibly the least reliable way to keep control of how your overall quarantine grows, but it is at least easy to understand and predictable for users. If the characteristics of your incoming spam change to include messages with lots of graphics and each message is 100K or more, each of these individual spams is 50 to 100 times larger than a more typical spam. Counting the number doesn't necessarily count size. And remember that hard drive space isn't elastic. Unless you have a large Storage Area Network with vast pools of readily available storage, you can't just add more space to an existing file system; instead you need to install additional hard drives.

I suggest a combined approach for managing your organization's spam quarantine. This way, available hard drive space is the driving factor, but you can also give end-users parameters for cleaning out quarantines that are easier for users to relate to. A combination of age and number of spams in quarantine permits the quarantine to fit in its allocated space with room for growth. For instance, you might delete all quarantined messages that are over 14 days old and also limit the number of quarantined messages per user to 1,000. These are numbers that your users can understand. (I didn't say *like*.) Then if the volume of spam increases, you can lower the age or quantity parameters temporarily and inform users that you have done so.

A final note: If you're wondering why I appear to be belaboring what appears to be such a simple point, it is because I have experienced a lot of pain over this matter and would like you to be able to avoid it. Getting users to understand storage constraints can be a difficult task, and I want you to have all the information available when trying to get the point across.

Managing Whitelists

Whitelists are lists of senders whose messages should never be treated as spam. When the spam filter receives e-mail from someone on your whitelist, that mail will never to go quarantine. Whitelists provide a way for you to turn filtering way up without ever missing an important e-mail from the people you do business with. You can imagine the converse, however, which is that poorly maintained whitelists require that you turn down the filters so they don't accidentally trap good e-mails in the quarantine or delete them.

Blacklists are lists of senders that you never want to receive mail from and whose e-mail should always be treated as spam. Because spammers nearly always hide who they are, blacklists have become nearly useless, and they're not worth maintaining.

If you make a list of everyone your company does business with and make that same list again three months later, your new list will likely include a lot of new names (and hopefully few or none of the old ones will be gone). The point is that in any active business, the list of important e-mail associates changes constantly, and your ability to keep the spam filter turned up to high is completely dependent on your ability to keep your whitelist current.

Whitelists come in two flavors: user whitelists and systemwide whitelists. I cover these in the following two sections.

Maintaining user whitelists

Some spam solutions allow users to maintain their own whitelists, which operate for only that individual user. In these cases, users must be responsible for how well spam filtering is working for them. Although this might seem like a good thing in terms of everyone being in control of his or her own destiny, from the company's perspective, it leaves a little too much up to the ability of each individual. Often, the same business contacts are important to several employees, not just individuals.

Encourage users to maintain personal contacts in their individual whitelists and submit business contacts to spam administration for inclusion in a systemwide whitelist. That way, if the individual leaves the company, the whitelist entry isn't lost when the individual's e-mail account is deleted. Further, if more people begin corresponding with the new business contact, the new contact's e-mail address is already in the systemwide whitelist.

Maintaining systemwide whitelists

The global whitelist for an organization is an interesting snapshot of who your company happens to be doing business with at that particular moment. To create that snapshot, you need to find the people in your company who have that information and extract it from them in the form of domain names and/or e-mail addresses that you should include in the whitelist.

Your sources for these lists depend on what business you're in, but talk to sales, marketing, and legal departments to start. (Thumbscrews may or may not be necessary.)

In maintaining the global whitelist, watch out for the following issues:

✓ **Entries that are too broad and thus allow lots of spam in:** For example, someone in sales might include `yahoo.com` in the whitelist because one of their important contacts uses a Yahoo! account. In this case, ask for the contact's specific e-mail address, such as `theactualcontact@yahoo.com`, because spammers frequently victimize Yahoo! users by using them in the `From:` address.

✓ **"Complicated" sender profiles that just don't seem to work as whitelist entries:** These profiles are often from folks who use nonbusiness accounts to send business e-mail. For instance, the whitelist entry may be for `businessname.com`, and the incoming e-mail seems to be coming from `billy@clientbusinessname.com`. But the mail is treated like spam. After you dive into the mail headers, you discover that although the `From:` address is `billy@clientbusinessname.com`, Billy is sending via his `yahoo.com` account while he's on the road. The spam-filtering software is doing its job in that it's refusing something that looks like spam from the domain `yahoo.com`, even though the sender name is set to something in the whitelist. Your spam filter may or may not have a way to deal with this specific problem, as it's a tricky one. Look for something called "relayed by" or "received from" in your whitelist options. Using my example, you would then create a whitelist option for `billy@businessname.com` which allows it to be "relayed by" or "received from" `yahoo.com`.

✓ **The inside address leaks to the outside world, throwing off your whitelist:** For example, you might run into instances where mail from `billy@clientbusinessname.com` actually shows up as `billy@mailserver.clientbusinessname.com`. Yeah, it's poor form for an e-mail system to do this, but it does happen.

Managing Filter Rules

Filter rules are the rules that determine what e-mail will be considered spam. Filtering products each handle filter rules very differently because for most spam-filtering companies, the rules are the secret sauce. Here's how you need to handle whichever situation you're in:

- ✓ **You don't even have any concept of how they do their filters:** About all you can do is make sure that your filter subscription is up to date and that the filter is downloading updates on some sort of regular schedule.

- ✓ **You *do* have insight into how the filters are set up, can influence how the filters work, or create your own filters:** You have more to do in terms of management. The following sections explain the details.

Avoid specific rules that solve specific problems

Avoid letting users convince you that a specific spam that's making it through the spam filter is something that you should create a special rule to get rid of just for them. Although that might be a nice thing to do and very customer-service oriented, after the thousandth such request, you have started down a path from which there is no simple return. What you're doing in this case is trying to keep up with the new dirty tricks that spammers are using to get past your filtering product. However, unlike your filter vendor, who has a whole team of programmers devoted to this task, you're all alone in this struggle.

The way the battle goes, spammers find a new way to get their spam in, resulting in user complaints. Instead of acting directly on those complaints, I suggest that you manage this problem as follows:

1. Listen while nodding your head and looking concerned. Practice your concerned look in the mirror if you need to. When the user finishes the complaint, say that you take this matter very seriously and you plan to see what can be done to prevent such a problem in the future.

2. Meanwhile, your spam filter's manufacturer is fully aware of the new spam technique and is working on a comprehensive solution, rather than the more specific filter that you would probably have written yourself. Wait for the new filter to arrive via an automatic update or feel free to bug the spam filter's vendor about it if you feel like you really need to be doing something.

3. After the automatic update is complete, stop by the user's office and ask how things are going. The user will be so happy that you've been so proactive in solving the spam problem that he or she will tell your boss you deserve a raise and more vacation time.

Let the vendor do battle with the spammers rather than engaging with the spammers directly. You're paying your vendor to provide this service, and you should take full advantage of that. You purchased the spam filter to rid yourself of this tedious business; otherwise, you have effectively raised the cost of dealing with spam, which is probably the opposite of the intended effect you had in mind when you acquired your spam filter in the first place. If you really have to create a rule to block something specific, keep an eye on the new rules arriving from your vendor. If the vendor solves the problem later, get rid of your rule. Maintaining your own specific filter rules is a little like maintaining source code: No sane person would choose to do it, given a choice.

Monitor how effective specific rules are

Check whether your spam filter can show you statistics on how many spams each rule is filtering. If you have such a tool, it can help you:

- ✔ Know what rules are effectively killing spam and thus what rule types are getting the most action.

- ✔ Focus the time you spend tuning the filter on the rules that get the most action.

- ✔ Determine the order in which rules get executed. If you move often-hit rules to the top of the list, your spam filter *should* run faster. The fewer rules the filter needs to try before eliminating a message, the sooner the filter can get to the next message.

Managing Updates

Updates to your spam-filtering product are essential to its operation. Both the software itself and the filters used are candidates for automated updates and are typically something that you would pay the annual fee for.

Updating filter rules

Updating the filter rules originally supplied by your spam filter's manufacturer is the key to your continued enjoyment of the filter's effectiveness. Any filter that you buy will become less and less effective over time without fresh updates to the base rules that came in the package. When applying filter updates, here are the important points to keep in mind:

- ✔ **For the most effective filtering, you want filter updates as soon as they're available.**

- ✔ **You also want the ability to back out any newly delivered filters that aren't behaving the way you want.** There's nothing quite like an update that makes everything worse, and in any situation where the updates are happening automatically, you want the ability to reverse the updates to get things back to where you were before.

Updates for most filters can be automated, and I suggest using the automated downloads. Because these happen without user intervention, they have little or no impact on IT, and the consequences of a bad new set of rules is usually limited to accidentally blocking good mail or missing some spam. In either case, no permanent harm is done.

Updating the software (or engine)

On a related topic, another kind of update exists that you'll almost certainly be interested in. The actual program that enforces the filter rules is usually called the *engine,* and over time, most vendors make significant changes to the engine to improve its ability to filter spam.

Sometimes these engine improvements are major leaps ahead in performance of the product. If your vendor makes a distinction between annual costs for filter updates and engine updates, you should carefully consider paying for engine updates as well.

Even more so than with filter updates, you want the ability to reverse software updates in case the new software doesn't work as well as the old software. Be careful to understand the mechanism for doing this before you upgrade your software.

Installing an updated engine is a lot like installing the program from scratch. Although some vendors might make the actual process very simple, you need to remember that the software itself is changing, and then plan accordingly. You will want to

- Wait for a while after the new version is released and see whether anyone else has problems with it. Someone out there will be brave enough to install it right away, and you can learn from that person's experience by watching message boards related to the product and waiting for patches from the vendor.

- If possible, install the new version in a test environment and see how well it behaves. You don't need to do the level of testing I cover in Chapter 9 because this product isn't completely new to you, and the basic rules of operation should be similar. Just make sure that the new software doesn't have any problems.

- Plan for an e-mail system outage and install the new software during the planned time frame. Remember to do good backups before the installation.

Chapter 12

Handling Thorny Issues

*I*nto everyone's life, a little rain must fall. A little rain now and then can be annoying if you're trying to have a barbeque, but an ever-increasing steady downpour starts to have all kinds of serious consequences over time. While spam started out as a trickle years ago, it now affects us all with both its volume and its general level of offensiveness.

In this chapter, I explain the various adverse effects spam has on organizations and individuals and how to handle them in ways likely to keep you out of hot water. Chances are, if you are responsible for limiting spam in your organization, you'll still see your share of hot water, but by reading this chapter, you'll have the tools to keep that hot water down to a pleasant hot-tub temperature.

Most of the time, your primary job is to help users understand the thorny issues that I discuss in this chapter, and work through their consequences. Users don't need the same level of understanding as information technology (IT) staff regarding these issues, and IT people don't need the same level of understanding as an Internet service provider. In this chapter, I provide the level of detail a typical IT person working on spam filtering needs to explain these issues to end-users.

Coping with Performance Issues

Come to think of it, you may have seen this exact heading in some of the spam you've received. In this case, I'm talking about the problems caused by the millions of spam messages flowing across and into every nook and cranny of the Internet each second of each day. Many years ago, I was shocked when an e-mail message took more than two or three seconds to reach its destination. Five seconds almost always meant that something was wrong. The playing field has changed, and a lot of things can slow down mail delivery between any sender and recipient.

The addition of spyware to the scene only makes computer performance worse. Most of it is written very poorly, and it inserts itself into the bowels of your operating system and Web browser. The combination of bad software and its deep integration into your OS means that individual machines that are infected with spyware often slow to a crawl or become unstable.

This section gives you some background on performance issues so that you can explain to your user base why they cannot rely on e-mail as an instant message service anymore and why they don't necessarily need new computers when theirs slow down to the point that they want to pitch their workstations in a dumpster because they can't get their work done.

Most end-users have no concept of the harmful effect that spyware and the enormous volume of spam is having on IT systems and mail delivery performance. Users pretty much expect things to work as well as they did three or four years ago, before the spam and spyware plague began. Although it's not your job to teach users lots of statistics that they don't care about and would quickly forget, it's good to have a grasp on what the numbers really are (and mean) when explaining the situation to management.

Dealing with interruptions in mail service

No system is perfect. Unless you are willing to spend about 2.5 times the typical cost for your mail, spam, and firewall solutions for perfect redundancy, occasionally some part of the mail system will be down for some length of time due to maintenance, hardware failure, or network outage. Deal with it.

During that time, all the mail that would have been delivered to your users' mailboxes is accumulating *somewhere*. If the outage is internal, it could be accumulating on the e-mail server, the spam filter itself, or even the virus gateway. When the outage is repaired in these cases, hundreds or thousands of e-mails that would ordinarily have been trickling into the system are now thundering in like a herd of buffalo at wire speeds. This can look like a very effective Denial of Service (DoS) attack based on mail flooding. The truly awful part is that if you use current ratios of spam to nonspam (or *ham*), about 70 to 80 percent of the incoming pile is useless spam.

The process of examining e-mail to see if the words, address, and demeanor are spammy is quite CPU-intensive, and in these situations, even a well-designed system can fall over gasping for air. It's important to set user expectations in times of an outage so that they don't expect that everything will immediately return to normal as soon as the outage is repaired. The nature of a spam-filtering *choke point* (the place where e-mail passes through and must be examined) is such that an outage of an hour or two could cause several hours of backlog that will be slow to completely clear out.

Law of Big Numbers

A friend of mine likes to talk about the Law of Big Numbers, and how it affects many aspects of our lives, including sales. The basic Law of Big Numbers states that when you're talking about large enough numbers, even statistically insignificant percentages or ratios will happen quite a lot. For example, the FBI says that the odds of any two unrelated people (identical twins don't count because they're related) having the same exact DNA are about 9.5 trillion to 1, given the number of genes in the human genome and the different ways of arranging them. Based on that, at one time or another, there have been at least six genetic duplicates in human history. The point of all this is that, because spammers can send millions and millions of their marketing messages almost for free, the very small percentage of people actually buying their wares still makes it a profitable proposition for spammers.

Combine the Law of Big Numbers for sales prospects with the same law applied to spam filtering, and you begin to see why the volume of spam sent as a percentage of useful mail will do nothing but increase.

The impact users' experience for e-mail is unfortunate: What once was an extremely reliable and rapid way to get messages from place to place is now, while still pretty reliable, sometimes questionable, especially in terms of timely delivery. I still have users that insist that their e-mail must be guaranteed to reach others immediately, at which point I explain the myriad uses of the telephone.

Dealing with loss of productivity from spyware infestation

As I write this chapter, catching spyware before it manages to infest a target machine is an imperfect science at best. Because of that, you often have to clean up after spyware has done its damage. You need to consider a few things in this situation:

- ✔ What sort of information was targeted by this spyware?
- ✔ Is there any chance that confidential information made it into the wrong hands?
- ✔ What confidential information did the spyware have access to through this computer and user login?
- ✔ Do I need to collect evidence from this computer before I make changes to fix the problem?

After you answer these questions, you can start the process of ridding the computer of the spyware you've discovered, and you can find more details on how to go about that in Chapter 2. Hopefully, the anti-spyware software that you're using is up to the task, but you should have some contingency plans in place just in case the spyware is one of the harder-to-remove ones. In Windows XP, try going back to an earlier restore point from before the infestation.

Setting Realistic User Expectations

The software is broken. At least that's how users can perceive new technology like spam and spyware filtering, blocking, or scanning that cannot achieve 100 percent accuracy. The fact is that there is no *perfect* way to detect whether a specific e-mail is spam or not spam. The very fact that some people actually buy things from spammers means that not even a human reading e-mail and deciding what is and isn't spam can be 100 percent accurate. (For the sake of argument, I'll say that people who buy from spammers are human. Because they are the real reason spammers exist, you might disagree.)

Spyware identification is a little more specific and generally yields very few false positives. But the fact that two separate spyware filters running on the same box almost always come up with different lists of spyware leads me to believe that anti-spyware technology still has a long way to go, too.

Understanding what goes wrong with these technologies is critical to explaining things to users when something isn't quite what they expected. A number of things can go wrong, each with associated user impacts that require explanation. Remember that although *you* may understand what's going on with users' e-mails, *they* almost definitely do not. And they can be a bit jittery about new technology that's going to be opening and examining their mail.

Chapter 1 discusses the sorts of legal problems that a company may experience when some types of spam reaches end-users. The best way of reducing the legal risk of this sort is to educate end-users about what they're likely to encounter and why. The fact that spam filters are imperfect is well established, so tell your end-users that and explain why. If this is accomplished both in official communication approved by your legal team and delivered by human resources as part of user training, users will start to see the problem as "us against them" and not "the company should be protecting me better."

Part of educating users about a spam filter is helping them understand how anti-spam measures can screw up in two ways:

- ✔ **False negative:** The anti-spam measures can fail to see spam for what it truly is, and let it through (called a *false negative*), thereby cluttering your inbox with unsightly gunk.

- ✔ **False positive:** The anti-spam measures can decide that a perfectly good e-mail is spam (a *false positive*) and feed it to the spam weasels.

Figure 12-1 illustrates the concept of false negatives and false positives for you visual folks.

Understandably, users are annoyed in both cases. However, by helping users understand how false negatives and false positives happen, you can help shift their annoyance away from you and the spam filter and toward the spammers. In the following sections, I offer tips for explaining just want your users need to know.

False negatives: "Your inbox won't be spam free"

Your user base has been through the trouble of learning to use a new spam solution, dealing with trial installations, and changing their own behavior to accommodate the expensive spam solution that you've put in place — and they're still getting spam. Computers are all ones and zeros, on and off, true or not true, so after you put some effort into blocking spam, it should all go away, right?

The problem here is that spammers are getting good at hiding their spamminess by using nonsense text to fool Bayesian filters, and by making their messages short and simple so that they're indistinguishable from the 50 or 60 messages users receive each day from associates and friends. Here's an example of a spam that made it through my filters recently:

```
Hi,

Drug developers figure they can charge a small fortune.
```

```
Buying overseas cuts costs.
Paste http://rx-factory.com/ into your address bar to recieve
          more info

Turn notifications off
http://rx-factory.com/u

Delores Mclain
```

So, given that I work with several biotech companies that develop drugs with large overseas markets, there aren't too many ways in which this spam message differs from important e-mail messages that I do want to see. In fact, if I changed the names and URLs, it could be a message from an important client of mine.

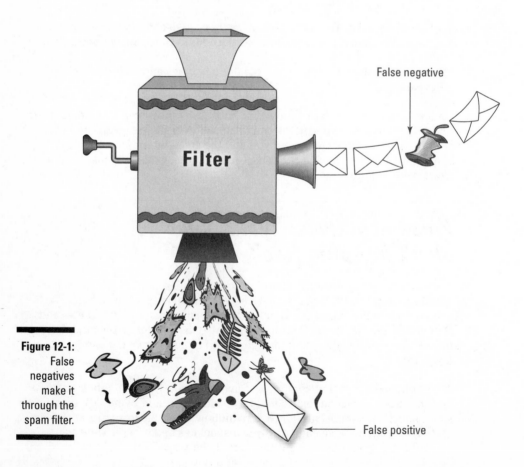

False negative

Filter

Figure 12-1:
False
negatives
make it
through the
spam filter.

False positive

Users need to understand the tradeoff between catching 100 percent of the spam (very simple to do, just block 100 percent of all e-mail) and trying to make sure that useful mail does get through almost all the time.

Work with users about where to set the dial

You can think of spam filtering as having a big dial that on the left points to 0 (zero), no spam blocked at all. On the right, it points to the highest position, 11, all spam (and lots of legitimate e-mail) blocked. At the 0 position, you have essentially no spam protection and everything is getting through. No good mail is ever lost to filtering in this position. At the 11 position, all spam is blocked, because all mail is blocked, including the good stuff. (That's why my spam filter goes to 11 and not 10.)

A setting somewhere in the middle is where you want to be, but that position is a decision to be made with the users and administration. If folks are starting to get too much spam, you can always offer to turn up the dial a bit, with the expectation that this could result in quarantining some of the legitimate e-mail as well.

Helping users recognize spam subject lines

Because this book discusses blocking spam for business, one interesting rule to apply to subject lines is that they should have something to do with the business you are in. For example, unless you work for ICOS, Pfizer, or Bayer/GlaxoSmithKline, you can (most likely) safely ignore subject lines that refer to Cealis, Viagra, and Levitra, respectively. If you do work for one of these companies, things get a little trickier.

Subject lines with misspellings of known spam words are a dead giveaway as well. I couldn't possibly go into all the known, purposefully wrong spellings of these words, but they are usually constructed so that you know the word and your brain mostly fills in the missing or incorrect parts. Some example words that spammers frequently misspell are the following:

- ✔ Refinance
- ✔ Drugs
- ✔ Pharmacy
- ✔ Mortgage
- ✔ Nearly any drug name you can imagine

User training should include guidance on how to delete spam before opening the message. Spam veterans can spot a spam e-mail from the smell of its subject line and sometimes from the apparent sender well before they might be tempted to open it. Teaching users what to look for in these areas can save you some grief.

Training the spam filter

Most new spam filters work better when trained to understand what is spam and what is not. Although users may be annoyed to receive spam after the filter is in place, they usually feel much better if they know that they can improve things directly by submitting a missed spam message as training material for the filter.

Different filters have different ways for users to report missed spam, but it usually boils down to just forwarding the offending message to a specific e-mail address, or clicking the This Is Spam button if the solution is integrated into the mail client. Either way, training users to use this helpful feedback tool is critical to training the filter, and it makes the users feel like they have some control over the solution.

False positives: When good mail looks bad

How many times have you had this conversation? It goes something like this:

> *Broker:* So, have you tied up the world supply of Lutefisk, like I talked about?
>
> *Me:* No, I don't recall you mentioning this.
>
> *Broker:* I sent you an e-mail about how lye supplies are low this year, and jellied cod will be in short supply! You could have made a killing!
>
> *Me:* Uh, let me check my spam filter and see if your message is in there.

Typically, I spend at least as much time tuning spam filtering to allow good messages through as I spend trying to keep the bad ones out. Although it may be annoying to receive spam, it can be disastrous to miss a time-sensitive e-mail. Because of this, most filtering programs have a mechanism called a *whitelist* that allows you to select either individual e-mail addresses like `joe@domain.com` or the entire domain `domain.com` as senders that will never be fed to the spam weasels.

End-users need to help create whitelists, or be prepared to deal with missing important e-mail. You can't really say that to your users, but it's a simple fact that if they don't pony up the e-mail addresses of people that they absolutely must not miss any mail from, the filter is on its own to decide, and it will sometimes make mistakes. One incentive for users is that creating comprehensive whitelists enables you to turn up the spam dial a few more notches, because important mail will still get through. Really complete whitelists mean less spam for everyone.

As you might expect, a *blacklist* is the exact opposite of a whitelist — a list of companies and people that you never want to hear from. Blacklisting is less useful than you might imagine, though, because spammers tend to hide who they are and where they are coming from. Don't make the mistake of confusing blacklisting with another useful spam-killing tool called blackholing.

Helping users explain RBL bounces to friends and colleagues

Real-time Blackhole Listing (RBL) is a way of telling spammers to go away before they even get a chance to send their spammy message. This method relies on a number of folks who keep track of the IP addresses of known spammers. Here's how the technique works:

1. When your mail system receives a connection for inbound e-mail, it checks with the RBL folks to see if this sender is on the list.

2. If the sender is on the list, your mail system refuses the connection before the message even begins to transmit.

Like any method for blocking spam, this approach has is pros and cons, which are presented in Table 12-1.

Table 12-1	Pros and Cons of Real-time Blackhole Listing
Pros	**Cons**
RBL doesn't require looking at the spam itself and uses less processor time to reject spam.	The lists sometimes include legitimate non spammers, and in some cases, it's nearly impossible to get off the list once you're on it.
RBL prevents 80% of incoming spam from ever clogging up your Internet pipe.	Because it's impossible to list the IP source address of every spammer in the world, RBL doesn't block all spam.

Even with these drawbacks, I like to use the Spamhaus Block List (SBL) at www.spamhaus.org (their more conservative list) because it prevents 80 percent of incoming spam from ever clogging up my Internet pipe.

The real user issue here is in explaining first to your own user, and then to the original sender, why an RBL-bounced message wasn't delivered. Almost always, you are treading on thin ice here. The message was bounced because a third party decided that the sender was a known spammer. The listing could be a mistake, or it could be that the sender's ISP isn't good about kicking off spammers and he or she is getting lumped in with spamming neighbors. For example, if you use the XBL (the eXploits Block List, which includes home machines thought to be controlled by spammers) from Spamhaus, a large portion of Comcast subscribers won't be able to send you mail because their DHCP (Dynamic Host Configuration Protocol) assigned IP address was once assigned to someone who was infected with a spambot, and so some Comcast addresses are on the list.

Understanding who really sent this e-mail

With a spam filter, you've just changed how e-mail is handled and caused some of it to not get delivered on purpose. For several weeks after a new filter is put into place, users will have many questions about what is happening with their mail. To help them understand what they see in their inboxes, or don't see as the case may be, you need to lay the pieces of spam on the dissection table and identify the parts.

What IT folks need to know about headers

Because the From: header of a spam message is usually faked, it can be much harder to spot spam just by looking at the sender information that your e-mail program presents. However, you need to know some important things about what users see on the screen versus reality.

The first thing to understand is what appears on the screen as the sender is actually taken from a mail header inside the message, the From: line. Because this is just a part of the message, the spammers can type anything they want, and your mail client will confidently report that president@ whitehouse.gov is sending you mail. It's important to note that this has no relationship to what's known as the "envelope sender." The *envelope sender* is what is used in the actual SMTP transaction used to deliver the mail message. While the envelope sender can also be faked, most anti-spam solutions have protections in place that prevent certain obvious fakes in the envelope. In the following example, you can see some complete examples of SMTP transactions, including the envelope information, and a mail server refusing some obvious fakes.

```
% telnet c1.conjungi.com 25
Trying 199.165.221.4...
Connected to c1.conjungi.com.
Escape character is '^]'.
220 c1.conjungi.com ESMTP Sat, 9 Oct 2004 07:45:47 -0700
        (PDT)
helo conjungi.com
250 c1.conjungi.com Hello c1.conjungi.com [199.165.221.4],
        pleased to meet you
mail from:<simon@conjungi.com>
250 2.1.0 <simon@conjungi.com>... Sender ok
rcpt to:<simon@conjungi.com>
250 2.1.5 <simon@conjungi.com>... Recipient ok
data
354 Enter mail, end with "." on a line by itself
Subject: Spoofing From headers
From: Your Best Friend <bestfriend@example.com>

I'm not who you think I am.

.
250 2.0.0 i99EjlVT022829 Message accepted for delivery
```

Compare the *envelope from* line (`mail from:<simon@conjungi.com`), which is a part of the SMTP transaction, with the `From:` header in the body of the message (`From: Your Best Friend <bestfriend@example.com>`).

The envelope from address is the one that is frequently checked by spam filters for basic correctness. By checking the envelope from line *and* the `From:` header, you know a few things:

- ✔ **What domain is connecting to you:** You know this because the filter does a reverse lookup on the IP address that connected to send you the mail. You can choose to refuse the mail if the envelope from address doesn't match the reverse domain. This is rarely done, because doing so blocks mail from any forwarding host that isn't part of the original sender's domain, and some of those forwarding hosts can be legitimate.

- ✔ **Whether the domain in the envelope address exists:** You can refuse to accept the mail if the domain in the envelope from address doesn't exist. This one is common practice, and therefore spammers rarely hide behind nonexistent domains.

- ✔ **If the envelope sender says that it's coming from someone inside the company:** If so, your filter should refuse to accept the mail. Because you know this message is coming from the outside, you also know that it couldn't possibly be from someone on the inside.

The `From:` header has no significance at all to the actual delivery of the mail, and neither does the `To:` header. It's best to think of these as essentially *data* in the message, not as any real indicator of where the mail came from or went to. Unfortunately, they have *everything* to do with what users see in their mail client. In Figure 12-2, you can see how the spoofed mail in the preceding example appears in my inbox. I could just as easily have spoofed the `To:` header, and because the envelope `rcpt to:` was to my correct e-mail address, it would have been delivered to me.

What users need to know about headers

I'm tempted to say "nothing," but the unfortunate truth is that users do need to understand certain header-related things.

Don't say the words *e-mail header* while explaining it, or you'll get the glassy-eyed stare way to soon. Talk in terms of *fake* `From:` *addresses* and *bogus* `To:` *lines,* and all should come out well.

Users need to understand that what shows up in the `From:` address or even the `To:` address doesn't have much to do with who might have sent the e-mail. Two of the most frequent questions I hear from users about spam that landed in their inbox are

"Why did I receive this? I'm not even who it was sent to."

"Did this really come from my friend Joe? I can't imagine him sending me *that.*"

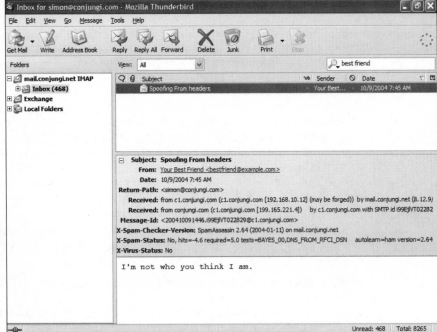

Figure 12-2:
Spoofed
e-mail
message as
seen by the
mail client.

This issue is especially sticky when the spammer is using another known inside addresses as the From: address and the message is offensive. The first ten times someone calls you in a panic about a lewd message from a co-worker advertising unspeakable items, it's amusing. After that, it gets old.

Restricting Web browser configuration

Although all Web browsers have security problems, the ones that spyware targets all seem to be in Internet Explorer (IE), so in this section, I talk a little bit about what you can do to help your spyware filtering out a bit.

Most of the really bad stuff that comes your way via IE is in the form of ActiveX, Java, JavaScript, and VBScript. Each of these have the ability to deliver executable code to your computer that, under the right circumstances, can do anything it wants to, including installing and running spyware.

IE is at least configurable for most of these options, and IT should have central control over the settings required. Under no circumstances is it a good idea to allow users to change their own browser settings to suit their convenience, because they are likely to turn on something truly awful like "initialize and script ActiveX controls not marked as safe." I'm not kidding; there really is such a thing that you can turn on in IE if you feel the need. The Microsoft Security Policy Editor enables you to prevent users from tweaking settings that you don't want them to tweak. Some of your power users will not be happy with this arrangement, but they are also some of the most likely to be infected with spyware in the first place.

Identifying and Handling Business Issues

Just as spam poses problems for the unfortunate individual who has to deal with it, spam has serious implications for the business as well. In this section, I help you identify some of the thorny problems that your business may face in dealing with spam, spammers, users reactions to being spammed, and the various folks that might be helping you deal with the spam.

Figuring out legal issues

When you insert a spam solution into the natural flow of business e-mail, you create a situation in which, at certain points, someone other than the recipient is more likely to read the e-mail. For instance, as an IT person with greater than normal access, you might end up having to read other peoples' e-mail when you're checking out the spam quarantine for a reported user problem. While this may happen in the old, unfiltered environment from time to time, the fact that you are now stopping some mail on its way increases the odds that mail will be seen by people for whom it was not intended.

When an anti-spam ASP (Application Service Provider) is involved, there are even more interesting issues regarding who may be reading what. For an ASP solution to work, *all* of the company's e-mail goes through the systems at the ASP. Unlike the Internet in general, where e-mail is just bits flowing through a few routers, at your spam ASP, the mail is collected, analyzed, and either forwarded or quarantined. Any employee with sufficient privilege at the ASP could potentially read your company's e-mail. The way to make this an acceptable risk is to make sure that your contract with the ASP addresses this issue very clearly, with sufficient penalties to make your own lawyers comfortable with the situation. The fact that many of my law firm clients use ASP-based spam filtering is proof that such arrangements are possible.

When you examine what is and isn't okay as you deploy a spam filter, you need to know something about wiretapping laws. Some debate goes on about when and where interception of e-mail becomes illegal interception, but in my conversations with folks in prosecutors' offices and federal law enforcement, the generally accepted principle is

> ✔ **It is illegal for a third party to intercept and read an "in transit" e-mail.** Such an interception would be a violation of the wiretapping laws.
>
> ✔ **The e-mail "at rest" — which is to say, delivered to the recipient — can be fair game,** if employees are told that e-mail on company mail servers belongs to the company and can be read at any time.

The whole "in transit" thing is troublesome, because it would seem to rule out doing any spam filtering or other invasive ways of looking at e-mail before it's delivered, such as virus scanning. I've asked everyone I can get to tell me what they think about this, and most of them suddenly have urgent business elsewhere. There's a good chance that automated systems, such as virus and spam filtering, would not be affected by wiretapping laws (although automated *telephone* wiretapping is, of course, still subject to the laws). However, in situations where a human gets involved in looking at e-mail before it's delivered to the intended destination, the legal waters become less clear.

If you are concerned about blocking spam and wiretapping laws, talk to your legal council.

When a company computer is infected with spyware, you risk far more than someone logging into your bank account and transferring money to their own. To get a proper perspective on this, imagine that a known extortionist broke into your office and had access to your still logged on PC for a few days, then left for a country with no extradition treaty with all your personal, corporate, and customer information in hand.

Most of the time, the spyware is really just interested in where you are going or what you are doing on the Internet, and but in some cases the nightmare above is the reality, with the small difference that you don't know about the plundering until you discover the spyware — or its effects, such as a sudden increase in the number of unfamiliar credit card bills addressed to you.

In case this happens, you need to understand the legal ramifications of your data, or data you are in possession of that is floating around in cyberspace, which could include

> ✔ Confidential information damaging to the company in the open, requiring civil action against the perpetrators
>
> ✔ Personally identifiable customer information in the open, requiring legal notification of the customers, and potential liability for identity theft
>
> ✔ Customer intellectual property stolen (think law firms) and millions or even billions of dollars worth of risk to the customer

Uprooting hidden costs

Hidden costs create a financial burden on the company without being easily recognized as associated with the spam or spyware problem itself. It is very important to identify hidden costs correctly for budgeting and risk assessment purposes. If you know how much it's really costing you to mitigate the problem, and you understand the risks the problem proposes, you can make valid business decisions about how much to spend on reducing the risk.

With any IT project that has any large impact on the organization, you have *soft costs* (those that aren't immediately apparent and are often hard to track) and *hard costs* (where actual money changes hands).

The soft costs are the most insidious types of costs, because nobody writes a check to cover them in the short term. Soft costs include items such as the following:

- ✔ Additional IT support time.
- ✔ Helpdesk and user training time.
- ✔ Lost productivity as users come up to speed on the new technology.
- ✔ Time spent dealing with legitimate e-mail that was marked as spam: In some cases, false positives can turn into hard costs, when important e-mail affecting sales or new deals is lost in the system.

Hard costs are easier to identify, but they can still be a bit surprising in some ways. For instance, because spam filters and spam are constantly in a war of escalation, a spam filter that works well today will be almost useless six months from now without constant updates. Some of the hard costs you need to plan for include the following:

- ✔ Software subscription and maintenance costs
- ✔ ASP annual or monthly fees
- ✔ Fees for changes to services (for example, DNS changes or rack space at the collocation facility)
- ✔ Annual maintenance on new hardware

Doing a good job of rounding up these less apparent costs and reporting them before the project starts is a great way to be on good terms with your boss and the accounting folks. Don't be afraid of scaring them away with the larger total cost — they already know these sorts of things will come up. Hearing it from you beforehand just makes them feel all warm and cozy.

Preparing for ASP outages

In the "Figuring out legal issues" section, earlier in this chapter, I briefly discuss the contract you create with your ASP, and how important it is that the contract reflects your business requirements for such a service. Contract terms are one thing; performance is another.

It's very important to establish and maintain a close working relationship with the ASP or reseller by communicating on a regular basis, so that when problems hit the fan, you know exactly who to call, and the ASP knows you and your company. Don't wait until you discover that all mail delivery has stopped to look for the support number.

Remember that with an ASP, if a problem is affecting you, it's probably affecting a lot of other people, and the ASP is getting a lot of calls about it. You want to be on the list of people the ASP knows and wants to talk to. In your communication with the ASP, always be courteous and accurate when you describe any problems you're having. That will distinguish you from the angry customers calling with vague descriptions.

You put forth the effort to establish a good relationship with an ASP, because even the best of the best will sometimes have a problem. (Chapter 5 covers checking references and even looking for bad reports on an ASP's performance.) You need to be prepared for some of the worst-case scenarios that you can imagine and be ready to deal with them organizationally because outages affect the entire business, not just IT. ASP outages of this nature are different from internal service outages in that you have little or no control over identifying and resolving the issue. Items to consider in planning for dealing with an outage at the ASP include the following:

✔ **Notification:** Be ready to tell users and administration what's up and what the impact will be.

✔ **Recovery:** Do you have control of your DNS and MX records? Can you point them back to yourself directly, thereby bypassing the ASP? Is the TTL (Time To Live) value in the MX record small enough so that direct-to-you inbound e-mail delivery will resume quickly? Organizations that regularly send you e-mail will not use the modified MX record until the TTL expires on their cached versions of your MX record.

✔ **Mediation:** Do you know what is happening to mail while the outage is occurring? What will happen when things come back online?

✔ **ASP/vendor lunch:** How nice of a lunch do they owe you after all this pain — steak, seafood, or burgers?

Developing skills to support the spam filter

You will need a number of new skills to support a new spam-filtering solution. E-mail coming into the company is getting messed with as never before, and when users come to you wondering why e-mails they need to send or receive aren't successful, it'll be your job to figure out what happened and why, given the barest snippets of information and working against the fact that spammers are doing their best to make that particular task difficult.

Two tools will help you in this effort to troubleshoot e-mail problems: the `Received: from` headers and the SMTP codes. The following sections explain the basics.

Tracking e-mail on your own

Tracking where an e-mail has been, and how it arrived in your mailbox, can be difficult in the best of circumstances, and the fact that spammers are trying their best to hide this information doesn't help. Listing 12-1 shows a typical set of e-mail headers from some spam I've received. For the purposes of tracking where this came from, the bold lines are really the only ones I can trust. Almost everything else in this header can be forged, and most likely is. The reason I can trust the bold entry is that it came from my own mail server.

Listing 12-1: Spam E-Mail Headers

```
Return-Path: <xaihvdhhcbd@losgatosfinancial.com>
Received: from c1.conjungi.com (c1.conjungi.com
        [192.168.10.12] (may be forged))
      by mail.conjungi.net (8.12.9/8.12.9) with ESMTP id
        i8QFLjqJ031039;
      Sun, 26 Sep 2004 08:21:45 -0700
Received: from 83.113.93.88 (ANice-151-1-
        25-88.w83-113.abo.wanadoo.fr
[83.113.93.88])
      by c1.conjungi.com with SMTP id i8QFKrVb014065;
      Sun, 26 Sep 2004 08:21:26 -0700 (PDT)
Received: from mdlxbkjfq.losgatosfinancial.com
        ([36.124.74.61]) (HELO
losgatosfinancial.com) by wcidqirbr.losgatosfinancial.com
        [83.113.93.88] with
SMTP; Sun, 26 Sep 2004 10:21:24 -0600
Message-ID: <000301c4a3dc$7c567530$3d4a7c24@XKVEMM>
From: "Hannah D. Dean" <xaihvdhhcbd@losgatosfinancial.com>
To: "Landon Lisa" <nookwrl@losgatosfinancial.com>
Subject: On a tall metal
Date: Sun, 26 Sep 2004 10:20:19 -0600
MIME-Version: 1.0
```

(continued)

Listing 12-1 *(continued)*

```
Content-Type: multipart/alternative;
        boundary="----=_NextPart_000_0000_01C4A3B2.93806D30"
X-Priority: 3
X-MSMail-Priority: Normal
X-Mailer: Microsoft Outlook Express 6.00.3790.0
X-MimeOLE: Produced By Microsoft MimeOLE V6.00.3790.0
```

The `Received: from` lines tell you what Mail Transfer Agents (MTAs) have handled this e-mail, and in what order. In the simplest case, you have only one of these lines, telling you what mail server delivered this e-mail to you. In most cases, at least one or two MTAs are in the middle routing your e-mail. When you read these lines, remember that the top entries are the last ones in the sequence, followed by each previous one. So in this example message, here's how you interpret the `Received: from` lines:

- ✔ The message makes one more hop when it reaches my firewall from the host `c1.conjungi.com` to the inside host `mail.conjungi.net`.

- ✔ The next entry down tells me which host actually delivered this mail to my firewall, giving me both the IP address 83.113.93.88 and the host name `ANice-151-1-25-88.w83-113.abo.wanadoo.fr`.

- ✔ Anything before the preceding entry is likely forged. I know that entry is correct because it's nearly impossible to forge an actual TCP connection source address across the Internet beyond the first packet or two. (Single packets are easy, as is UDP, but TCP connections require that the apparent source address be online and responding correctly, not spoofed.) Note here that the `From:` and `To:` lines don't list me as the recipient; those are both forged, and this message did come directly to my e-mail address.

Understanding SMTP standard response codes

As administrator of a spam filter, you need to spend time looking at rejected mail. Mail gets rejected for all sorts of reasons, and if you look closely at the rejection, it almost always tells you something about why. Often, an outright rejection of e-mail occurs during the SMTP transaction and is accompanied by an SMTP status code. You find these codes as described in Table 12-2 in the header of an e-mail; the codes look something like this:

```
550 5.1.1 User unknown
```

The reply codes are all three-digit codes. The first digit indicates what kind of response this is, as explained in Table 12-2, and the other two digits tell you more details about the response. For example, note the difference between 550 and 552 in Table 12-2.

Table 12-2	SMTP Reply Codes	
If the First Digit Is	**It Means**	**Example**
1	Commands are pending, waiting to be confirmed. You'll almost certainly never see this.	By definition, this code is used only in extended SMTP, and no examples of subcodes (numbers following the 1) are given.
2	Normal completion of SMTP transaction.	This is common. 200 is a standard code that means everything is okay, and that the command is completed.
3	Things are okay in this SMTP transaction, but the mail host is waiting for more stuff to complete the command.	354 is an indicator that the request to begin the data portion of an e-mail is accepted and the mail host may proceed to deliver the data portion.
4	The command failed, but for reasons that might eventually go away.	452 means that there was not enough system storage to accept the attempted e-mail.
5	The command failed and will never work.	550 means that the intended recipient doesn't exist. Spammers see a lot of these, but they ignore them for the most part. 552 means the remote mailbox is full (of spam, most likely).

If you look carefully in rejected mail, you find examples of these codes, which tell you exactly what happened when the mail tried to get delivered. I use the 550 responses all the time when I need to explain to users that they have the wrong address for the person they are sending to, and their message isn't being swallowed by a spam filter.

The full list of reply codes is way too long (and boring) to publish here but they're explained in excruciating detail in RFC 2821 (see www.faqs.org/rfcs/rfc2821.html). The juicy parts are in the section titled, "Reply Code Severities and Theory," so just skip everything else, unless you're having trouble sleeping.

What about when spam actually works?

When users respond to spam that arrived in their company e-mail inbox, they aren't putting just themselves at risk. For instance, if a user purchases an illegal drug using your company's computer and Internet connection, it can cause liability problems for the company.

It's temping to believe that none of your users would consider buying from a spammer or responding to a phishing scam, but remember the Law of Big Numbers: Of all the people reading this book, several of you have users who are getting ready to place orders from spammers right now, putting their identities at risk for theft and putting the company in a difficult legal position.

Getting involved with a forensic study of a user's hard drive and e-mail store to help the police figure out how the user's identity was stolen, or worse, is among the worst jobs I've ever had to do. It costs the company piles of money in lost time, productivity, and even hardware if the hard drive is taken as evidence. It's well worth spending a little time to explain to the user population what seems obvious — that placing any sort of order with a company that just appeared in your e-mail one day is likely to be trouble.

I guess that it's possible that a few spammers out there are actually selling legitimate products, charging reasonable prices, and acting in their customers' best interests, but the bulk of them seem to be selling snake oil for more than snake oil prices. It may be useful to remind mail users that:

- ✔ If it sounds too good to be true, it is.
- ✔ The only things that alter size or shape of a body part are muscle, fat, and cosmetic surgery.
- ✔ "Generic" forms of drugs are still patented, and they are dangerous and illegal.
- ✔ There's no such thing as 2.3 percent financing for your home.

The best-case scenario for most of the stuff advertised in spam is that you pay the spammer and the goods never arrive. Worst cases range from them having your credit card number and using it in unexpected ways, to receiving the generic Viagra and risking a heart attack by taking it.

Some of the scams that are arriving in e-mail are subtler than the obvious illegal drugs and too-good-to-be-true offers. I used to tell people to deal only with companies that they had some prior association with if the offer comes to them in e-mail, but that's exactly the sort of trust that phishing spammers (which I discuss near the end of this chapter) are using to get users to click links and enter personal information. The best rule now is to never buy from someone who's using e-mail as his primary advertising scheme, and to never click any links that you receive in e-mail that you weren't expecting to receive.

Supporting spyware filters and scanning

Spyware has a number of ways that it can get into your networks and computers including e-mail, Web browsing, and deliberate download. Because of this, and the fact that it usually installs itself very silently and then covers its tracks, it can be difficult to figure out what the user did to become infected. If you can't figure out where the spyware came from, it can be really hard to make sure that it doesn't happen again.

Most of the current technology in anti-spyware is centered on scanning and removal, but both of these are after-the-fact solutions, and just assume that the initial infection with spyware will happen. Because of this, if you have chosen a solution that doesn't do on-access scanning or filtering at the gateway, you need to really focus on user education (telling them what *not* to do) and locking down the workstations to make it harder for spyware to get a toe-hold.

Another problem with many of the current spyware solutions is that maintaining spyware signatures is rarely centralized and usually relies on individual users to occasionally click the Update button. If your solution supports it, have it download new signatures on a schedule at least, so you don't have to rely on your users remembering this important task.

Lastly, spyware seems to come in flocks. If you find that you have an infected workstation, there is a good chance that there are multiple spyware atrocities on that same workstation. What I like to do is have another spyware scanner on CD or floppy that I can run on any workstation that comes up positive for spyware. After you've run the resident spyware scanner and your own from floppy, you should have most of the gunk cleaned up.

Stopping Deliberate Attacks

In the somewhat sleazy world of people who send billions of e-mail messages each month trying to get you to buy questionable products, which they often don't deliver, some of those people are obviously not very nice. Some spammers get very angry when anyone makes it hard for them to send spam, or even accuses them of doing wrong. As it turns out, the seedy spam business attracts sociopaths that behave badly in all sorts of ways.

Your users should be aware that some of the attacks mentioned in the following sections are direct attacks against individuals, usually because the attacking party is angry about something in an e-mail or posting of another sort. The attack that may result from this anger can have lasting effects on your company in the form of denial of service attacks, increased spam loads, and compromised confidential information by using the means I discuss in the following sections.

Block Web bugs and other malicious content

Web bugs have been around for a while now, and they are also known as *Web beacons, pixel tags,* or *invisible GIFs.* The basic idea is that most e-mail clients display HTML-formatted e-mail, including image tags that reference URLs on the Internet somewhere. So, if a spammer sends you an HTML-formatted e-mail with an image tag that points to a 1-pixel-by-1-pixel white image on its Web server, there's a good chance that you won't notice because the tiny image is not visible. However, the spammer will notice the moment that you open this e-mail because its Web server logs will record that your e-mail client downloaded and displayed that tiny image. The spammer can even get tricky and have the Web server logs reference a CGI script with your e-mail address as a parameter, so that the spammer can keep a running tally of exactly who opens its spam.

Spammers pay actual money for lists of people to spam. Any given list contains a large number of bad addresses that reach nobody, people behind effective spam filters, and folks who just don't bother reading their spam. Imagine how valuable the address of someone known to both exist and read spam is. Users that are bitten by this method go on special lists, and they'll receive even more spam than usual. In the following sections, I explain the key vulnerabilities in e-mail clients and how you can close some of the backdoors that let Web bugs and the like into your business.

Message preview is bad

Message preview, shown in Figure 12-3, is a way of looking at an e-mail message without actually opening it in a new window. In effect, message preview automatically displays any e-mail highlighted in the inbox in a pane within the e-mail program's window. Outlook, Outlook Express, Mozilla Thunderbird, and other e-mail programs utilize message preview.

For a number of reasons, users should turn off message preview, or any other mechanism that essentially opens mail by just selecting it in the incoming mail list. By disabling message preview, you prevent Web bugs from calling home to add your users' e-mail addresses to spammers' lists, and you create a roadblock for other virus laden spam that exploits holes in HTML-enabled e-mail clients — unless the user opens the e-mail on purpose.

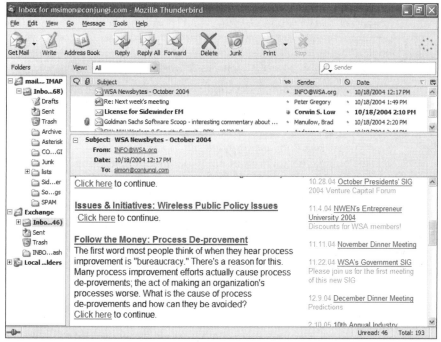

Figure 12-3:
Messages
preview
with HTML.

Your mail client is a Web browser

Although turning off the preview pane will keep the spammer from being noti-fied when a user just selects the message for deletion, if the user chooses to open the mail to see if it's really spam, the only help is to have HTML render-ing disabled entirely in the e-mail client, or in more sophisticated mail clients, to disable rendering remote HTML tags. The ability to turn off HTML render-ing is available in most e-mail clients and should be done for the whole com-pany to prevent this problem.

Whether you're using Microsoft Outlook, Eudora, or Mozilla Thunderbird for reading your e-mail, in some respects, your mail client is a Web browser. It will, if asked, render HTML just like a browser, and if the basic code that ren-ders these pages has a flaw that spammers can exploit to their own benefit, they will. Unlike Web bugs, which rely on standard operation of the mail client to do their dirty work, this kind of mail gone bad uses any of the several dozen known security problems in the HTML rendering libraries in Windows to track your usage, install spyware, or otherwise compromise your computer.

In the case of spammy content that exploits security holes, the only defense is to never view the e-mail in the first place, either in the preview pane or by opening it. This sort of attack is generally based on flaws in the operating system, the mail client, and/or the HTML rendering engine, so keeping a good antivirus program patched and running helps. But if you are the first on your block to receive the new spam, virus, phishing e-mail, or Web bug, patching and antivirus can't help you. The Flea.A virus is an example of this method, but there are now several others in the wild.

Even more reasons to not open spam

Like you needed more reasons. . . . The Microsoft GDI (a standard Microsoft device-independent library for rendering graphics in the Windows operating system) vulnerability opened up a somewhat new category of Bad Stuff happening on your computer. The GDI problem is new in that the virus, spyware, or other bad code is not delivered in any form that looks like a program. It's just an image with a program embedded in it, and the Microsoft GDI library can be induced to run the bad code. The short version is that if you view an infected image by using a vulnerable viewer, the virus can infect your computer. Because of the specific way the GDI vulnerability works, both Internet Explorer and Outlook are vulnerable. But you can't count on the next vulnerability of this nature sparing browsers and mail programs. Because even images and nonprogram content can be used to infect your computers, users need to learn to treat spam like a plague-carrying rat: Get rid of it from as far away as you can.

Forensic dumping

The science of digging through a computer to look for evidence in a criminal case is practiced with varying levels of expertise by certain law enforcement agencies. *Forensic dumping* is the practice of placing incriminating evidence, usually photographs, onto the target computer without the knowledge of the user. If you think about what Web bugs are doing (which is getting the mail client to download images without the user's knowledge or consent), you can see that Web bugs are one way of doing forensic dumping. The idea has been used as a successful defense in more than one case by just showing that the incriminating images *could* have been placed on the computer in this way. In relationship to spam, the delivery technique is spam itself. The person doing the dumping sends large amounts of incriminating evidence to the victim, knowing that even if it's all deleted, the images or text can still be recovered from the hard drive, and then the person dumping the images calls the police with a hot tip.

Clearly, having illegal images placed on your company's computers by these means poses a problem for the company. Although there is no way to be completely protected from this, good spam and spyware controls are the best way to minimize the risk.

The only defense against this is to have a better forensic team working for you than the one on the other side. It should be simple to show that the incriminating evidence came into the computer via e-mail and was in no way solicited by the user. In one case in the U.K. where this concept was used as a successful defense, the defendant's team showed that the computer had a remote-control Trojan on it, so the person controlling the Trojan could have planted the files.

Don't make yourself a target for Joe Jobs

I've heard a few different definitions for the term *Joe Job* (on the Internet, everyone is an expert), but by the common definition, Joe Jobs work something like this:

1. I annoy some spammer by reporting him to his ISP. The ISP terminates his Internet connection.

2. The spammer retaliates by sending 14 trillion really, really disgusting spams with my e-mail address as the return address, from some other link. (Spammers always have a lot of connections to the Internet.)

3. About 14 trillion people get upset with me. (Yes, I know the human population on Earth is 6.4 billion or so, but I'm pretty sure that spammers are annoying people on other planets at this point.)

4. I have to change my name, buy some llamas, and move to eastern Oregon or Peru.

In the "Understanding who really sent this e-mail" section, earlier in this chapter, I explain that the apparent sender of a spam is usually not the actual sender. Even though falsifying the sender of an e-mail has been illegal in the U.S. since January 2004, the law doesn't affect U.S. spammers sending you e-mail through their ISPs in Korea. The law still applies to them, but it's harder to prove who they are.

If you want to complain about a particular spam you've received, your best bet is to send it to your own ISP and see if it will help you report the spam to the proper places. If your users feel the need to escalate a spam problem, make sure that they bring it to you, and you handle the issue by working with professionals who track Internet attacks and fraud. In the case of fraud or damage to your business, local or federal law enforcement may get involved.

Taking matters into your own hands will almost certainly result in persecution of the wrong individual, possibly the intended victim of a Joe Job.

Prevent spammers from verifying or listing e-mail addresses

For spammers looking to build a list of e-mail addresses to send spam to, what could be more attractive than a place to look up valid e-mail addresses on your own network? Although nobody would be so foolish as to just publish a list of e-mail addresses for the world to see, spammers have a number of ways to check whether a list of common names contains valid addresses at your site.

Sendmail, the oldest and still most common e-mail server on the Internet, responds to a number of commands beyond just the ones needed to identify sender and recipient. Eric Allman wrote sendmail back in the early 1980s, when the Internet was a much friendlier place, and it includes a command called VRFY that allows someone to verify that a specific address actually exists at the destination. A spammer can take advantage of this facility by running through a large list of potential e-mail addresses with the VRFY command and seeing which addresses exist at your site. In the following example, you can see an example of how VRFY works, returning the success code 250 if an address is guessed correctly, and a failure code 550 when the guess is wrong.

```
$ telnet mail.example.net 25
Trying 192.168.120.10...
Connected to example.net.
Escape character is '^]'.
220 mail.example.net ESMTP Sendmail 8.12.9/8.12.9; Sun, 10
        Oct 2004 16:36:16 -0700
VRFY <spamvictim@example.net>
250 <spamvictim@mail.example.net>
VRFY <notarealuser@example.net>
550 <notarealuser@example.net>... User unknown
```

Because running through thousands of combinations of new names costs spammers almost nothing, they have no reason *not* to use this sort of directory discovery attack. A similar sendmail command called EXPN does the same thing, only for lists of users.

If your mail server responds to the VRFY command in this way, you need to turn that feature off. Explaining how exactly to make that change to your sendmail configuration is beyond the scope of this book, but if you're going to dive in, know that what you need to set is the option called PrivacyOptions and add the directive goaway to it.

You might imagine that this same technique could be used for any service that will return yes or no to the question, "Does the user Mary exist?" and you would be correct. Other services to carefully hide from these prying eyes include LDAP, NIS, and NDS. If you're responsible for these services, however, you know that allowing outsiders access to them poses large security problems, and they should be hidden already.

Make the Web spiders starve

Spammers also use *Web spiders*, little programs that crawl around your Web site and look into every page to harvest every single mailto: link on your Web site. If you are on the receiving end of a mailto: link on the company Web site, just expect a lot of spam to come your way.

To prevent Web spiders from harvesting addresses, replace a simple `mailto:` link with a form that visitors fill out on the Web site to send mail to sales, or whoever needs the Web site feedback. This method doesn't expose any actual mail addresses to the spammer's Web spider but still enables visitors to send e-mail from the Web site to the right people inside the company.

Although spammers could certainly write a program to fill out the form and send mail that way, the form would be different for each Web site, and not worth their time to customize the program to deal with different forms. It's all about volume for them.

Viruses — don't be part of the problem

While it doesn't really qualify as a deliberate attack, it's worth mentioning another way (remember Joe Jobs) that you can get blamed for sending spam when you had nothing to do with it. As I write this chapter, several viruses out there, including W32.Bagz.B, W32.Mydoom.AC, and W32.Beagle.AR, take the time to read the infected victim's electronic address book, and then send themselves (including spam or virus or both) to every person in the address book, apparently from another person in that same address book. In these situations, it doesn't pay to be popular, because the more address books your address is in, the more likely you are to get blamed for sending spam or viruses.

One of my favorite situations is when the infected person has a couple of mailing lists in his or her address book, and the virus/spam sends itself to someone on vacation with an auto-reply setup, using the mailing list as the reply address. The resulting confusion is nearly impossible to untangle.

Out-of-office replies are another way spammers verify that e-mail addresses go to real people, but there's really no way of avoiding this problem, unless you can tell your mail server only to reply to messages from people on a specific list.

Shut out the robot army

Possibly the most serious threat facing the Internet today is the massive collections of home computers that have been taken over by various persons and organizations (referred to as *bots* or *zombies*) through lack of good virus protection, firewalls, and/or up-to-date patching. These machines are taken over using worms, viruses, Trojan horses, and even direct attack and then used to perform all sorts of evil deeds, including providing an untraceable source for sending huge amounts of spam. By some counts, zombies are being recruited at the rate of 30,000 per day. In many cases, the bot wends its way to users' computers through spam. That's nearly 1 million new zombies per month, all recruited with evil intent.

These bot zombie armies have a major impact on end-users in a number of ways:

- ✓ **The bot can harvest users' passwords and e-mail addresses:** If a bot has been installed on your computer, don't plan on anything you might have had on that computer staying private for long. It's not the primary purpose of the bots to read your private correspondence, but there are a few things that they might take a look for, including any passwords you might be using with Web banking or brokerages (even if these are encrypted when they hit the Internet, someone with control of your computer could intercept *before* the information is encrypted). Also, one of the first things the zombie does is harvest the address book. If you've never given an address to anyone except friends and co-workers but are suddenly receiving lots of spam, your computer or the computer of someone you know may have become a bot.

- ✓ **The zombie bot makes the user's computer the spammer's virtual hideout and makes the user look like a spammer:** The person or organization in control of a bot army can use each enslaved computer to send thousands of e-mails to their list of spam victims, without any chance that the source can be effectively blocked, noticed, or traced back to the spammer. If any recipients care enough to check, the owner (and now victim) of the zombified machine is the one that gets the call, and could potentially be cut off by his or her ISP because spamming is almost always a violation of the service contract.

- ✓ **The bot recruits users' computers in Denial of Service (DoS) attacks and other unsavory activities:** If spammer want a Web site to go offline for some period of time, they can directly hire the services of bot armies to perform a DoS attack. In such an attack, the bots are told to send legitimate-looking traffic to the Web site until the sudden overload of traffic paralyzes the site's ISP and operations staff. With the number of bots available for this sort of attack, nobody is safe. Many of the largest and most capable sites on the Internet have been taken down with a DoS attack in this way.

Some individuals own bot armies that number in the hundreds or thousands, and armies owned by organized crime are substantially larger. Payment for the use of these armies varies from cash to stolen credit card numbers to free access to pay-for Internet sites. There are even wars conducted between the folks who recruit these armies for the control of vast numbers of computer zombies. Never assume that your activities or low profile keeps your computer safe from recruitment.

Needless to say, you want to make your organization's computers as inaccessible to these bots as you possibly can. Keeping computers patched and running virus scanners and anti-spyware software is your first line of defense. But one of the most effective ways of preventing your PC from being used to spam others is to tell either your software firewall or your hardware broadband firewall (you *do* have a firewall, right?) to prevent inbound *and* outbound TCP connections on port 25 (the SMTP port), except when talking to your actual mail server.

Although protecting port 25 isn't perfect protection (because the bot could also use your mail server to spam), most of the bots out there try to send spam directly from the user's infected workstation, rather than through your mail server.

Many times I've been looking at firewall logs for some other reason, and spotted user's workstations that were clearly taken over, but failing to accomplish their spamming goals because the firewall blocked their connections. It's better to not get infected at all, but if you're infected, it's really important not to do damage to others. Permitting *only* your mail server to send and receive e-mail on SMTP (port 25) is a good way to not become part of the spam problem by accident. Your company's legal department will be happier, too, because you won't be exposing your organization to the downstream liability problem.

Educate users about spammy NDRs

When you accidentally send mail to `nill@microsoft.com` instead of your close friend `bill@microsoft.com`, you typically receive a response from the mail system at Microsoft that says something like "The user you are sending to: `nill@microsoft.com` does not exist at this server. Please check your spelling blah blah blah." And after that, the message includes the text of the original message that you sent. This is called a Non-Delivery Receipt, or NDR.

In their desperation to originate mail from anywhere except their own ISP, spammers are now using the NDR to send spam through unsuspecting victims. The process works something like this:

1. The spammer picks a username that doesn't exist at the victim's company.

2. The spammer sends the spam message to the nonexistent e-mail address, with the intended recipient (a real e-mail address at the company) in the `From:` address.

3. The victim's e-mail server sees an e-mail to a nonexistent person, from an actual user, and rejects it.

4. The mail server sends back the entire message (including the spam content) to the apparent sender (the user's e-mail address that the spammer falsified in the From: address of the original mail they sent out).

From spammers' perspectives, this isn't perfect, because the message comes in with a subject line that looks something like "Rejected, no such user: Buy MeatShakes, delivered to your door!!!!" with a From: address of something like Mailer-Daemon. It does fulfill the mission of getting the spam into the hands of the person they are spamming and possibly getting past blacklists or even misusing a whitelist if they choose the NDR victim carefully.

Users should be taught to recognize an NDR that didn't result from any mail that they sent and to understand why they get them. I have to admit that the first few times I saw an NDR resulting from mail that I didn't send in the first place, I thought someone might have broken into my computer and sent e-mail as me. It's a confusing new tactic that the spammers are using, and if you can explain it all in advance to your users, you'll receive fewer panicked phone calls.

Protect users from phishing scams

The only effective way to combat phishing attacks is user education. Your user base needs to understand that no legitimate brokerage or bank is *ever* going to send them e-mail asking them to log in to their account by clicking a link, for any reason. These days, phishing spam is very well constructed and looks professional, using the actual logos and Web site graphics from the company the phisher is pretending to be. Even the links are constructed in such a way that it takes an expert to unravel what's been done and understand that the message is not from the company it pretends to be from.

The example phishing e-mail in Figure 12-4 shows a well-constructed fake, with what appears to be a legitimate link to the Smith Barney Web site at the bottom. The whole e-mail is actually an image map (a picture that's linked to a Web site), and the text shown on the link has nothing to do with the actual URL where the unsuspecting user is taken to if he or she clicks the supposed link.

Phishing is another place where I encourage the use of the telephone. If a user is really concerned that his or her bank account is about to be terminated for some unclear reason, he or she should look up the phone number in the phone book (don't call any number in the e-mail!) and call the bank. The user only risks mild embarrassment for bothering the bank's customer service staff, but that's better than dealing with identity theft and a cleaned-out bank account.

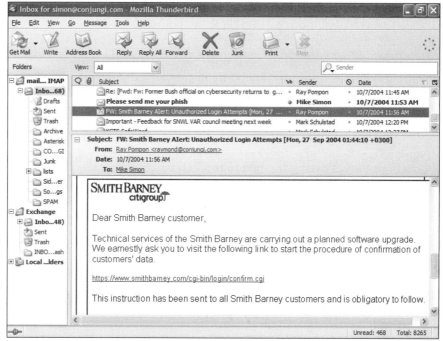

Figure 12-4:
A fake Smith Barney phishing e-mail.

Be aware of single-target spyware

So far, I haven't talked about deliberate attacks via spyware, and that's because the way spyware propagates, it's pretty hard to get specific hosts infected in specific places. Sometimes though, if the perceived payoff is great enough, spyware writers put together something specific for a company or industry and do their best to place it on specific desktops.

Usually, these are delivered via e-mail, looking like spam or something from an associate, but the really determined ones I've seen actually hack into Web sites that they feel the target might frequent and place the spyware there (often not changing the look or function of the Web site at all). This level and sophistication of attack is rare, but not completely unheard of. If your company is an attractive enough target, it's possible you might see this.

Chapter 13

Defense in Depth: Providing Layers of Protection

*U*tilizing a defense-in-depth strategy to guard your enterprise against malware and related threats is essential if you are to succeed in your mission of protecting the organization's information assets and information processing capabilities. In this chapter, I explore the concept of defense in depth and cite some examples.

Understanding Defense in Depth

The analogy of the castle and its varieties of defense is worn out and no longer serves as a decent defense-in-depth model. A better analogy is *your* castle: your home or apartment, for example.

Protecting you and your home are several layers of defense. These layers might consist of, from the outside in:

✔ Wood or chain-link fence

✔ Thorny bushes under the windows

✔ Locked windows

- ✔ Solid core door with deadbolt lock
- ✔ Intrusion alarm (electronic)
- ✔ Intrusion alarm (canine)
- ✔ That big candelabra in the dining room
- ✔ Those wickedly sharp knives in the kitchen drawer

An intruder must overcome *all* these obstacles if he is to successfully invade your home. What is important to understand is that each layer of defense is different — it isn't merely seven layers of chain-link fence, nor is it lots of candelabras, dogs, or kitchen knives. The *variety* of defense is important here. If a skilled intruder knows how to slither over or under chain-link fences, those fences are ineffective. Similarly, if he is impervious to knives, that knife collection is useless. If he has steaks for the dogs, the dogs will probably forget all about defending you. However ineffective one layer of defense might be, other layers — when properly designed and implemented — will still protect you.

The layers and variety of defenses comprises the concept known as *defense in depth*. Defense in depth refers not only to layers of defense, but to a variety of independent defenses. The layers slow down intrusions, and the variety protects against a wider range of threats.

My point: You can't depend solely upon a spam filter to remove all spam-related risks, or on anti-spyware programs to remove all spyware-related risks. Each will significantly reduce — but not eliminate — the risk from specific types of harm. Only the application of multiple layers of protection against each of these threats can reduce the risks associated with spam and spyware to acceptable levels.

A wide variety of good practices provides considerable protection from common — and not-so-common — threats. The remainder of this chapter delves into the details of these practices.

Deploying Security Patches

The role of security patches as part of a holistic strategy to protect the enterprise cannot be overstated, but I try. There have been so many holes discovered in Microsoft Windows, Internet Explorer, IIS, SQL Server, Outlook, and Office products in the past several years that an entire cottage industry of patch-management and configuration-management products has sprung up, and none too soon. The fact is that a large number of the hooks that spyware uses to get into your systems are based on vulnerabilities (some that are there by design, others that are errors in programming) in the operating system and browser.

Patches eliminate vulnerabilities

The role of security patches is simple: They are remedies that are designed to eliminate specific vulnerabilities in software that, if left unpatched, could allow a successful attack, the compromise of confidential information, or even the complete destruction of the computer's information. A vulnerability can even permit an intruder (electronic or human) to attack and compromise *many* systems in an organization. The legendary Internet worms such as Nimda, Code Red, Blaster, Nachi, and Sasser are the superstars of malicious code that successfully exploited known vulnerabilities for which security patches were readily available.

The infamous worms I mention here *were all preventable.* In every case, Microsoft had published security patches that eliminated vulnerabilities — and those patches were available for months! Had most servers in the world been patched, none of these worms would have made headlines — they would barely have been noticed at all. You do your organization and world a colossal favor by keeping your systems up to date with patches.

Keeping pace with viruses and worms

A troublesome phenomenon that is challenging IT departments everywhere is the fact that hackers are developing new exploits such as worms and viruses faster than ever before. Until around 2003, a new worm or virus might be released six months after Microsoft published a security patch. However, after around 2003, this "mean time to exploitation" had shrunk to less than a month, and in some cases the exploit actually *preceded* general knowledge of the vulnerability and the patch came out after it.

This is putting tremendous pressure on IT organizations that are forced to consider changing their patch-management processes in order to get critical systems patched in a few weeks or even days. Given larger organizations' complex life cycle processes (which include analysis, configuration management, testing, more analysis, and more testing), deploying critical patches in a matter of days has become the subject of many debates in academia, research organizations, and businesses.

Smaller organizations often have it somewhat easier: Their infrastructures are smaller and less complex, and there are often fewer processes that encumber what I would call "progress." As a result, smaller organizations generally are experiencing less pain with regard to the rapidity needed to patch systems.

Patching made easier with dedicated tools

The need for organizations to more quickly deploy critical patches to vulnerable systems has spawned a new breed of patch- and configuration-management products that consider the big picture of patch management and elevate it to configuration management or vulnerability management.

Many of these products include a variety of functions that together enable an organization to more effectively manage its Windows-based servers and workstations. Some of the features that can be found in many of these products include

- **System inventory:** One of my pet phrases is, "You cannot manage what you cannot measure." In terms of managing dozens or thousands of servers and workstations, if you don't know what you have and what software is running on them, you can't hope to effectively and successfully manage those systems. And if you can't manage the workstations, you can't adequately protect them and your enterprise as a whole.

- **Vulnerability scanning:** Many patch-management solutions now include network-scanning tools that are used in two ways: They aid in identifying vulnerabilities that are present in servers and workstations, and they help to discover previously unknown (and probably unprotected) systems on the enterprise network.

- **Patch installation:** The heart of patch-management products, patch installation itself has improved. Increasingly sophisticated products are able to "dribble" patches to workstations with slower network connections, and even to workstations that frequently connect and disconnect from the network (for example, dialup and mobile users). These products are also capable of performing "silent" installations of patches so that the user remains blissfully unaware.

- **Software upgrade installation:** Many an organization has, at one time or another, encountered a new security patch that it couldn't install because the systems weren't at the required service pack or release level. Many patch-management products have responded to this problem by including the ability to install not only patches over the network, but also operating system and application service packs, upgrades, and features on enterprise servers and workstations, with the same ease and rapidity as a patch installation.

- **Configuration:** In addition to installing patches and software upgrades, organizations increasingly need to perform other configuration changes on their servers and workstations. This may include replacing or modifying files, changing software configurations, and making changes to the Windows Registry. Greater numbers of patch-management toolsets include the ability to make these and other types of changes to enterprise servers and workstations.

These extra features address the fact that just pushing patches to thousands of workstations no longer cuts the mustard, or the cheese. Organizations require greater visibility and control of their entire inventory of systems in order to effectively manage them, especially in times of impending crises.

Some of the companies and products that offer these features include

- ✔ **Altiris:** This is a full-featured toolset that includes hardware and software inventory, patch management, software management, software usage, and configuration management. Information is available at `www.altiris.com`.

- ✔ **Marimba:** This product performs automated patch-management functions, as well as patch testing and auditing. Information is available at `www.marimba.com`.

- ✔ **Shavlik HFNetChkPro:** A simple tool focused on security patches. Shavlik makes it easy to obtain trial versions. You can find out more about Shavlik HFNetChkPro at `www.shavlik.com`.

- ✔ **Novadigm (from HP):** This full-featured product includes several functions, including life cycle management, OS deployment, application maintenance, and — oh yeah — patch management. You can find information at `www.novadigm.com`.

- ✔ **PatchLink:** This is a more specialized product that performs patch and inventory management. Find out more at `www.patchlink.com`.

I should hasten to mention that Microsoft itself has been improving its own system management tools and developing new ones as well. SMS (Systems Management Server), SUS (Software Update Service), and WUS (Windows Update Service) have been developed and improved, not quite to the level of performance and capability of most of the third-party toolsets, but nonetheless to higher levels of flexibility and control. Also, as more organizations implement and discover the power of Active Directory as a systems-management tool (primarily through Group Policies), these organizations gain a higher degree of control over their Windows systems.

Managing Anti-Everything

The wide variety of threats on the loose these days requires a multifaceted strategy that includes several defensive measures. Stopping spam and spyware isn't enough — it never was. The following sections discuss the various solutions that are available.

Antivirus

The mainstay of malware-blocking tools, antivirus software still offers a strong defense against viruses and worms that attempt to enter a system via enterprise and Web-based e-mail, Web sites, instant messaging (IM), thumb drives, downloads, PDA synchronization, Bluetooth, you name it. Antivirus programs utilize signature databases (data files that contain "signatures" of known viruses) in order to detect and block known viruses, Trojan horses, and worms, as well as heuristic detection to block new viruses just based on how they behave.

Antivirus solutions are often deployed in a number of places in order to provide the greatest likelihood that any virus or other malicious code will be caught. The usual ways that antivirus solutions are applied include

- ✔ **End-user workstations:** Because end-user workstations have the ability to communicate to both the enterprise and the outside world in a wide variety of ways (e-mail, Web, FTP, IM, IR, MP3 players, USB drives, and so on), the end-user workstation continues to be an important defense point for detecting and blocking malicious code. End-user workstations are becoming increasingly difficult to manage, however, because of their portability: Corporations are buying more laptop computers than desktop computers, resulting in corporate workstations not always being connected and manageable and not always being protected by enterprise firewalls and other defenses. This increases the risk of exposure and infection of internal networks, as well as complicating the defense strategy for organizations by making end-user workstations more difficult to reach and control.

   You may be asking yourself now, "If I can adequately protect the enterprise by protecting end-user workstations (where all the problems are anyway, right?), why do I need to bother with antivirus *anywhere else*?" In a nutshell, the answer is this: You *cannot* any longer adequately protect the enterprise from viruses by protecting only end-user workstations. In addition to the increasing problems of management, the end-user workstation is not the sole entry point for malicious code. Other systems may be the targets of malicious code, including those in this list.

- ✔ **File servers:** Someone who is thinking "defense in depth" should consider corporate file servers as another place to implement an antivirus defense. This is a popular choice, primarily because an end-user workstation with out-of-date, faulty or nonexistent antivirus software can permit malicious code to implant itself (and many known instances of this exist). If the malicious code present in an executable or document file is copied to a file server where other users may download it to their own workstations, the malicious code has an opportunity to spread to other systems. Hence, antivirus on file servers prevents viruses from sneaking through an end-user workstation and spreading through the organization via a file server.

✔ **E-mail servers:** Since the mid-1990s, e-mail has been a transport of choice for viruses and worms. It therefore makes sense for e-mail servers themselves to have their own antivirus capability. The argument for antivirus on e-mail servers is not unlike that for file servers: If a virus can be caught on the way into an organization at the e-mail server, the likelihood that the virus can reach an unprotected end-user workstation and attempt to spread is practically eliminated.

✔ **PDAs:** As I write this chapter, PDAs and cell phones are becoming targets of viruses and worms. As PDAs and cell phones increase in popularity, they too are an attacked platform. More widespread use of PDAs also creates more opportunities for malicious code that infects PDAs in order to spread. Further, Windows-like operating systems on PDAs and cell phones mean that Windows file formats cross these boundaries, making embedded viruses in Word macros and Visual Basic scripts a potential for interspecies viruses (that is, viruses that can infect more than one type of computer system).

✔ **Web proxy servers and filters:** Businesses use these tools to manage and control inbound and outbound Web traffic. These devices or systems seem like a natural place to set up antivirus measures that prevent the download of malicious content from the Internet to an end-user inside the organization. The problem with this method is that viruses often are transmitted in a form that makes them hard to spot; compressed with a password (with the password included in the mail message in the form of a graphic image, preventing the antivirus program from opening the Zip file to check for viruses). Proxy servers and filters need to unwrap many or all levels of encoding to see whether a particular file is a virus, and are not as reliable as end-point scanning for this reason.

✔ **Other servers:** It would be difficult to find an organization that has *not* implemented antivirus on its Windows-based servers. Arguably, viruses and other malicious code can compromise servers, even when no end-users use it. An example of this is the Code Red worm that attacks systems running Microsoft Internet Information Server with Indexing Service; Code Red spread from system to system with no user invention required.

Many organizations also use antivirus tools on some UNIX servers. Although malware has rarely attacked UNIX systems themselves, those same UNIX systems may be used to transmit data to or from Windows servers or Windows end-user workstations. In these instances, implementing antivirus on UNIX systems provides a layer of defense in depth that protects the more vulnerable Windows-based systems in the enterprise.

✔ **Antivirus firewalls:** Advances in hardware technology have facilitated the advent of firewall appliances that perform other functions (such as VPN termination, e-mail gateway, spam filter, and antivirus functions), thereby protecting the entire enterprise against viruses at the network boundary. Firewall scanning has the same limitations mentioned above for Web proxy servers and filters; they may not see an encoded virus on the way through.

Using these antivirus solutions in various combinations provides an effective antivirus defense-in-depth that maximizes the likelihood that viruses will be apprehended *somewhere* in the enterprise before they have a chance to take hold and disrupt business operations.

Anti-popup

Popup windows were designed into Web sites to perform many legitimate purposes such as logging in, getting help, or seeing a closer view of a picture. But, like most other technologies, people have created other uses for popup windows, such as advertising and generally annoying users with lots and lots of windows.

Popup-blocking programs are popping up all over the place. Well over 100 popup-blocking programs are available, most of them free, and I'd personally stay away from nearly all of them. So many popup-blocking programs are available because blocking popups isn't all that difficult — anyone who has taken a six-hour training course from the *University of Close Cover Before Striking* can write his or her own popup-blocking program. Additionally, the newest versions of most popular browsers have popup blocking built in.

In case you're using an older browser (and, for some reason, you want or need to stay with that older version), a number of good popup stoppers are available. I list a few choices for you here:

- ✔ **Yahoo! Toolbar:** This is my personal favorite (but perhaps there's no accounting for taste, eh?); I use the Yahoo! Toolbar anyway, so when they added a popup blocker, I was glad to use it. This is strictly a user-controlled program with no management visibility. Get it at http://companion.yahoo.com.

- ✔ **Google Toolbar:** This is a good product, essentially the same as the Yahoo! Toolbar. It too has no management control or visibility. Download it from http://toolbar.google.com.

- ✔ **Pop-Up Stopper:** Here is a popular popup blocker that has been in use for several years — almost as long as those irritating popup ads have been around. You can find Pop-Up Stopper at www.panicware.com.

Filtering incoming e-mail attachment extensions

Most malicious code enters business networks in the form of e-mail attachments. The attachments are usually program files that run if the user tries to open the attachment. New strains of viruses are often variants of existing viruses, and they still arrive in the form of program files.

Many enterprises have deepened their defenses by unilaterally blocking several file types in attachments, including EXE, COM, PIF, VBS, and others. When all such attachment types are blocked, the business has essentially protected itself against most any new virus that would arrive in that manner. This is especially important in instances where a virus arrives in a network prior to its signature in antivirus programs.

Even if enterprises choose not to block these types of e-mail attachments, newer versions of Microsoft Outlook block them automatically so that they can't be opened. Rather than consider this an excuse to avoid blocking certain file types as attachments at the e-mail server or firewall, think of this feature as an *additional* layer of defense. I suggest you do both.

As you deepen your defense against malicious code, the more difficult — and unlikely — it will be for a malicious attachment to infect a user's workstation.

Turning off VRFY on your e-mail server

One of the methods that spammers use to obtain e-mail addresses is to launch directory attacks on e-mail servers that support the SMTP VRFY command. The VRFY command permits a spammer to ask the mail server whether a particular e-mail address exists without having to actually send a mail message to that address.

To find out whether your mail server still supports VRFY, and what to do if it does, please turn to Chapter 12.

Managing Firewalls

For many years, the focus of defense from Internet-based threats has been the corporate firewall. Although the perimeter has eroded to the point that the firewall looks more like a giant block of Swiss cheese than a castle's drawbridge, the firewall is still an important deterrent in a company's arsenal.

Intranet firewalls

One new firewall fashion that's in vogue this year (and for many years hence, I hope) is the notion of implementing firewalls *within* the enterprise network at logical boundaries. Here are some good uses of firewalls *within* an organization:

- ✔ **Test and development labs:** Test labs — whether IT's or one used for product development — should be logically isolated from the rest of the enterprise so that experiments in the lab can't leak into the corporate environment. And likewise, in order for a test environment to remain pure, corporate network traffic should not be allowed to just flood into the lab.

- ✔ **Data centers:** Servers and other centrally located systems should be isolated from the rest of the corporate environment. Why? With worms, viruses, and Trojan horses occasionally infiltrating end-user environments, you'd sure want to be able to isolate corporate servers from the ravages of workstations scanning for more Blaster (or insert the name of your favorite worm here) victims.

- ✔ **Geographic or functional divisions:** A large national or multinational company would do well to provide at least a modest amount of segregation between its headquarters, or domestic, network and its regional, or international, networks. This helps to isolate different parts of the organization, which further helps to contain incidents and provide another layer of access control. Imagine fire doors in large commercial buildings that prevent fires from spreading from one part of the building to another.

- ✔ **Regulation:** Because of increasing regulations such as Sarbanes Oxley, HIPAA, and Graham-Leach-Bliley, many companies are now segregating accounting and other functions from the rest of the company to assert more control over access to sensitive information.

- ✔ **DMZ:** Of course, there's the traditional DMZ (demilitarized zone), the network containing servers that are directly exposed to the Internet. Firewalls are used to isolate those servers from the Internet, and also from the internal network. In the event a hacker is able to successfully compromise a server on the DMZ, the second firewall protects the internal network by treating Internet servers as *external* (potentially hostile) systems.

Filtering inbound as well as outbound

In ancient times (the 1990s), most firewall administrators blocked all inbound traffic except for the few inbound services that were actually needed, for instance SMTP to the mail server, HTTP to the Web server, DNS to the domain server, and so on. However, many sites placed no restrictions on outbound traffic. That's no longer (and really never was) a good practice.

A site that doesn't block outbound traffic implicitly permits instant messaging (IM), peer-to-peer file sharing (with Kazaa, Napster, and so on), IRC (chat rooms), and everything else that is good, bad, and ugly. Furthermore, if a server or workstation becomes infected with a virus or worm, the infected system can freely propagate the infection not just inside the organization, but anywhere on the Internet, as well. (This is reminiscent of a funny sign I once saw in a restaurant washroom that read, "Employees are required to wash hands *before* using the washroom.")

Today's best practice is to block *all* outbound traffic except for that which is explicitly required. Some examples include

- ✔ Outbound SMTP (e-mail) is permitted *only* from corporate mail servers.
- ✔ Outbound DNS queries are permitted *only* from site DNS servers.
- ✔ Outbound HTTP is permitted *only* from the Web proxy server.
- ✔ Telnet and FTP are permitted from any user workstation. (The burden of security for telnet, ftp, and other protocols rests with the owner/administrator of the far-end telnet/ftp server.)

Business processes are as important as technology

All the security technology in the world is of little value if the organization using it lacks the proper business controls and processes to govern and manage their use. Here are a few examples:

- ✔ If the rule changes made on a firewall are not traceable back to a requestor (and, hence, a true business reason), it would be difficult to later determine the reason for the rule change and whether it was still needed.

- ✔ If a system administrator made configuration changes to a server without documenting the change or getting advance approval for the change, the configuration changes could lead to problems that could have been avoided.

- ✔ If various network engineering groups in a multinational company took it upon themselves to determine IP addressing and routing, the organization's network could become troublesome and difficult to manage.

- ✔ If user accounts were created or access controls changed without proper approvals, there would be problems of accumulation of privileges and unauthorized access to information.

These are just a few examples. The key elements to building proper processes around technology and security are

- ✔ All changes should be made only when approved by someone in authority.

- ✔ All requests should be documented, regardless of outcome.

- ✔ All changes should be documented, with a given reason for the change.

- ✔ All approvals should be documented.

- ✔ All changes must be traceable back to the requestor, request date, reason for the change, and who performed the change.

Examples of changes include changes to firewall rules, creation or modification of user accounts, configuration changes on servers or network devices, and any other nonroutine changes that are performed.

I hope that you recognized the preceding as the core of a Change Control process. If you did not recognize it as such, I suggest you reread this sidebar and meditate on this topic for a while.

Keeping One Eye on the Future

Right now, nearly all the effective spam and spyware filtering that's available on the market either filters based on content, or (in the case of spam) refuses mail based on known sender IP addresses or domains. These methods are not 100 percent effective, and where there's a need, the market will try to fulfill it.

To provide defense in depth, your challenge is to learn about new threats that try to cripple your business, new layers of protection that augment what you already have, and new technologies that may make your current solution obsolete. In areas causing as much pain to everyone as spam and spyware, you can bet that a lot of creative people are thinking of interesting ways to keep them out of your environment, just as there are creative people thinking of new ways to defeat or side-step your defenses and get into your environments anyway.

Watching the spam-filtering market as it matures

As with any product that your company depends on, you need to keep an eye on developments in the market. You don't want to be caught unaware when your vendor goes out of business or starts heading down some path that will ultimately burn you and your company.

Markets for new technology follow fairly predicable patterns:

1. A new market sparks innovation. Small agile companies make splashes in the market, which result in many unique offerings.

2. The market begins to mature as dominant technologies start to take hold and less-dominant technologies drop by the wayside (along with their creators).

3. A mature market settles in, dominated by the big players, who are actively purchasing smaller companies as a way to update their product lines and eliminate competition.

IT managers trying to stay on top of the spam problem need to pay attention to the key characteristics of the developing market. You don't want to be stranded on your own little lonely island of technology, so I discuss these characteristics in more detail in the following sections.

Consolidation

In 1985, dozens of viable IP router solutions were available on the market. A request for proposal (RFP) to build a large routed network would yield at least half a dozen viable alternatives, all with interesting differences in approach. That same RFP today would yield possibly three serious contenders, vastly similar approaches, and at the end of the process Cisco would win the business. For those of us who bought Wellfleet routers in ancient times (1987), we watched Wellfleet, Synoptics, and Bay Networks all merge into a large happy pile (Nortel) only to be completely eclipsed by Cisco's market dominance.

Because the spam-filtering/reduction market is still somewhat new and the spyware-filtering/scanning market is still *very* new, the consolidation process has just barely begun. A number of smaller players are still out there, each building new innovative products, but that number will start dropping pretty quickly as traditional security product manufacturers start buying up all the interesting technology and rebranding it as their own. *Why* those traditional security companies — with their large R&D budgets — couldn't come up with these ideas themselves is left to the customer to ponder.

A side effect of this process is that some perfectly good technologies are purchased and killed off just to eliminate competition with current offerings from the big players. Just because a particular technology is better than its competition, that doesn't mean it will survive the consolidation phase of a growing market. Talk to Sony about Betamax format or LaserDiscs. . . .

The largest purchase in this space so far has been Symantec gobbling up Brightmail for a mere $370 million all cash deal. Activestate was purchased by Sophos (a large antivirus vendor based in the U.K.); Network Associates acquired Deersoft; NetIQ acquired MailMarshal; and the list goes on. In some cases, where there is little or no perceived competition between the two companies, such as Trend Micro, an antivirus-software-only company, and Postini, a spam-filtering ASP, the deal is about licensing the technology rather than purchasing the company.

I expect that many of the currently free spyware-blocking products such as Ad-Aware and others will receive offers that they can't refuse in the coming months from large commercial players. The once-free software will then transform into paid-for products.

Almost all the big names that currently have a spam-filtering solution bought their technologies from early market entries rather than developing them in-house late in the game. Expect to see another "buying other technologies to eliminate competition" phase start up very soon.

Innovation

In such a new market, don't assume that the best ideas are already on the table. As more money is brought to bear on research and development in the area of stopping spam and spyware, you can expect to see new products that have little or no resemblance to the products you're using now. As new, disruptive technologies enter the marketplace, their appearances can have adverse affects on existing companies and business models.

Don't forget that hackers (and spammers, crackers, vxers, and so on) are innovating on their own. This, too, is likely to spawn new cottage industries of products designed to stop the latest threats.

When someone comes along with a new "Active Spam Defense" that deletes spam on the spammer's hard drive before he can send it, your vendor will need to adapt, license the new technology, or invent a better one (maybe one that alters the DNA of spammers to turn them into something more savory, like bread mold). The truly good ideas that take hold will be adopted by all the major players, including *your* vendor, I hope. If your vendor misses the boat, it may be time to start shopping again.

Emerging standards

Speaking of innovation, a fair number of people and companies are looking into new ways to stem the flow of malware. The list of such companies is ever changing, and is probably mostly outdated by the time you read this, but it should be interesting to look at this from a historical perspective. Note, for example, that most of the proposed anti-spam solutions center around making sure that the spammers are correctly identifying themselves, not in detecting spam per se. Although that may keep spammers honest about where they're sending from, it almost certainly doesn't prevent them from sending messages.

Yahoo! "authentication"

Yahoo! proposes, much like some other proposals here, to use DNS (Domain Name Service) as a way to deliver important information regarding the identity of a particular sender. Yahoo! proposes that the sender deliver a secure private key in a message header in the e-mail. The receiving host would do a DNS lookup for a specific record type from the sender's registered domain, which should return a public key. If the public key is able to decrypt the private key in the message header, the sender is deemed to be authenticated.

So, this is a nearly foolproof way of knowing who is sending the spam, and some would argue that either spammers without anonymity will tuck tail and run for the hills or you can block them because you know who they are and they can't lie about it.

Personally, I don't buy it. Spammers can get new identities like I can buy pretzels by the bagful. For the most part, they don't really care that you're aware of their true identities, which they've hidden behind a pile of dummy corporations anyway. Did you think they'd use their home addresses and telephone numbers?

Microsoft's "caller ID"

Having caller ID for e-mail sounds like a good idea, and Microsoft's Caller ID for Email proposed standard uses DNS to deliver information about the sender's domain, only instead of exchanging a cryptographic key, a recipient's mail server is just looking up a list of hosts that are allowed to send mail for that domain, and if the sender is on the list, he or she can send mail. If the sender is not in the list, additional scrutiny is applied to the incoming e-mail, including possibly just refusing the e-mail or running it through additional filters.

Microsoft has been lobbying the Internet Engineering Task Force (IETF) to adopt a combination of their technology and Sender Policy Framework as a new standard, but the IETF has rejected this idea, partially due to the fact that Microsoft has patented parts of Caller ID for Email, and anyone wanting to use the new standard would have to license it from them. Although Microsoft says that this license would come at no cost (today), not everyone at the IETF was comfortable with this.

Sender Policy Framework

SPF works much like what I describe for Microsoft's proposal in the preceding section. It does DNS lookups of the domain of the sender's IP address, determines from that list who is authorized to send mail from that domain, and allows or disallows the mail based on that lookup.

SPF has the advantages of not being encumbered by patents or licensing structures and should accomplish the goal of identifying a sender domain before allowing it to send mail. It does still suffer from the same problem that all the ID-based solutions do: Spammers will happily ID themselves, using a "real" ID, and then send you spam.

Assigning a cost to the transaction

Although I know of no specific initiatives in this area, a number of folks are looking into the idea of assigning a cost to the SMTP transaction, albeit a small one, and killing off spam one penny at a time. The cost doesn't even have to be a hard cost in money. One of the most promising avenues I've heard discussed is that of requiring the sending computer to calculate a computational puzzle (something that takes them a few seconds at least) before they are allowed to deliver mail. What this does is greatly reduce the amount of spam any one host can send, as they are spending all their time solving computational puzzles. It's not a huge imposition on everyone else, because waiting another few seconds for a single e-mail isn't a big deal. For a spammer, the extra wait might be the difference between a viable spam business model and getting a real job.

Although the computational puzzle idea has some real potential, it seems unlikely that it will catch on anytime soon. The changes to MTA (Mail Transfer Agent) software required would be large, and everyone would have to make the changes at once for it to be very effective. On the plus side, I'd love to see what gargantuan computing problems might be solved if someone could assign little parts of the problem to several million e-mail servers throughout the world, each solving it a little bit at a time. That's not the intent of this potential spam solution, but an interesting opportunity.

Methods that involve actually charging some finite amount of cash to send e-mail would be very effective in curbing spam, but are even harder to get incorporated into the infrastructure. This idea would require a universal method for requesting payment, making the payment, and verifying funds that would all take place before the e-mail is sent.

Watching the maturing anti-spyware market

Because the methods used for detecting, blocking, and removing spyware are so similar to those used by antivirus programs, my thought is that the stronger anti-spyware tools will be acquired by the antivirus companies, leaving the weaker spyware-blocking tools to wither and die out.

In a few short years, the elimination of spyware will be completely integrated into antivirus programs, so much so that you might even see the disappearance of the term spyware altogether. The only remaining distinction might be that spyware will be treated as "unwanted content" (indeed, McAfee uses the term PUPs, or Potentially Unwanted Programs), where there may be various options available as to which types of spyware should be blocked and which should be left alone.

However, I also feel that as spyware blockers become commonplace, spyware and scumware techniques will evolve (if you can call it that) to stay one step ahead. And eventually, a new form of badness blockers may emerge to rid the Internet of new evils.

Part V
The Part of Tens

The 5th Wave   By Rich Tennant

"Drive carefully, remember your lunch, keep your spyware blocker updated, and always check your e-mail quarantine for messages from your mother."

In this part . . .

Ten fingers; ten digits in our numbering system; and ten items in each and every Part of Tens chapter (except for Chapter 15, where Peter got carried away).

In these chapters, you can find basic facts and features of various products that make each stand out from its brethren. You also find my favorite ten or so ways to make your spam or spyware projects completely unnoticed in every way (that's IT talk for successful).

Chapter 14

Ten Spam-Filtering Solutions for the Enterprise

A lot of anti-spam products are on the market now, and the list is growing quickly. While the market is starting to see some large antivirus and security companies buying small anti-spam entrepreneurs, there is still room for innovation, and small players can still play a part by keeping the larger companies from getting complacent.

I don't have room in this book to talk about all the spam-filtering products on the market, so I've chosen ten products, based on market prominence and personal experience. The products listed in this chapter are ones that you are likely to run across when you start looking for a spam-filtering solution, and they're products that I have personal experience using. In this chapter, I present some basic facts about each product, as well as anything that's unique to that product. Note that many of the products listed here have won awards from various organizations. While the kind of award won and from whom can provide some insight into the product, I never take them very seriously, and rely on independent reviews for comparison. Thorough review articles on anti-spam (and, any other) products can provide additional insight, but in my opinion, you'd be making a mistake if you consider awards in your selection criteria *at all.*

I'm leaving out client-based products from this list because they are typically not aimed at business use. Spam solutions that run at the client level are fine products, but in a business environment, because you need central control of the product behavior that doesn't include touching every workstation in the company. While the central control problem is solvable, I also dislike installing nonmanaged software on every workstation in the enterprise when I don't have to.

Please note that almost all the vendors with anti-spam products listed here also sell antivirus products as well. In this chapter, I only include an antivirus product if it's a part of the anti-spam product. In the cases where I don't list an antivirus product, it is almost certainly possible to purchase antivirus from that vendor as well and integrate it into the spam filter.

If you're coming straight to this chapter in hopes of getting the jump on spam-blocking solutions, great. However, if you aren't yet familiar with the various *kinds* of solutions available (hardware, software, ASP), then you should book-mark this page and read Chapter 4. You want to be an educated shopper, especially if you're impulsive.

Brightmail AntiSpam 6.0

Brightmail started out as a small company with a good idea and was recently purchased by Symantec to extend its scope of security and antivirus products to include spam filtering.

One of the more interesting aspects to Brightmail AntiSpam is that Symantec maintains a network of 2 million-plus decoy e-mail addresses that are used to train and extend spam-filtering rules for Brightmail AntiSpam users. The decoy network extends over 20 countries and receives tens of millions of spam e-mails each day. Brightmail AntiSpam also has a feedback mechanism built in to allow users to submit missed spam (false negatives) back to Symantec to further improve the filters.

Brightmail AntiSpam updates the filters for you about every ten minutes (wow!), based on Symantec's analysis of current conditions, via a secure connection to its four operations centers worldwide. In theory, this provides very current filter rules and makes it hard for spammers to defeat your protection for more than a few minutes.

Maker	Symantec
URL	`http://enterprisesecurity.symantec.com`
Virus scanning included	No
ASP or in-house	Both, licensed ASPs or in-house available
Gateway or integrated	Both, integrates with Exchange or standalone or appliance
Auto-update	Yes
Blacklist	Yes, both central and personal if a desktop plug-in is used
Whitelist	Yes, both central and personal if a desktop plug-in is used
Quarantine	Yes, user-accessible spam folder

Postini Perimeter Manager

Postini is a well-established spam-filtering ASP. It offers two different solutions that interest most businesses: the Standard Edition, which is the basic inbound filtering of spam and viruses, and the Enterprise Edition, which includes outbound content and attachment and virus filtering as well.

Postini is privately owned and funded, so it's hard to look at the company's internal resources in terms of stability or long-term viability, but the company has enjoyed steady growth since 1999 and boasts 5 million users as of first quarter 2004, processing 1 billion e-mails per week. It's hardly a garage startup.

Postini doesn't publish information regarding its service infrastructure, so it's also hard to say anything about redundancy and global coverage. Any serious look at an ASP solution should include a look at how many data centers are available and how scattered around the globe they are. You don't want a single site catastrophe to interrupt your inbound e-mail, and a highly redundant, globally dispersed infrastructure ensures this doesn't happen.

Maker	Postini, Inc.
URL	`www.postini.com`
Virus scanning included	Yes

(continued)

ASP or in-house	ASP
Gateway or integrated	N/A
Auto-update	Yes
Blacklist	Yes
Whitelist	Yes
Quarantine	Yes, Web based

CipherTrust IronMail

The IronMail appliance is a pretty complete e-mail security appliance, which includes more than just filtering spam and viruses. IronMail offers "policy and content compliance," which includes the following:

- ✓ **Attachment blocking:** Quarantine or reroute the message based on sender or recipient

- ✓ **Domain blocking:** Create what is essentially a blacklist for domains

- ✓ **Encryption:** Enforce encryption based on sender, recipient, or other policy

- ✓ **Message review:** Quarantine outbound messages until they have been reviewed, based on questionable content

As a product designed with security (not just spam and virus filtering) in mind, the IronMail gateway also provides some levels of security against mail server-based intrusion and noncontent-based attacks that may be launched against your mail system.

Maker	CipherTrust, Inc.
URL	www.ciphertrust.com
Virus scanning included	Yes
ASP or in-house	In-house, appliance
Gateway or integrated	Gateway
Auto-update	Yes, with feedback to CipherTrust
Blacklist	Yes
Whitelist	Yes
Quarantine	Yes, Web based

FrontBridge TrueProtect Message Management Suite

FrontBridge TrueProtect Message Management suite is an ASP solution with a major emphasis on stability and availability. FrontBridge has seven data-centers worldwide currently, with plans to open four more. Its service guarantees include 99.999 percent availability, with 100 percent availability to date.

TrueProtect spam filtering is based on proprietary algorithms that do black-listing, *fingerprinting* (comparing current mail to known spam directly), and rules-based scoring. Like all the other ASP solutions and some of the gateway products, FrontBridge relies on information gathered from the billions of spams that it filters to block the few thousand headed for you.

To ensure that you don't miss e-mail that's important to your business, TrueProtect processes outbound mail, too. If you choose to send your outbound mail through FrontBridge, the solution learns that those people you are sending mail to are most likely not spammers when it sees mail coming back from them. This means your whitelists are at least partly automatically generated.

FrontBridge virus scanning employs scanners from Sophos, Symantec, and Trend Micro so that it doesn't have to worry about who has a signature for the newest virus first. Whoever wins the race that day is put in place for virus scanning.

Maker	FrontBridge Technologies, Inc.
URL	www.frontbridge.com
Virus scanning included	Yes
ASP or in-house	ASP
Gateway or integrated	N/A
Auto-update	Yes
Blacklist	Yes, global (whole enterprise) only
Whitelist	Yes, global (whole enterprise) only
Quarantine	Yes, Web based

Trend Micro Spam Prevention Solution

The Trend Micro Spam Prevention Solution is interesting in that it's packaged as an in-house version of the software used by an all-ASP provider — Postini. From some reports, the same software Postini uses in its ASP doesn't do quite as good of a job in this in-house version, due to local tuning versus Postini's professional tuning based on vast spam-filtering experience.

This gateway solution allows administrators to assign different spam-filtering sensitivities to specific user groups, so that groups such as IT can receive things like activation keys (which always look like spam because they are short and full of junk that doesn't look like normal text), and other groups can remain more protected.

Trend Micro has an excellent gateway virus scanner with support for more than just Windows as a platform, which might be helpful if you are not using a strictly Windows environment. The company's continued support for Solaris and Linux with this product means that you can integrate your spam filter with mature virus scanning software on whatever platform you are comfortable with.

Maker	Trend Micro, Inc.
URL	www.trendmicro.com/en/products/gateway/spam/evaluate/overview.htm
Virus scanning included	No
ASP or in-house	In-house, software for Windows, Solaris, and Linux
Gateway or integrated	Gateway
Auto-update	Yes
Blacklist	Yes, global
Whitelist	Yes, global and per user
Quarantine	Yes, end-user accessible

McAfee SpamAssassin

McAfee has taken an interesting approach to how it acquires spam-filtering technology: It's licensing a mature open source software product called SpamAssassin. This is a host-based (loaded onto the mail server itself) solution for either Microsoft Exchange or Lotus Domino servers, which is interesting, considering that SpamAssassin was originally written for UNIX.

Like many other providers I mention in this chapter, this product comes from a company with a history of providing antivirus tools. McAfee is a well-known and respected name in antivirus software, which is why the parent company, Network Associates, decided to adopt the McAfee brand as their new corporate name. McAfee's choice of a well-established open source package like SpamAssassin is interesting as an experiment in moving software from the open source realm into corporate sales.

Maker	McAfee, Inc. (formerly known as Network Associates, Inc.)
URL	`www.mcafee.com`
Virus scanning included	No
ASP or in-house	In-house
Gateway or integrated	Integrated, Microsoft Exchange and Lotus Domino
Auto-update	Yes (perpetual license)
Blacklist	Yes, global and per user
Whitelist	Yes, global and per user
Quarantine	Yes, multiple options including user folders or global

Sophos PureMessage

Sophos wins the prize for the most platforms supported by an integrated solution, though for some reason its UNIX support seems slightly better than Windows. (For UNIX, I see support for personal whitelists and blacklists, but this support doesn't appear to be available for Windows.)

PureMessage handles the disposal of spam somewhat differently from most other products: It allows administrators to discard, quarantine, modify subjects, or add hidden headers based on a calculated probability that the specific message is spam. Based on this, a sophisticated internal mail system could have multiple quarantine areas:

✔ One with messages that are most likely spam

✔ Another for messages that are probably spam but that a user might want to examine for false positives from time to time.

Maker	Sophos Plc.
URL	www.sophos.com/products/pm
Virus scanning included	Yes
ASP or in-house	In-house
Gateway or integrated	Integrated, Microsoft Exchange, Linux, Solaris, HP-UX, FreeBSD, and AIX
Auto-update	Yes
Blacklist	Yes, global on Windows, per user only on UNIX
Whitelist	Yes, global on Windows, per user only on UNIX
Quarantine	Yes, optional end-user accessible Web interface

Tumbleweed MailGate

For part of its spam filtering, MailGate uses a proprietary artificial intelligence technology that the company calls Intent-Based Filtering. According to Tumbleweed's literature, this technology "recognizes spam like a human reader would." That should work fine, until spammers start sending spam about bigger, better interfaced RAM.

The other part of MailGate's filtering is the more traditional approach, using matching based on known spam to block stuff that's already been recognized as spam.

Tumbleweed has taken time to deal with a problem that many spam filters have: classifying legitimate bulk e-mail (like newsletters that you have opted-in for) as spam. MailGate allows individual users to decide how to handle bulk e-mail, and hopefully eliminate the false positives for newsletters and other opt-in bulk e-mail sources.

Maker	Tumbleweed Communications Corp.
URL	www.tumbleweed.com/products/antispam/mailgate.html
Virus scanning included	No
ASP or in-house	In-house
Gateway or integrated	Gateway, appliance
Auto-update	Yes

Blacklist	Yes, per user
Whitelist	Yes, per user
Quarantine	Yes, user accessible through clicking on links in a spam digest e-mail

Proofpoint Messaging Security Gateway

Proofpoint offers modular mail protection services either as a software package running on a provided hardened Linux OS with the Messaging Security Gateway, or as an appliance in the Protection Server.

The Proofpoint solution really wants to be on the edge of your network (outside of the firewall, where other mail servers connect directly to it), in order to perform some of its connection-based testing. For example, Proofpoint does DNS and MX-level checking on the connection and on the From: address, as well as a dynamic check with its own database of known bad senders (basically, a private real-time blackhole list).

 The other interesting thing about this solution is Proofpoint's "corporate lexicon" adapter that allows you to adapt the solution's checking to your particular industry. That's handy if you happen to be in certain industries that have some relationship to products typically sold by spammers, such as home loans or prescription medications.

Maker	Proofpoint, Inc.
URL	www.proofpoint.com/products/msg.php
Virus scanning included	No
ASP or in-house	In-house
Gateway or integrated	Gateway, appliance or software
Auto-update	Yes
Blacklist	Yes, global and per user
Whitelist	Yes, global and per user
Quarantine	Yes, user accessible by clicking links in a spam digest e-mail

MailFrontier Gateway Server

MailFrontier is the only company I've seen that correctly identifies phishing as a separate category of bad e-mail from spam, and deals with it in a completely different way than it deals with regular spam. Incoming e-mail can be classified as fraud, rather than just spam, when that label applies. Combining this with integrated virus scanning and e-mail policy enforcement makes MailFrontier Gateway Server an interesting all-in-one appliance.

MailFrontier has also given considerable thought to the user experience and provides a number of tools to make spam filtering individualized, both with personal whitelists and blacklists and how aggressively to handle potential spam based on category and language. Like some other products, MailFrontier Gateway Server delivers a *spam digest,* which is basically a listing of recent spams received that gives you the option to click links in the e-mail to receive false positives. The product also provides direct Web access to the quarantine, in case a user doesn't want to wait until the digest is sent out to receive a false positive.

Maker	MailFrontier, Inc.
URL	www.mailfrontier.com
Virus scanning included	Yes
ASP or in-house	In-house
Gateway or integrated	Gateway, appliance or software
Auto-update	Yes
Blacklist	Yes, group and per user
Whitelist	Yes, group and per user
Quarantine	Yes

Chapter 15

Ten Keys to Successful Spam Filtering

This chapter discusses some simple ways to make sure that your new spam filter's rollout is successful and causes as little disruption as possible. Read on for my ten best suggestions for successfully mitigating your spam problem.

Knowing Your Users

Not every company or group of users is the same, nor do they have the same needs and expectations when it comes to spam filtering. Although the goal in each case might be similar — stop the spam — the way that you go about it should take into account how your users work and what they expect from a spam filter.

For example, while all companies these days rely on e-mail, service companies that derive *revenue* from e-mail activities (such as law, accounting, or consulting firms) might choose to loosen up the rules a little bit and be very careful about whitelisting the people and organizations they do business with. That's because whitelisting helps ensure they don't miss e-mails from those people and thus don't miss any business. In contrast, schools or organizations that deliver e-mail to children might turn all the filters all the way up, because protection in their cases will be a high priority.

Don't make these decisions in a vacuum. As you set criteria for the selection and operation of a new filter, get your users involved. Talk to representative groups about their expectations and fears regarding filtering spam, and be sure to address them in your requirements.

If you know *only* your IT department users, then you really don't know your users. IT people take to new technologies far easier than people in accounting, marketing, sales, legal, and so on. IT users are also more tolerant of invasive and disruptive technologies such as spam filters. You need to walk a mile or more in the shoes of e-mail users in other departments.

Keep in mind that IT departments typically have completely different goals for this sort of project than normal users. IT might look at spam filtering from the viewpoint that spam reduction will result in lower infrastructure costs, whereas the users look at increasing productivity and improving their work environment. If these goals are ever in conflict, it's time to broaden your planning scope a bit to include management with a high-level view of what's best for the company.

Spam isn't just a technology problem; it's a business problem, too. Keep this in mind during all phases of your anti-spam endeavors.

Knowing the Product

It's always tempting to learn just enough about a new product to deal with whatever is required at the time, and no more. Just-in-time (JIT) learning works fine as a support strategy until you don't perfectly predict the next issue with the product, and your learning happens just *after* the moment you needed it. (Why do you think they have flying lesson videos in airplane cockpits?)

I've seen enough mail administrators figure out how to restore a mail server *after* the mail server ate itself to realize that sometimes knowing the product better *in advance* can save time, sanity, and let you get more sleep. Say, it might even help to *prevent* some problems from occurring in the first place, and enhance (or preserve) one's career. Some overworked system administrators are run so ragged that thinking in proactive terms is a foreign concept.

After you select a product, complete whatever training is offered, but also talk to other people who have been using the product for a while. Get an idea from them about the ins and outs of the system, what parts to concentrate on knowing well, and what you can safely ignore.

At the very least, the appropriate responsible person(s) in IT should know how to do the following with the spam-filtering solution:

- Back up and restore system databases (quarantine, mail stores, and so on).
- Recover the system from hardware meltdown.
- Administer global settings, user settings, and user accounts.
- Read (and be able to interpret) all log files.
- Follow e-mail through the system and explain the steps to anyone who asks.

In addition, you want to know other details that are specific to the product you choose, but you get the idea. Expect things to go wrong, and be prepared. Sometimes that's the best way to make sure nothing actually *does* go wrong.

Matching the Product to the Users

So many choices are available in the spam-filtering market right now that you can be picky about the features you want, and to some degree, tailor your selection to meet your specific needs. For instance, MailFrontier Gateway Server doesn't just have two buckets — spam and not-spam — but classifies what kind of spam it thinks any particular e-mail might be and allows you to apply rules to that category specifically. If your user base is very large, and you can't imagine a one-size-fits-all rule applying across all categories to determine if an e-mail is spam, such a product might be the best choice.

When evaluating the products available, take time to see if there's a feature set that closely matches your users and how they behave. To do this:

- You have to *know your users,* as I mention earlier in this chapter.
- Understand the profile of the e-mail your company receives. Is it primarily known clients with fixed addresses, or do you receive lots of mail from random sources?
- Talk to vendors about what makes their products unique. The unique characteristics that each vendor brings to your attention give you an impression of the vendor's philosophy regarding its spam filter and its capabilities. Knowing how your vendor thinks about filtering will give you a good idea of how the vendor will adapt and grow.

When you understand how your vendor is likely to adapt to the changing requirements of spam filtering, you can start to see how well that matches your users so that you can provide the best possible match between their needs and your vendor's projected direction.

Training Users and Admins

Many IT professionals skip over training when installing a spam-filtering solution, much to their regret later. Most users see training as a major impact on their time, as well as a boring, thankless task that nobody wants to attend anyway (especially those in IT).

However, the problems that untrained users create are a large drain on IT resources in the form of helpdesk calls, helpdesk escalations (where the helpdesk is unable to handle the call and must hand it off to a more senior person within, or outside of, the helpdesk department), and even database restoration activities if things go too far south (or north, depending upon the influence of the Coriolis effect where you live).

Users who aren't familiar with the new spam filter and have to fight through it are a major productivity loss for the organization as well. Along with the loss of productivity, the resulting frustration with the product can taint the user experience from that point on. The last thing you want is for the spam filter to have a reputation that's worse than the spam itself.

When the IT administrative staff is well trained, they're able to keep the new system running smoothly and ready to report anything anomalous in plenty of time to prevent larger, harder-to-solve problems. An in-depth understanding of the spam filter also helps them spread the burden of providing an escalation path for the helpdesk and quickly dealing with problems that rise to that level.

Chapter 7 covers training users and administrators in more detail.

Preparing to Troubleshoot

You can safely assume that not everything will work perfectly all the time in your spam-filtering environment. When things *do* go wrong, you want to have as many troubleshooting tools in your toolbox as possible.

Troubleshooting tools are, to some degree, a matter of personal preference, and no two people have exactly the same toolbox. But I suggest that you have some familiarity with the following:

- ✔ SMTP protocol and return codes (see Chapter 12 for more details)
- ✔ Log files for all servers and services involved with e-mail
- ✔ A network sniffer with protocol decodes for SMTP
- ✔ Mail headers and their meaning (see Chapter 12 for more details)
- ✔ DNS, especially MX records (see Chapter 12 for more details)

With these tools, as well as some understanding of how your spam filter works, you can figure out what's happening when things aren't quite working the way everyone expects.

Preparing a Backout Plan

While I'm on the subject of things not working as expected, I'd like to introduce the idea of a backout plan. Specifically, you might want the ability to return your entire e-mail delivery system to a prespam-filtering state in case the installation and rollout of the filter go really wrong.

If you launch into a spam-filtering installation and rollout without having a quick way of putting things back the way they were in case of disaster, you might find yourself in a situation where the new filter is failing in some catastrophic, not easily fixable way, and you have no way to get back to normal e-mail delivery. For instance, if your solution requires installing software on the mail server, you may discover that you can't completely uninstall only that software after the installation fails. Getting back to your preinstallation state will require restoration from backup of the mail server itself at that point. If you didn't make a backup just before installing, you might even lose e-mail at that point.

In the case of an ASP solution, the task of backing off to where you were is usually just a matter of pointing the DNS records back to your mail server rather than to the ASP. For in-house filters, you need to be able to remove the filter from the inbound mail path.

Although it's a good idea to document the backout plan, I strongly urge you to actually try it out. Otherwise, how can you be completely sure that it will work?

Revisiting Your Policies

Helmuth Karl Bernhard von Moltke said, "No battle plan survives first contact with the enemy." Keep that in mind while you engage the spammers in what will be a never-ending battle. Spam is a cat-and-mouse game, but with spam, there are *lots* of mice. Your original assessments of your filtering policies and procedures need to be adapted as required by intelligence on the ground (in the server room) and new strategies that are brought to bear.

Here are some examples of how to check out whether your spam filter is working and fine-tune it:

- ✔ If you turned up the filters to try and catch as much spam as possible, and you are actually catching quite a lot of good mail in the quarantine, it's time to turn down the filter a notch, generate better whitelists, or make specific adjustments in filtering rules to resolve this problem.

- ✔ If your spam filter supports fine-grained control based on spam type, look for certain kinds of spam that are still getting through and see if you can target that spam for stricter filtering.

- ✔ If your automated quarantine cleanup is deleting messages before users get a chance to look at them, then you need to either increase the time that quarantine messages are kept or train your users to read the quarantine more often.

Creating a Global Whitelist

I don't usually bother much with blacklists. Spammers fake the `From:` address anyway, and sometimes they fake the source domain as well, so it's really not worth trying to keep track of everyone you don't want to get mail from. To be truly effective, your blacklist would have to contain *all possible e-mail addresses* except those from whom you *do* wish to receive e-mail from. Merely storing this blacklist would probably cause catastrophic climactic shifts and melt the polar icecaps.

On the other hand, for almost any company, there's a list of individuals and other companies that you most definitely do want to receive mail from and never miss. The way to be certain that nobody ever misses a single piece of mail because the spam filter grabbed it is to produce and maintain comprehensive whitelists that tell your spam filter to permit mail from those senders to pass.

Whitelists can be either global, for the entire organization, or personal, for just an individual. Spam-filtering solutions can support whitelists that are global, personal, and sometimes both. I suggest you don't rely on individuals creating their own whitelists and maintaining them, because the highest levels of management will ignore this task and then get upset when they miss important e-mail.

Make the process of gathering important business contacts a productive exercise for everyone by finding a way to maintain that list into the future. One way to accomplish this would be to have whoever is in charge of new business relationships update the whitelist as a part of adding contact information to the global address lists. Asking users to submit all of their entries for the global whitelist every six months just isn't practical and will lead to mail getting lost in quarantine because entries aren't updated often enough.

If you have a fairly relaxed work atmosphere, you can even encourage participation in the process by adopting a "no complaining about lost e-mail" policy if that user hasn't added the sender to the whitelist.

A nice-to-have feature in a spam filter is the ability to observe all *outgoing* e-mail and automatically add all recipients in outgoing messages to the whitelist. If you are sending mail to someone, it's unlikely that mail coming back from that person is spam.

Testing the Solution

The better you test things, the better your experience will be after testing. That is, the more complete your testing, the better you know how everything will perform in production.

Completeness in testing is a large amount of ground to cover, so I don't try to cover everything involved here, except to say that you should try and think up all the crazy things that might happen to your spam filter, perpetrated by users, spammers, administrators, or even custodial staff (power cords and cleaning equipment collisions are almost always deadly), and throw all that at the system while you're testing.

If you are creative enough, you get pretty complete testing coverage, and no surprises when you roll out the solution to users and administrators. Don't worry too much about this, though. If you miss something, one of these groups will help you to find what you've missed in testing and explain the critical nature of your mistake in detail.

Monitoring after You Deploy

The first few days after you deploy a new spam filter are critical. During those days, users see their new, cleaner inboxes for the first time, and wonder if possibly you're deleting important stuff, because they're pretty sure they used to get more nonspam e-mail than they are getting now.

Though users would never admit it, after receiving all that spam for so long, your users will miss the sheer volume of e-mail and have vague feelings that they are missing something important. Time will heal this.

Aside from the psychological trauma of spam deprivation, you should watch for some specific things to understand how the deployment is going:

- ✔ **Support call volume:** Should be high to begin, and taper off quickly.

- ✔ **Support call topics:** Specific topics with high call volumes are trouble areas.

- ✔ **Hardware stats:** Is the quarantine growing too quickly? (In other words, is it filling up the space allocated to it before it can be deleted?)

- ✔ **Maintenance time:** How much administrative time is being spent operating the solution?

Epilogue: Reviewing Your Original Business Objectives

As your spam project materializes, clearly document the business objectives that the moneychangers agreed to when they decided to fund your project. Print those objectives and put them on your wall where you'll see them often. Then, as your project progresses through the life cycle of requirements, evaluation, selection, implementation, and so on, always keep those original objectives in mind. Whenever you have a decision to make — big or small — ask yourself whether that decision contributes to the original objectives.

Chapter 16

Ten Spam-Related Issues Most Enterprises Face

In This Chapter

▶ Encouraging users to follow new procedures

▶ When spam technology attacks

▶ Handling real company e-mail that smells like spam

*I*n the war against spam, there is occasionally collateral damage in that the spam solution may frustrate your users, slow the delivery of e-mail, and make a real dent in your already overtaxed IT budget. This can happen because things don't quite work the way you expect, users don't behave the way you expect, and the enemy doesn't even cooperate and just go away. In this chapter, I discuss ten of the most common issues that you are likely to face in the war against spam.

Users Don't Check Their Quarantines

Putting spam e-mail in a quarantine folder, where users can inspect at their leisure and retrieve any good mail that accidentally wound up there, all sounds good in theory. But if you have a good spam filter, you will have a very low number of *false positives* (good mail marked as spam), which means that 98 percent of what winds up in quarantine is trash that nobody wants to read in the first place. With those kinds of odds, many users don't ever look at their quarantine until there's a problem, and by then, they may have forgotten even how to do it.

Spam quarantine hygiene isn't fun. It's tedious, and it exposes you to the very spam that you were trying to get away from in the first place. If you don't occasionally take a look, however, you might miss important mail that was misclassified or end up with a mountain of spam to sift through when you *do* need to retrieve something.

If your spam filter uses a rating system, see if you can sort the spam by its score, and just wholesale delete all the stuff with really high scores. If someone sent you important mail that received a really high score, there's a good chance you didn't want to read it anyway. Most of the false positives will have just barely scored high enough to get classified as spam, so it's pretty easy to separate those legitimate messages from the crowd if your filter supports that.

Alternatively, if you are *really* good about maintaining *whitelists* (lists of people and companies that you *never* want marked as spam), you can just dive into the quarantine and delete everything every few days or so. You'll never miss mail from anyone on your whitelist, but you might delete mail from random people you handed your business card to.

Users Don't Manage Their Whitelists

The number one tool to ensure that users aren't stung by false positives is the proper use of a whitelist. Whitelists can be either global for the whole company or local for a single user. For example, the whole company doesn't need to whitelist my sister's e-mail address, but I would add her to my personal whitelist to be sure I receive her mail. My sister is a restaurateur, and she could at any moment send me a new recipe for Spam Musubi from her last visit to Hawaii. I wouldn't want to miss that!

The problem is that a whitelist is something new that each and every user needs to maintain, or the user risks missing e-mail. A user like me who's been using e-mail since 1985 or so will find establishing new e-mail habits a bit hard to do.

It's helpful to let users know that if they maintain really good whitelists, they won't have to spend nearly as much time sifting through the piles of junk in their quarantine folders. The mail that they really care about is going to get through without any problems. To help these users along, when a user complains that the spam filter blocked an e-mail that it shouldn't have, you can provide the gentle reminder that if that sender had been in his or her personal whitelist, mining the manure pile of the spam quarantine would have been unnecessary.

Too Many Helpdesk Calls

Although a deluge of calls to the helpdesk frequently occurs just after installing a new spam filter, this deluge isn't inherent to spam filtering. Almost always, the problem is either due to poor user education, or because something is truly broken.

At the beginning of a rollout for any technology, you can expect to get a fair number of calls to the helpdesk. Most of these calls will be in the following forms:

- ✔ I didn't know there was a new filter coming. What's going on?

- ✔ I deleted the instructions on how to get into my spam quarantine, and I think I'm missing e-mail.

- ✔ I have read my quarantine and my regular mail, but I have an uneasy feeling that I'm still missing some e-mail.

- ✔ I want my spam back. It was how I knew my e-mail was working.

- ✔ My computer is now spitting sparks out of the CD-ROM drive. Could that have something to do with the new spam solution?

Be sure to prepare your helpdesk workers for these calls, and make sure that you are around to help them with the first few rounds on the first day after you deploy a new spam filter. That way, if something is really wrong, you can react quickly and fix the problem.

Important Messages Lost or Delayed

No matter how you slice it, after you have a spam filter in place, a computer is making decisions about what e-mail you get to see and what you don't. You've also introduced a new point of failure into the mail delivery system, which could behave in all sorts of annoying and unhelpful ways.

The very fact that a computer is now reading your e-mail to make the spam/not-spam determination means that your e-mail is delayed more than before. In the best of all circumstances, that delay is small, but if for some reason you suddenly have a high spam volume, regular mail might be delayed more than usual as well.

There may be e-mail that your company depends on that must not be delayed or stopped. In these cases, at the very least, put the sender(s) into the whitelist and check this by sending a test spam from those senders. (See Chapter 8 for the GTUBE test spam, or take a look at `http://gtube.net` for a simple way to do this.)

You may also want to consider routing critical e-mail along a totally different path from your regular e-mail, which bypasses your spam filter. To do that, you'll probably want to route that e-mail to a subdomain within your organization, such as `username@critical.example.com` instead of `username@example.com`, and publish a different *MX record* (or Mail eXchanger DNS record, which tells mail servers where to send mail for your company) for that subdomain.

Truly lost mail, with no clues to what might have happened or where it might have gone, is quite rare, but it can happen. Now that more than just a couple of servers are talking to each other and delivering the mail, the chances for lost mail have increased, but almost always, a log, bounced e-mail, or something is left behind to tell you what might have gone wrong. Get to know the log files on your mail server and spam solution. You'll be using them to ferret out these problems.

The Filter Vendor Exited the Market

In Chapter 13, I talk about what happens in a maturing market for any particular technology and how companies closing their doors or just getting out of the spam filter market are commonplace. The market for spam-killing technology is pretty new, and it's quite common for vendors and manufacturers to fail or to be purchased by another player in this market. If that vendor is your chosen solution, you will need to make some changes.

If your solution is an ASP

In the case of an ASP (Application Service Provider — see Chapter 6), hopefully the vendor gives you some warning before disappearing or changing, and you have enough time to put a new solution in place. Even if you receive no warning at all, quick action on your part could mean that no e-mail is lost or returned.

When a mail host on the Internet is unavailable, the sending mail host will keep trying to deliver the mail for a while, typically five days, before it returns the message to the sender. Within those five days, you can change your DNS so that the MX records no longer point to the failed ASP, but either back to yourself or to a new ASP. When the senders see the new MX record, the queued mail will deliver and only be somewhat delayed.

Have a plan in place in case something similar happens to you, and be ready to make the DNS changes (or have your ISP make them). A little preparation and documentation here can save you a lot of grief and time.

If your solution is in-house

Chances are that you still have a functional solution; even though your vendor has abandoned you, there's no need to panic. Over time, your spam filter will become less and less effective without updates from the manufacturer, and you just never know when the software will do something unexpected, so you do need to start looking around for a new solution at this point. Use the same process you did last time, with the possible exception that you take a closer look at the health of the vendor or manufacturer.

Your Filter Is No Longer Effective

Spammers are constantly trying to figure out how to get past spam filters. In many cases, they already own the same spam filter you have, and they test each of the items they want to send you through that filter before sending it. Over time, any filtering technology will become less effective in blocking the new spam strains.

A good vendor constantly adapts its technology to meet new challenges from spammers. For some, that means a subscription-based approach, much like virus scanners, so that you constantly have the latest ideas in filtering. For others, this adaptation takes the form of software updates, which refresh the whole software package a few times each year. In the worst case, your vendor's approach is a dead end, and there's no way for it to update or refresh other than starting from scratch with a new approach. Be sure that you understand what you are getting in terms of software upgrade support from your vendor. Most contracts that really keep you up to date cost about 20 percent of the purchase price each year in software support.

An ASP-based solution avoids the issue to some degree because this spam-filtering approach doesn't require a customer to deploy new software and technologies. The ASP provider just installs these at the data center and rolls out quickly to all customers as needed.

Spam That Makes It through the Filter Is Still a Liability

You have reduced the amount of spam that gets into your organization, but not stopped it entirely. All the dangers and pitfalls of receiving spam still apply to your company, only now in significantly reduced numbers.

Because you can't rid yourself of the spam problem entirely unless you completely shut off e-mail (if you do that, let me know and I'll bring a video camera), you need to protect yourself from the remaining threats in other ways. Take a look at Chapter 13 for more details about the protection mentioned here:

✔ **Legal:** Make sure employees know that you can't protect them from everything, and that you are following industry best practices to protect them from as much spam as you can.

✔ **Virus:** Spam and viruses are linked more now than ever. Make sure that your virus protection is up to date. For help on that subject, you can always refer to *Computer Viruses For Dummies* by Peter Gregory (Wiley), and support one of the authors of this book at the same time.

✔ **Spyware:** I talk about the threat that spyware poses in Chapter 2, and I cover how to deal with it in the rest of this book. But it's worth mentioning here that much spam includes spyware payloads, and you need spyware blockers on the desktop to catch and remove anything that gets by the spam blocker.

✔ **HTML bugs:** If your e-mail clients support it, turn off downloading external links automatically.

Although you have reduced your spam problem, almost all the potential problems associated with receiving spam are present, even if you receive only one spam message.

Mail Delivery Becomes More Complex

When e-mail isn't working correctly, it's hard enough to diagnose the problem without throwing new places to fail into the picture. But that's just what you've done with a new spam filter.

Get to know the mechanics of how your spam filter receives and delivers e-mail. Know how to interpret the log files and explain what they're telling you. Also, if you aren't already familiar with the rest of your e-mail infrastructure and how to troubleshoot problems within it, you need to get up to speed, because you'll be using this knowledge more in the new environment.

Log file management in this area is your key to success. If you can trace an e-mail all along its path — both outside the company and inside — by examining its traces in your log files, you can handle most of the mail delivery problems that come your way.

If you're up for a challenge, spoof e-mail using *telnet* (the standard remote terminal program for the Internet, used to establish a command-line interface on another computer over a network). Spoofing e-mail isn't that hard, and the process of spoofing e-mail can tell you a lot about what part of your e-mail infrastructure is having problems. Here's an example of a spoofed e-mail session using a telnet client. In the following code, lines in bold are the lines that you type. The other lines are what the remote mail server returns in response.

(Note the SMTP, or Simple Mail Transport Protocol, port number at the end of the first command — 25.)

```
$ telnet 192.168.30.11 25
Trying 192.168.30.11...
Connected to 192.168.30.11.
Escape character is '^]'.
220 clyde.conjungi.com Microsoft ESMTP MAIL Service, Version:
        6.0.3790.211 ready at  Tue, 26 Oct 2004 15:13:10 -
        0700
helo conjungi.com
250 clyde.conjungi.com Hello [192.168.30.9]
mail from:<simon@conjungi.com>
250 2.1.0 simon@conjungi.com....Sender OK
rcpt to:<simon@conjungi.com>
250 2.1.5 simon@conjungi.com
Data
354 Start mail input; end with <CRLF>.<CRLF>
Subject: Test mail
Test Test test

.
250 2.6.0 <CLYDEJR6DUZL35Vyddh00000004@clyde.conjungi.com>
        Queued mail for delivery
```

The only commands that you need to use, in order, are `helo`, `mail from`, `rcpt to`, and `Data`. Note that in this case, I was sending mail to myself, from myself.

Your Internet Connection Seems Slow

After you have an in-house spam filter in place, you can easily forget that all the spam that was clogging up your pipes before you set up the filter is *still* getting delivered. The fact that you're not seeing the spam anymore can mask how much spam is still coming in. For example, when a new spam network comes online, incoming spam can spike, increasing by 400 percent in your organization. But because the filter siphons away most of the spam, this increase doesn't impact your inbox.

The increase can affect your Internet connection by simply filling up your connection with incoming spam because you don't have the opportunity to reject it until it's already been delivered. In some cases, spammers are sending to hundreds of nonexistent addresses at your company and the *bounces* are filling up your connection as well!

If your spam filter generates statistics on how much it's blocking versus the overall volume of e-mail, keep track of those percentages. It's even better if your spam filter can graph this sort of information over time because you can use these graphs to see spikes in spam delivery, as well as trends in how much e-mail and spam the company receives. Trends can show you when you will need to increase the capacity of your Internet connection or your mail infrastructure or both.

If your spam filter is an ASP, or even hosted off-site, this particular problem will not afflict you, because the ASP stops the spam before delivering your good e-mail across your connection. Keep in mind that over time, higher and higher loads probably burden the ASP, and so it may have performance problems if it isn't proactively gearing up.

My Company's Products Smell Like Spam (Or, I Work for Hormel)

This scenario is a bit more rare, but it happened more than once in preparing the text of this book. The first two times I e-mailed Chapter 12 to the publisher, for example, it was silently digested by the publisher's Spam Eating Weasels. Another good example of this is what happened recently when I refinanced my home loan. I thought my chosen bank was being really unresponsive, and they thought the same of me. It turns out that my own spam filters were picking up on the words "refinance" and "interest rate" and saving me from what looked a lot like spam. I was able to resolve the problem, but not before getting pretty annoyed at a very nice and quite responsive loan officer. The unfortunate truth is that spammers and phishers are starting to do business in areas that also are home to legitimate businesses, such as finance, banking, real estate, medicine, pyramid schemes, and software sales.

If your company's legitimate business overlaps with the spammers' and you use e-mail for anything marketing-related at all, you have a problem. Even if you send e-mail only to people who have opted in (by signing up for an e-mail newsletter, for example), there's a good chance that the spam filters at the recipient are catching and deleting your e-mail.

There's almost as good a chance that your own filters will catch and kill incoming e-mail referring to your product, unless your filter has the flexibility to be taught the difference between spamlike and spam.

When sending out information that might look like spam to a filter, one of your best methods to avoid transmission problems is to send a short e-mail with a link to the information on a Web site, but avoid the phrase "click here," or anything like that. Your customers can figure out what to click, and if they are interested, they will.

Chapter 17

Ten Spyware-Filtering Solutions for Businesses

The anti-spyware market is both older and also less mature than the anti-spam market. The problem with the commercial market for anti-spyware products is that spyware is stealthy and quiet. So, when an anti-spyware pioneer like PestPatrol came out with a spyware-killing tool a few years back, most people said, "So what? I don't have any spyware on my PC." The funny thing was that even back then, every time I ran anti-spyware tools on a supposedly clean PC, it came back with lots of nasty stuff. So, while anti-spam tools took the limelight, getting rid of much of the spam from your inbox, anti-spyware tools didn't really find much of a market until recently. Not only has the nature of spyware been changing and becoming more intrusive, but people are also becoming more aware of and concerned with online privacy issues.

Because I can't cover *all* the spyware products currently on the market, I've chosen ten completely at random . . . well, not totally at random. I've chosen some of the most popular anti-spyware products, some solutions that look like they have a bright future, and some products that I've used myself.

Note that because the anti-spyware market is still pretty immature, some of the products that I mention in this chapter are in a state of flux. For example, PestPatrol, which was developed as a standalone product, was recently purchased by Computer Associates International and incorporated into its eTrust suite of products. You can expect a lot more consolidation as the market matures and smaller players with innovative products are purchased by the big spam- and virus-blocking vendors that need to fill the spyware hole in their product lines.

Ad-Aware Professional SE

Lavasoft has been around since the mid-1990s, and the company focuses solely on anti-spyware products. While Lavasoft has a number of versions of the basic product, including a personal edition, the following table shows the features of the business-focused edition, Ad-Aware Professional.

Ad-Aware is an example of a product that has outgrown its name. Because nearly all early spyware was about stuffing advertising into your computer, forcing you to look at it, and tracking your surfing habits, some of the products show these origins in various ways, including their names. In the case of Ad-Aware, don't let the name fool you: It's a complete anti-*spyware* package with registry scanning, centralized configuration management via Windows file shares (all clients can see the central configuration file via a Windows file share), and automated background operation.

Notes on terminology

Three ways to detect spyware exist at this time. A *gateway* or *filter* is placed in the network path to watch for spyware entering the network. An application on the workstation discovers spyware by scanning the hard drive and memory periodically (client). An application on the workstation can watch what is happening on the computer and block spyware as it tries to install itself. Some spyware filters on workstations detect in real time, but not all of them do, so I make the distinction in this chapter in the tables. Take a look at Chapter 19 for a more detailed explanation of criteria you can use to evaluate anti-spyware products.

Maker	Lavasoft
URL	www.lavasoftusa.com
Also a virus scanner	No
Client or filter	Client
Auto-update	Yes
Real-time detection	Yes
Logging	Yes
Scheduled scanning	Yes
Price	$39.95 (volume discounts available)

SpywareBlaster 3.2

SpywareBlaster takes a preventative approach to spyware, focused on spyware's main entry point, your Web browser. When you load SpywareBlaster, it detects your Web browser(s) and gives you the option of protecting each browser from downloading and installing all the known spyware problems for the browser.

This product is strictly about preventing spyware from a very specific channel, your Web browser. It has no facilities for scanning your hard drive for stuff already downloaded and running and no facilities for removing spyware that is already on your system. If you prevent spyware from arriving in the first place, you don't need removal tools, right?

There are so many delivery mechanisms for spyware these days that I can't see something that is strictly browser-and-prevention focused as a *complete* solution for any business, but it could easily be a part of a defense-in-depth strategy that employs lots of tools and filters to keep spyware at bay.

Javacool Software has recently changed to a freeware-for-all policy with SpywareBlaster, charging only for *automatic* updates to the known spyware database (although manual updates continue to be free).

Maker	Javacool Software LLC.
URL	www.javacoolsoftware.com
Also a virus scanner	No
Client or filter	Local filter
Auto-update	Yes (for a yearly fee)
Real-time detection	Yes
Logging	No persistent logs
Scheduled scanning	None
Price	Free, auto-update for about $10 per year

SpyBot - Search & Destroy

SpyBot - Search & Destroy (you see it most often shortened to Spybot-S&D) is a great program that I've been using for quite some time. Spybot-S&D is especially helpful when I need to check out a computer that I suspect is infected with spyware and I don't have a commercial anti-spyware package at hand, because Spybot-S&D is free and quick to download.

Spybot-S&D does the typical manual scan for spyware on your computer's memory and hard drive, but it also includes some interesting features that allow you to automatically delete the "most recently used" lists from myriad places on your computer that keep track of what documents you have opened, what movies you have viewed, and what Web pages you have visited.

Spybot-S&D does have real-time spyware blocking, but it's turned off by default and isn't easy to find. To find it, you must have the menu in advanced (expert) mode, and then you must choose Tools⇔Resident. After it's activated, it does work nicely and remembers block or don't-block decisions you've made so that it won't pester you every time you load the ActiveX controls that you know are safe.

An interesting and cautious feature of this product is that when you click the button to fix (mostly delete) what it has found, Spybot-S&D automatically creates a restore point when running on Windows XP before it makes changes. That way, if deleting anything it found creates a problem, you have a known restore point that you can get back to.

In keeping with the general privacy theme, Spybot-S&D also includes a built-in file shredder that will permanently remove files of your choosing. Because dragging files to the Recycle Bin does nothing more than mark these files as deleted and doesn't really delete any information, you need a file shredder if you want to get rid of the contents of a file and know that it's really, really gone.

One last note about this product is that it supports 33 languages. That kind of extensive language support is rare for a free product, and it helps make Spybot-S&D a widely used tool.

Maker	Patrick M. Kolla / Safer Networking Limited
URL	www.spybot.info
Also a virus scanner	No
Client or filter	Client, some local filters
Auto-update	Manual or on startup
Real-time detection	Yes
Logging	Yes
Scheduled scanning	Yes
Price	Free

eTrust PestPatrol Anti-Spyware

As I mention in the introduction to this chapter, PestPatrol was one of the early commercial anti-spyware products, back when not very many people saw spyware as the threat that it is today. Computer Associates International has added the PestPatrol product to its eTrust suite of products, which also includes antivirus, firewall, vulnerability management, and intrusion detection products.

eTrust PestPatrol Anti-Spyware is a mature product with features in the Corporate Edition that will be appreciated in medium to large enterprise environments, such as centralized deployment, logging, and management.

Computer Associates International's considerable resources behind an already great product should produce a strong, long-term contender in this market.

Maker	Computer Associates International, Inc.
URL	http://ca.com
Also a virus scanner	No
Client or filter	Client, local filters
Auto-update	Manual or on startup
Real-time detection	Yes
Logging	Yes
Scheduled scanning	Yes
Price	$36.80, volume discounts

Norton AntiVirus 2005

I include Norton AntiVirus from Symantec in this chapter as an example of a product that stakes claims in both the antivirus and anti-spyware areas. Like many of the products that essentially "bolt-on" new functionality, there are some problems with functionality and documentation for the new features.

The Web page for Norton AntiVirus contains two sentences regarding spyware, both of which essentially say that Norton AntiVirus also prevents spyware, key loggers, and adware. In the users' manual, the word *spyware* doesn't appear at all. Yeah.

From personal experience running Norton AntiVirus and a dedicated spyware checker on the same computer, I know that Norton AntiVirus will miss a number of things that most anti-spyware software will pick up.

So, why include Norton here at all? Because I'm convinced that antivirus and anti-spyware products should be combined and given a new name (something like anti-malware or anti-bad-stuff), and I like the fact that Symantec has started down this path. To be fair, I have had this product catch spyware, and catch it earlier than any of the other products I have access to, so I'm looking forward to what's next in the spyware part of this program.

Maker	Symantec Corporation
URL	www.symantec.com
Also a virus scanner	Yes
Client or filter	Client, local filters

Auto-update	Manual, on startup and scheduled
Real-time detection	Yes
Logging	Yes
Scheduled scanning	Yes
Price	$199.95 for a five-user pack ($40.00 each), volume discounts

McAfee Anti-Spyware Enterprise Edition Module

McAfee is a long-time leader in the antivirus space, but the company has been a little slow to recognize spyware as a significant threat and a potentially large additional market. This entry shows that McAfee wasn't just sitting around watching other companies gobble up market share, but was working on an anti-spyware module that integrates with its current strong suite of central management and reporting tools. McAfee Anti-Spyware Enterprise Edition Module is not an independent product, however, and it requires VirusScan Enterprise to be already installed on the target system.

This is quite a different approach from what Norton is doing, because McAfee is providing a separate spyware-focused product with integration into its virus-scanning product line. Although either approach seems valid, I think that eventually the lines between viruses and spyware will blur, and most folks will be looking for a single product to make it all go away.

McAfee includes protection against PUPs in its anti-spyware, so you can feel safe from hordes of cute little furry canines running amok on your computer. Actually, McAfee defines *PUPs* as Potentially Unwanted Programs. These are programs that might have some sort of beneficial purpose, like indexing your browser cache for quick searches, but also have an adverse effect on the security of your computer or your privacy. Many users install these programs on purpose because their negative effects are seriously downplayed or hidden.

On the downside, Anti-Spyware Enterprise Edition Module is not an independent program and requires that VirusScan Enterprise be installed first. If you're operating in a McAfee shop already, that's not really a problem, and you'll benefit from the integration of the two products.

Maker	McAfee, Inc. (formerly Network Associates Technology, Inc.)
URL	www.mcafee.com
Also a virus scanner	No
Client or filter	Client, local filters
Auto-update	Manual, on startup and scheduled
Real-time detection	Yes
Logging	Yes, centralized
Scheduled scanning	Yes
Price	Bundled pricing with VirusScan Enterprise, volume discounts

Panda Platinum Internet Security 2005

Panda Software has taken the idea of putting antivirus and anti-spyware in the same package and taken it to its (somewhat) logical conclusion. The name says Internet Security, and Panda Software included everything it could think of for the security of your workstation (except perhaps explosive bolts on the network adaptor or the nuclear fusion 10,000-year backup power supply, but nobody but my friend Ray has those).

In this single package, Panda Software includes a firewall and filters for viruses, spyware, phishing, and Web content. Although that's a pretty big load for any one product, Victorinox has done well with the Swiss Army knife, so maybe this all-in-one product will catch on, too. The convenience of only managing one product is certainly a plus, and tight integration between all the security products on a system means that the content filter can start blocking a site that you just received spyware from.

Maker	Panda Software
URL	www.pandasoftware.com
Also a virus scanner	Yes (also a firewall with spam and phishing filter)
Client or filter	Client, local filters
Auto-update	Manual, on startup and scheduled
Real-time detection	Yes

Logging	Yes
Scheduled scanning	Yes
Price	$49.95 per PC

SpyHunter

SpyHunter by Enigma Software Group claims to be the fastest scanner on the market, though I haven't been hearing people complain that their spyware scanners are too slow. SpyHunter comes with a popup blocker to get rid of annoying popup ads when browsing, and it has rollback capabilities so that you can undo any previously deleted spyware. (In case you made a mistake, and it wasn't really spyware.)

According to the advertisements, the user interface was "designed to be as simple as a Fisher-Price toy." I'm not sure what that means, but I'm hoping that I don't have to insert a bunch of blocks into their respective holes before the timer runs out and the spyware runs rampant on my PC.

Maker	Enigma Software Group, Inc.
URL	www.enigmasoftwaregroup.com
Also a virus scanner	No
Client or filter	Client
Auto-update	Manual, on startup and scheduled
Real-time detection	Yes
Logging	None
Scheduled scanning	On boot
Price	$29.99 per PC

Yahoo! Anti-Spy Toolbar

Yahoo! is now offering an anti-spyware toolbar for Microsoft Internet Explorer. This seems to be the very beginning of the toolbar wars, with Google and Yahoo! just starting to duke it out to see which one can provide the most attractive additional browser functionality and drive more searches its way.

The actual anti-spyware engine offered on the Yahoo! Anti-Spy Toolbar is the same one that PestPatrol from Computer Associates International uses (I discuss PestPatrol earlier in this chapter). But the delivery mechanism is unique enough that I thought it was worth mentioning.

Browser toolbars are nothing new. In fact, some of the spyware out there passes itself off as a helpful toolbar doing something that you might want, like posting your search to multiple search engines and sorting out the duplicates. In reality, these toolbars are also snooping where you go on the Internet and what you search for and sending all that information off to their masters.

The Yahoo! Toolbar is just what it says it is, a simple toolbar with a spyware checker embedded in it. While Yahoo! is so nicely helping you out with your spyware problem, it's also providing one-click access to the Yahoo! search engine and various other Yahoo! sites, such as e-mail, games, and shopping. I don't think I'm going too far out on a limb when I say you should expect to see similar anti-spyware offerings from other major search site players, such as MSN and Google.

Still, I can't help but wonder if Yahoo! Toolbar will block its own advertisers' spyware (or at least what other, *neutral,* programs you would call spyware). This seems like kind of a fox-and-henhouse situation to me.

Maker	Yahoo! Inc.
URL	`http://toolbar.yahoo.com`
Also a virus scanner	No
Client or filter	Client
Auto-update	Manual
Real-time detection	No
Logging	None
Scheduled scanning	No
Price	Free

Microsoft Windows AntiSpyware

In December 2004, Microsoft purchased Giant Company Software, Inc. for an undisclosed sum. Giant produced three products: Spam Inspector, Popup Inspector, and Giant Antispyware, but Microsoft's interest seems to be almost entirely in the anti-spyware technology. In January 2005, Microsoft made a beta version of the Microsoft-branded Giant product available for download.

So why look at this as one of the top ten spyware-filtering solutions? Based on the fact that Microsoft will be making this available in all its upcoming operating systems, the technology in Giant will quickly become some of the most widely used anti-spyware technologies out there. What I do here is talk a little about what Microsoft has provided in the beta release and what it is likely to provide in the future, according to its grand plan to save us all found at www.microsoft.com/athome/security/spyware/strategy.mspx.

Here's a quick look at the features (or lack thereof) the Microsoft Windows AntiSpyware product currently offers as I write this book:

- ✔ **An anti-spyware tool:** This tool scans your hard drive and memory for known spyware and helps you delete the spyware it finds. It also includes prevention technology that watches 59 checkpoints for spyware trying to install itself to keep your computer from getting infested in the first place. All these offerings are similar to those of other products mentioned in this chapter.

- ✔ **Spynet:** This is a 100,000-member community whose members report new spyware as they find it, adding to the list of detectable badness. Spynet is included in the beta product, and according to Microsoft's roadmap, it plans to maintain Spynet in some form.

- ✔ **No form of central management:** It would be surprising if Microsoft doesn't add this in the near future. Microsoft understands the need for central management of security infrastructure, and I definitely expect to see enterprise-friendly changes to the Giant product in the near term.

Based on Microsoft's strategy document, it plans to combat spyware using a combination of technology, consumer guidance and education, industry collaboration, legislation, and law enforcement. Each of these areas is important to start turning the tide on this threat, but the following list focuses on technology you might expect in the future from this product:

- ✔ **The same or similar monitoring software:** The product will continue to use software agents that monitor Internet, system, and application settings for unauthorized attempts to make changes.

- ✔ **Extend the product to provide more *system explorers,* which allow users to see exactly what is running in the system and choose to eliminate stuff they don't want:** System explorers are intended for experts who can examine a detailed list of software and files and make informed decisions about what should and shouldn't be on the system.

- ✔ **Complete user control over what is loaded and starts running on the Windows operating system:** This is more of a long-term strategy, and the Giant Company Software acquisition is a move in that direction for Microsoft. I think it's critical to mention this here because whatever Microsoft chooses to bundle for free will have a major impact on all the other commercial offerings.

Maker	Microsoft Corporation
URL	`www.giantcompany.com` and `www.microsoft.com/athome/security/spyware/default.mspx`
Also a virus scanner	No
Client or filter	Client with local filters
Auto-update	Automatic
Real-time detection	Yes
Logging	Yes
Scheduled scanning	Yes
Price	Unclear at this time, maybe free?

Chapter 18

Ten Online Resources for Resolving Spam and Spyware

Something to keep in mind regarding spam and spyware resources on the Internet is that, in most cases, spammers and spyware writers see these resources as active impediments to their business model. Because of that, many of these resources are constantly under attack in one form or another by nasty folks who are using any means that they can think of, both legal and illegal, to eliminate the resource.

Be kind to the people and organizations running these sites, because they are doing their best to help the rest of us deal with the real threat of spam and spyware on the Internet. And remember — the fact that they are being attacked is a good indicator that they are on the right track.

The Spamhaus Project

www.spamhaus.org

Spamhaus is a U.K.-based site that provides a number of information resources regarding spammers as well as a well-respected Real-time Blackhole Listing (RBL).

One of the information resources on this site is the Register of Known Spam Operations (ROKSO) list. This is a list of 200 known spam operations that Spamhaus says are responsible for 80 percent of the spam you receive. This list isn't specifically an end-user resource, but this site is really fascinating reading if you are interested in just how bad some of these spammers are.

The other valuable resources that Spamhaus provides are two Real-Time Blackhole Listings. Spamhaus maintains two listings, because the project tracks two specific kinds of spam sources:

- ✔ **The Spamhaus Block List (SBL):** The SBL is the list of verified spam sources, including spam sending servers, spam friendly ISPs, and probably a few unwitting victims that don't have mail relay blocked on their mail servers. (See Chapter 3 for details on how spammers use servers to relay spam e-mail.)

  This list is devoted to the semipermanent home bases for spammers and is very accurate. I've used this to block millions of e-mails to hundreds of thousands of users with no complaints of a false positive (blocking a nonspammer) yet.

- ✔ **The Spamhaus Exploits Block List (XBL):** The XBL is a list of known IP addresses that have been compromised in some way, such that spammers can use them to send spam. Although this list is also verified, there are problems using it in some environments. The only thing that you know for sure about a host that's trying to send you e-mail is its IP address. So, these lists always use IP address as the identifier in the database to see whether you should block the incoming mail (see Chapter 12 for details on how this works). The problem in the XBL is this: Many hosts that spammers have hijacked are people's home computers, and these computers are assigned a new IP address from time to time by their ISPs. The IP address that these computers used last week, when they got infected, is now assigned to some innocent broadband user, potentially causing the innocent user problems sending e-mail.

  Strangely enough, this rarely causes a false positive, because most businesses use fixed IP addresses and will not be on the list. If you have home users who insist on sending e-mail directly from their home addresses without an intervening server, XBL can be a problem, though.

Coalition Against Unsolicited Commercial Email (CAUCE)

www.cauce.org

The Coalition Against Unsolicited Commercial Email Web site is an all-volunteer organization devoted to providing as much helpful information as possible about spam and actively lobbying for better spam laws. CAUCE offers free membership to any person or organization, which gets you nothing but a happy feeling that you are contributing to lobbying efforts by raising membership numbers. Membership statistics are one of the items that CAUCE uses when speaking before the U.S. Senate and the Federal Trade Commission about spam and the horrible effect it has on people's lives and businesses.

For those of you who like to take an active part in solving society's problems, CAUCE would be a good place to consider donating some of your time and energy.

Internet Privacy For Dummies

www.internetprivacyfordummies.com

Well, I couldn't really pass up the chance to point out the online resources associated with *Internet Privacy For Dummies,* now could I? Spyware, spam, and viruses are all mixed up with your privacy online today, and the Web site for *Internet Privacy For Dummies* contains a lot of information regarding current issues in online privacy, and even some tutorials on useful stuff such as tracking spammers.

Of course, the Web site is really a supplement to an excellent book, so if you are interested in privacy issues on the Internet and how to protect your privacy, you should run down to the bookstore now and get a copy of *Internet Privacy For Dummies.* I'll wait.

The SPAM-L Tracking Spam FAQ

www.claws-and-paws.com/spam-l/tracking.html

SPAM-L is a listserv mailing list created in 1995, devoted to discussions on ways to prevent spam. The FAQ, as you might expect, is a list of the most asked questions over the last ten years, along with well-considered answers. Dedicated spam warriors should consider subscribing and contributing to the mailing list, but for most of you, the online resources that SPAM-L has compiled are what you will be interested in.

The folks involved in the mailing list are (mostly) well informed, and the entries that were accepted for the FAQ list are all top-notch information, with a lot of knowledge and experience behind them. Among all the entries on the site, you might be interested in these:

✔ Many of the more mysterious tools used in tracking down what's up with spam are explained on these pages, such as `tracereoute`, `nslookup`, or `whois`.

✔ In addition to the tool descriptions and usage, there are also some very practical how-to pages here on subjects such as "How do I track down the point of injection?" and "What does *forging* mean?"

✔ A number of other spam-related FAQs are listed at this site, including one on blocking spam, which is accurate but a bit shallow.

✔ The miscellaneous FAQ has some good advice about contacting people when you are really upset regarding some spam you received.

Federal Trade Commission (FTC)

www.ftc.gov/spam

The U.S. FTC is taking spam and phishing very seriously, and this Web site is intended as a resource both for consumers and businesses, with specific sections for both. For an authoritative look at what U.S. law says about spam, you'll want to take a look at this site. The site is updated pretty regularly and frequently, and it often has something interesting in the Hot Topics list.

My very favorite part of this site though is the File a Complaint link, which does exactly what it says — it enables you to file a specific complaint with the FTC regarding spam that you receive. I wouldn't expect a call from the FTC enforcement squad anytime soon after filing such a complaint, but it makes me feel better just knowing that I can.

SpywareInfo

www.spywareinfo.com

Sometimes spyware just doesn't cooperate when you try to kill it. Sometimes after two or three days of messing with registry entries, deleting executables, and reinstalling programs, you feel like it's going to take a couple of pounds of TNT to eliminate the spyware. (In case you're on the brink of doing so, remember that computers are expensive and there's lots of licensing and certifications around the use of explosives . . . although that method would work.)

If you're frustrated by some persistent spyware and want help, this Web site is a great place to look for answers. It has the usual links to software and other resources, but it also has forums that have "trusted advisors" reading and posting on them. More than once, I've found the answer to a spyware problem by hanging around on the forums. This site is also home to the most comprehensive explanation of browser hijacking that I've seen yet, complete with equally comprehensive instructions on how to unhijack your browser.

Spychecker

www.spychecker.com

Spychecker is the site I use for locating new or interesting software to deal with spyware. The site acts as a collection point for information about nearly every anti-spyware program that's available for download (32 at last count), along with a brief description of how each program operates, a link to the author of the software, and the price (if it's not freeware). There's not much to say about such a simple site, but it's a great resource when you are looking for spyware, virus, spam, and security tools that you can download in a pinch. The folks who run Spychecker also say that they have tested every piece of software listed on the site, but you're downloading software from the Internet for goodness sake — be careful!

GetNetWise

www.getnetwise.org

The GetNetWise Web site is an information portal brought to you by a lot of large companies whose best interests include keeping your Internet experience safe from spammers and spyware. The entire list of supporters is too long to list here, but the Sponsoring Committee includes Dell, Microsoft, and Verizon. As you might expect with so many large corporations supporting such a site, there's a ton of really useful content, though some of it seems centered around solutions friendly to the sponsors. That doesn't mean that the tools aren't useful — they are. In fact, these sponsors' customers likely total a sizable percentage of the Internet as a whole; so any way you slice it, this is a useful site.

The GetNetWise site really covers almost all aspects of security, privacy, and safety online, including some that are not part of this book, such as children's online safety and online shopping safety, but the spam and spyware sections have a lot of great content. Just read it after reading the industry sponsors' page for perspective.

ScamBusters.org

`www.scambusters.org/spyware`

The ScamBusters.org site is focused on helping people protect themselves from Internet-based scams of all kinds. It just so happens that spam and spyware are two of the ways that scammers get access to your computer, so this site is a helpful tool in understanding the actual contents of some of these items as they make their presences known.

This sort of resource can be really useful when you get the call from a user (and you know you will) that goes something like: "Hey, I, uh, thought I could get a great deal on my home mortgage, and so I, uh, clicked on this link I got in e-mail, but. . . ." This site can be a good place to discover the details of the particular scam hapless users have succumbed to and help them assess the potential for harm.

Anti-Phishing Working Group

`www.antiphishing.org`

I've saved one of my favorite Web sites for last. The Anti-Phishing Working Group is a really helpful site with just about any information you might ever want about any kind of phishing scam. The site also has what may be the most impressive list of sponsors I've ever seen for a Web site. The group's membership includes eight of the top ten U.S. banks and four of the top five ISPs, as well as a who's who of security software vendors.

The Anti-Phishing Working Group site publishes monthly Phishing Activity Trends reports in PDF format, which describe a fair number of statistics about phishing for the current month, as well as trends for the last few months. In terms of justifying an anti-spam project, these numbers are invaluable (see Chapter 4 for more about calculating return on investment). For instance, the average rate of increase for phishing scams was 50 percent for the year previous to July 2004. If that rate continues to be sustained, the Internet would soon be crushed under the enormous load of phishing scams alone.

The Anti-Phishing Working Group site has a really fascinating collection of phishing scam e-mails that people have submitted to the site. The Phishing Archive comes in handy for me every time I'm preparing a presentation for a bunch of executives who think I'm making up the term, and that it's not really a very big problem. The handy thing about the samples in the Phishing Archive is that you can see just how creative and skillful some of the phishers are in creating something that looks like it really did come from your bank or ISP. I use the archive for slides on a regular basis.

Chapter 19

Ten Keys to Successful Spyware Filtering

*Y*ou won't find a Secret Sauce for installing spyware filters, but the tips in this chapter are about as close as you can get. Follow these ten commandments — er, common-sense guidelines — and your installation is sure to go more smoothly.

Understanding the Problem

Blocking spam is relatively simple: Watch all inbound e-mail messages, and filter those that match specific criteria. Similarly, blocking viruses (as well as worms and Trojan horses) is a matter of monitoring all file reading and writing while scanning for signatures of known viruses. However, blocking spyware isn't so straightforward, because spyware is an inclusive term that includes many forms of malware that affect a user's workstation in different ways.

A program that successfully blocks spyware must watch several things at one time:

- ✔ **Cookies:** Files placed on your computer by Web sites that you visit. Cookie files can be used to track your Internet-browsing activity.

- ✔ **The HOSTS file:** Also known in Windows as the lmhosts file. This can be used to fool your computer into browsing to a site that you didn't intend to visit.

- ✔ **Browser helper object (BHO) installation:** A program that changes the behavior of Internet Explorer. Because BHOs have complete control of a user's browser, they're used to track Internet usage, steal information, and remotely control *(zombify)* computers.

- ✔ **Home page and search page settings:** Changing these settings is a common spyware tactic to increase the number of hits for a selected Web site. These are also changed by spyware to increase traffic to chosen search sites.

- ✔ **ActiveX and JavaScript downloads:** ActiveX and JavaScript are programs delivered from Web sites to your computer; they can do anything the programmer intended when writing them. ActiveX has no security controls other than a signature, which identifies the user who wrote the program. JavaScript is designed to be more confined in what it can do while running on your computer. In other words, ActiveX is unsecure by design, and JavaScript is unsecure only if a software bug is discovered and exploited. Because several security holes in both ActiveX and JavaScript have allowed programmers to bypass these controls, spyware authors use both of these tools to take control of your computer.

- ✔ **Windows Registry access and changes:** The Windows Registry is where most of the default settings for Windows operations are stored. Spyware authors use registry entries to autostart their spyware at boot time (or at login), as well as to change Windows parameters to suit their purposes.

- ✔ **Standalone executable programs:** Any executable program may be spyware or have spyware embedded in it. Spyware authors can sometimes trick users into executing programs that they download, and then use these programs to completely control the computer they're executed on.

The threat level of various types of spyware ranges from trivial tracking cookies that enable Web servers to know where you've been browsing, to surreptitious e-mailing of your confidential files to the spyware author. Remember that the whole purpose of spyware is to spy on you and your company and send reports back to whomever wrote the spyware in the first place.

Educating Your Users

Nowadays, blocking spyware takes place primarily on end-user workstations, and many spyware-blocking programs still rely on frequent user interaction in order to keep signature files and software up to date. If your organization is going to have any chance at winning (or at least, not getting involved in) the spyware wars, your users had better know what to do and how to do it. As much as I hate to go there, users should also be aware of the consequences of *not* keeping up on scanning and updates — infection by spyware and potential reprimand for not following corporate security guidelines.

More than that, users need to know — at least on a rudimentary level — what spyware is all about. The reason for this is that spyware-blocking tools are not 100 percent effective, so diligence on the part of users is another important factor that helps prevent spyware from breaking into your environment. If you can't get users' attention regarding protecting the company assets, you might also point out that spyware doesn't discriminate between company data and personal data.

I cover training in a lot more detail in Chapter 7.

Updating Your Policies

If blocking spyware is important enough to devote budget and man-hours to the effort, then it should be important enough to update your organization's policies.

Specifically, I'm talking about your organization's Internet usage policy. In brief terms, a typical Internet usage policy would include the following:

- ✔ **All Internet usage should be for business purposes only.** The rationale for this is multifold: Employees are being paid to work, so they ought to be conducting only company business, and employees are using company-provided workstations, so those workstations should be used only for company business.

- ✔ **Employees should not download programs from the Internet.** A variety of problems result from employees downloading and installing programs:

  - Unsupported programs may interfere with IT-supported programs.

  - Downloaded programs could include potentially harmful or intrusive spyware.

  - Downloaded programs may cause performance or stability issues and result in higher support costs for the entire organization.

> ✔ **Information created on, downloaded to, and stored on company work-stations is the property of the company.** There is plenty of legal precedence for this: The employer paid for the computer, so the company can stake a viable claim on any information stored therein. In fact, in some states, no search warrant is required if the employer grants police access to the workstation, because both the computer and the data on it belong to the employer. Exposing the computer and/or data on the computer to spyware through negligence is treated the same as it would be for any other company property.

The purpose of the example policies mentioned here is to alter employees' behavior in order to reduce the risk of introducing spyware into the company's environment. The presence of spyware blockers should not give employees license to surf the Internet recklessly any more than the presence of antivirus software be sufficient excuse to open all manner of e-mail attachments. With a company policy, the limits of employees' behavior are more clearly defined, so that everyone knows what the rules are.

Choosing Products Wisely

As I mention throughout this book, the spyware-blocker market is immature and likely to merge with antivirus products in use today. For this reason, any investment in spyware blockers should be made carefully, because the market is likely to change significantly over the next several years.

In Chapter 17, I cover several different spyware-blocking packages using most of the following criteria. Although some of these items (such as user friendliness and broad coverage) are subjective and might not even apply to all products, they're important to consider when they do apply and can be reasonably evaluated. When you compare spyware-blocking solutions, consider the following criteria: automatic updates; schedule scanning; proactive blocking; central management, control, logging and reporting; broad coverage for detecting spyware; and user-friendliness. (Chapter 6 covers how to evaluate these features in more detail.)

I'm willing to bet that whatever spyware-blocking program you purchase, you'll be shopping again in three years or less, and you'll find that spyware-blocking programs will have changed a lot since the last time around. Depending upon a number of factors, you might consider your first purchase of spyware-blocking software as an interim solution while everyone waits for the products to mature.

Planning the Installation Judiciously

In organizations of nearly every size, a number of things can go badly during the installation phase of an IT project — things that are often not considered beforehand. If you prepare yourself for the following issues, you should have a smoother, more successful installation:

- **Unavailable resources:** The people whose time you so carefully planned are fighting fires or have been pulled into some other important project, so they aren't available for the expected number of hours each week to help with the anti-spyware project. As a result, the schedule suffers. I cover resource planning in Chapter 8.

- **Inadequate training:** The people who are performing the installation aren't familiar enough with the product, and they run into problems during installation. This is more likely in organizations that have several versions of Windows. You can read more about user training in Chapter 7.

- **Installation is taking too long:** If initial testing was inadequate, you might have underestimated the length of time that's required to install the product and ensure that it's working properly. Multiply that by dozens or hundreds of users, and that can add hours or days to the schedule. I include information on testing in Chapter 8 and initial installation in Chapter 9.

- **Unprepared users:** In settings where users need to perform scans or updates themselves, many users may have ignored the e-mail messages, the posters, flyers, voicemails, singing telegrams, and apparently all other sensory input. Now they are taken entirely by surprise and don't know what to do.

Keep in mind that the people around you are doing their best, and the problems that I list here are typically the fault of bad luck more than anything else. Careful planning can help you make luck less of a factor in your success.

Testing Your Solution Thoroughly

Spyware blockers need to reach deep into a workstation — the same parts where spyware may wrap its little tendrils around your system. Thus the blockers keep their eyes on browser configuration, system files, parts of the Windows Registry, downloaded files, and perhaps more. The controls are coarse (if adjustable at all), and given the blocker's reach, there is a slight chance that a spyware-blocking program will have an adverse effect with something in your environment.

To head off problems with a spyware blocker at the pass, I recommend that you test every aspect of the spyware-blocking software, including

- **Installation:** Does the product install properly on all of the types of workstations in your environment? If you are using a distribution tool such as Microsoft Systems Management Server (SMS) to install the spyware blocker over the network, does the product install properly each time on the supported systems?

- **Automatic functions:** Do updates and scans work silently and properly on all types of supported workstations?

- **System management:** If your anti-spyware tool includes any centralized management, do all of those management functions work properly? If you have another system management layer (SMS, SUS, WUS, or a third-party tool such as Patchlink, HGNetChkPro, Novadigm, Altiris, and so on), does it work properly?

- **Local customization:** Do your anti-spyware software and any custom configurations (such as customized IE security settings) get along?

- **Third-party software:** Do any third-party software programs on user workstations play nicely with your spyware blocker?

- **False positives:** While browser helper objects (BHOs) are often spyware in disguise, you may be using a legitimate one that an over-enthusiastic blocker calls spyware. While rare, I have also seen random files that I know are not spyware cause some blockers to act up.

Personally, I don't like testing, and most of you probably don't either, but testing has to be done anyway. If you don't test and discover problems in your lab, your users will discover your problems for you — and there goes your credibility. For details about testing, see Chapter 8.

Equipping the Helpdesk

The helpdesk needs to be prepared for the volume or types of calls that come in from users in the first days and weeks of a product rollout. Four ways to keep the helpdesk prepared are

- Get the helpdesk staff involved in the spyware-blocking project from the get-go.

- Offer training so the helpdesk staff can become familiar with the types of problems that users are likely to encounter.

✔ Help them prioritize calls about spyware (for example, handling a transient printer font problem versus helping someone whose spyware blocker is telling him that his computer is infected).

✔ Prepare for high call volumes.

I cover helpdesk training in considerably more detail at the end of Chapter 7.

Monitoring after Implementation

The job isn't over when your spyware-blocker programs are installed everywhere — you're just entering the next phase of the life cycle. You need to monitor many things, including

✔ **Central management and reports:** If you selected a spyware blocker that includes centralized management and reporting, you need to be watching the dashboard and any reports that give you performance data. Are all user workstations properly updating, scanning, and detecting spyware? Are any users modifying, tinkering, or removing the spyware software from their workstations?

✔ **Helpdesk:** Find out how many calls the helpdesk is getting, and what those calls are about. Spending time at the helpdesk will give you a good feel for the pain that users are feeling, especially in the first few weeks after installation.

✔ **Talk to users:** Personally visit some end-users and ask them about their experiences with the new anti-spyware program.

Reporting to Management

To get your spyware project off the ground, you had to convince upper management that your organization needed to invest in spyware-blocking software. Providing useful information (keep it nontechnical) will let management know whether this was a good investment. Provide high-level stats if they're available, such as the number of hits (identified spyware infestations) there have been, as well as how frequently systems are being scanned, whether there are any failures to scan workstations, and how complete your anti-spyware coverage is.

It may not be obvious to management (unless you point it out) that the investment in a spyware blocker may pay for itself with just one incident by blocking the right thing at the right time. For instance, if your only reported hit for the month is that the spyware blocker stopped some spyware from installing on the CFO's machine, and the known behavior of that spyware is that it searches the workstation and file shares for documents and mails them out, there's a good chance this investment paid for itself right there.

Watching the Product Market

The spyware-blocking product market is changing rapidly and is expected to do so until anti-spyware software is wholly consumed by antivirus software. (At least, that's what I think will happen.) Because of this, you need to keep a watchful eye on things, including

- ✔ **Which anti-spyware vendors are being bought by antivirus (and other) companies.**
- ✔ **Which features are included in new spyware-blocking programs.**
- ✔ **What is happening with *your* anti-spyware vendor.** If you purchased from an independent vendor (one that has not yet been purchased from one of the major companies), is your vendor still independent?

I'm sure that, no matter which solution you choose, you may be returning to the market in two to three years to upgrade to a newer version of anti-spyware software, whether from the same company, another company, or as a part of an antivirus solution. Either that, or Windows will become immune to viruses and spyware. Personally, I'd keep an eye on the market.

Appendix A

Spam- and Spyware-Filtering Project Plan

*P*lanning makes the difference between a project that comes together well and a never-ending project that consumes all available resources. What I provide in this appendix is a simple project plan that touches on all the areas of putting together an IT project for spam reduction. For the most part, the plan is applicable to many different kinds of IT projects, so you can use it for spyware or even for unrelated projects if you make changes to the spam-specific parts.

Many of the items in this plan (see Table A-1) may not be the same for your environment, but the basic plan should be similar. The time required for each of the phases is almost certainly inaccurate because of considerations such as the size of your company, the staff implementing the project, and even budget cycles. The times for each task should be fairly accurate *relative* to other tasks though, so they can give you a starting point.

Table A-1	Project Start
Step	*Task*
1.0 Definition	**Define the parameters of the project.**
1.1 Analysis	Examine the problem to be solved and outline what you want the project to accomplish.
1.2 Identify stakeholders	Identify the sponsors in the organization who will provide the budget, the working hours, and the authority to support the project.

(continued)

Table A-1 *(continued)*

Step	Task
1.3 Identify participants	Identify the individuals in the organization whose time will be required to complete the project. Identify the manager or director who will clear roadblocks and manage resources; the project manager who will oversee the day-to-day progress of the project and perform recordkeeping; and engineer(s) or administrator(s) who will perform the project's design, development, testing, and implementation.
1.4 Customize for your organization	Identify unique characteristics of your organization that will require special attention when designing a spam solution. For example, some companies that deal with healthcare may have filtering requirements that allow anatomical terms through the filter.
1.5 Report	Write up the analysis as a preface for the design document.
Total time required for phase 1	3 days
2.0 Requirements	**Define the requirements and objectives of the project.**
2.1 Identify participants	Select individuals from the technology and business-stakeholder departments who can dedicate the time necessary to develop requirements.
2.2 Develop requirements	Develop an initial set of requirements for review by all stakeholders.
2.3 Review requirements	Circulate requirements to stakeholders and gather feedback. Hold one or more interactive meetings for the participants to discuss the requirements.
2.4 Identify prospective vendors	Search the market for available vendors and select those that appear to have a product or service that will fulfill your requirements.
2.5 Send requirements to vendors	After securing any necessary NDAs (Non-Disclosure Agreements), send your requirements to vendors. Answer any questions or concerns brought up by the vendors.
2.6 Evaluate responses	Evaluate each vendor's responses. Narrow the list of prospective vendors to two or three.

Step	Task
2.7 Choose a vendor	Closely analyze the responses from the final two or three vendors. Dig deeper and ask more questions about implementation, operations, support, and so on. Consider cost as a selection criteria.
2.8 Select a vendor	Select the vendor. Finalize and sign any contracts, purchase, and support agreements.
Total time required for phase 2	10 days
3.0 Design	**Design a solution to the spam problem, based on the analysis and requirements.**
3.1 Choose an architecture	Based on network infrastructure, business requirements, and price, choose between ASP, hosted, appliance, or software solution.
3.2 Integrate design with current network architecture	Based on the spam architecture chosen, design a method for fitting it in with the current network.
3.2.1 Identify changes	Identify changes to the current network that will be required for the chosen solution.
3.2.2 Assess impact	Examine the impact of the required changes to the network architecture and notify stakeholders.
3.3 Allocate resources	Determine hardware requirements, if any. Estimate personnel time for all aspects of implementation, including training and support. If the product will be purchased (hardware or software or both), determine budgets and timing. Show that existing personnel can meet support requirements or that you require additional workers. If you need additional help, factor that cost into your budget.
Total time required for phase 3	6 days
4.0 Acquisition	**Acquire the solution, including all hardware and software required.**
4.1 Evaluate	Evaluate competitive products, and then select the best fit based on your requirements.
4.2 Purchase	Choose your purchasing channel (for example, direct, VAR, or retail); negotiate the price; and then purchase the product.

(continued)

Table A-1 *(continued)*

Step	Task
Total time required phase 4	3 days
5.0 Assemble the solution	**Put together the complete solution for testing, and then install hardware/software into the test environment.**
Total time required for phase 5	Dependent on solution chosen.
6.0 Training and Education	**Develop all necessary training and support materials.**
6.1 Assemble team	Meet with everyone that will be involved in supporting the new solution regarding training schedules, rollout, and installation.
6.2 Develop support scripts	Develop troubleshooting procedures and solutions for expected common scenarios.
6.3 Develop user training materials	Develop materials needed for informing and training users. Such materials may include e-mail messages, slide shows, flyers, tip sheets, FAQs, and so on.
6.4 Schedule	Develop a training and messaging timeline: Schedule classrooms, messages to users, and the release of other materials over the first several months.
Total time required for phase 6	2 weeks
7.0 Testing	**Perform testing on the solution in a test environment.**
7.1 Develop test plan	Using the requirements document as a guide, develop the test plan. Generally, each technical and functional requirement should be testable.
7.2 Unit testing	Isolate and individually test each functional unit of the new spam-filtering solution.
7.3 Integration testing	Test the complete solution in the test environment, including all components.
7.4 Helpdesk support	Involve helpdesk staffers during testing when difficulties arise; doing so tests their support scripts and gives them initial experience supporting the solution.
7.5 Evaluate test results	Make changes to the solution if testing shows that changes are required. Repeat phase 7 until you're satisfied with the results.

Step	Task
Total time required for phase 7	8 days
8.0 Train personnel	**Train IT, the helpdesk staff, and the users.**
8.1 Train IT	Train IT on system maintenance, operations, and troubleshooting of the new system.
8.2 Train helpdesk workers	Familiarize the helpdesk staff with the new system and diagnostic procedures.
8.3 Train users	Train users on operation and user maintenance of the new system.
Total time required for phase 8	2 weeks
9.0 Deploy to test group	**Deploy the spam filter to IT, the helpdesk, and the administrative staff.**
9.1 Create back-out plan	Create a plan to revert your mail system to its original prefilter state.
9.2 Cutover IT	Move IT personnel to the new filter.
9.2.1 Test function	Make sure that solution is working as expected.
9.3 Cutover Helpdesk and Admin staff	Move helpdesk and admin to the new filter.
9.3.1 Test function	Make sure that the helpdesk and admin solution is working as expected.
9.4 Test back-out plan	Test the back-out plan from Step 9.1 by reverting IT back to using the old unfiltered mail system.
Total time required for phase 9	4 days
10.0 Deploy	**Move the whole company over to the new solution, repeating the process used for the trial cutover of IT, helpdesk, and admin staff.**
10.1 Party	Just kidding.
Total time required phase 10	1 day
11.0 Evaluate	**Evaluate user experiences.**
11.1 Collate helpdesk calls	Determine from helpdesk traffic what problems people are having.

(continued)

Table A-1 *(continued)*

Step	Task
11.2 Interview sample users	Choose people from several different e-mail profiles. Ask them how the solution is working and what they're having problems with.
Total time required for phase 11	2 weeks
12.0 Adjust	**Make changes to the running system to deal with problems discovered in phase 9.**
12.1 Repeat phase 11 until perfect	Okay, you don't have to keep going until the solution is perfect, but try to come as close as you reasonably can.
Total time required for phase 12	3 to 4 weeks
13.0 Party	**I'm not kidding.**
Total project time	**15 weeks (not including partying)**

Appendix B

Spam- and Spyware-Filtering Project Requirements

*I*f you're at the beginning stages of a spam or spyware filter project, you need to begin thinking about many details, including what features you require in the product. I recommend that you review the suggested requirements in this appendix before developing requirements for your organization.

The bigger the potential sales price, the more time a vendor will take to respond to a requirements document. Conversely, vendors will sometimes completely ignore a long, complicated requirements document if responding to it in detail would eat all the potential profit from the sale.

I use some terms used here that you can commonly find in requirements documents:

- **Solution:** This is the spam or spyware filter product or service that you are shopping for.
- **Customer:** This is your company.
- **User(s) or end-users:** The people in your company who will be using the solution.
- **Administrators:** The people in your company who will be managing the solution.

Remember that no vendor will be able to answer affirmatively to every requirement. (If the vendor does, you may want to look very closely. Sometimes vendors answer yes when they really mean the requirement is an add-on that's going to cost more.) You will have to evaluate each vendor's responses in order to narrow down your list of potential products to two or three, and then discuss requirements with each finalist in order to better understand how their products work.

Other things to think about with respect to creating a requirements document:

- ✔ If you haven't decided which type of solution you want to use (ASP, software, or hardware), make sure that your requirements don't automatically eliminate any of these types of solutions.

  You can, however, have special sections in your requirements that are relevant only for ASP, hardware, or software-based solutions that cover those specific solution types, in case you choose that type.

- ✔ Avoid the temptation to use a likely product as a template for your requirements. Although this method may be a shortcut to a workable requirements document, it almost certainly eliminates competitors that may have a better solution for you.

- ✔ Some companies like to add a column to their requirements that explains the rationale behind each requirement. This may give potential vendors more insight about *why* each requirement is important to you, and this should aid vendors as they respond to you.

- ✔ Give vendors *soft copies* of your requirements (meaning it's in a document or spreadsheet format) so that they can easily and conveniently respond. Be sure to have each vendor sign a Nondisclosure Agreement before you send your requirements and before any discussions where you share details about your technical or business environment. Contact your company's legal department and get guidance from them.

- ✔ Tell vendors how much time they have to complete these requirements. Make sure the time allotted is reasonable. Ask them whether they think they can respond in time.

- ✔ Require that vendors not simply answer yes or no to requirements; if an answer is yes, have them explain why or how. Likewise if the answer is no, have them explain why, as well as any alternatives or other information that would be helpful.

- ✔ If a vendor asks a question about a requirement, respond to the vendor in a timely manner in writing (usually e-mail will suffice — make sure the vendor's spam filter does not block your reply). Then send the vendor's question and your response to all other vendors. This helps to keep the playing field level.

Common Requirements

The requirements in given in Table B-1 are generic, and you can adapt them for use in a spam or spyware-filtering project, as well as other types of company-wide software-deployment projects.

Table B-1	Common Requirements
Category	*Requirement*
Functional Requirements	Functional requirements address the core function of the solution. This is where you define basic features that you require for your business.
Requirements for end-user interface and functions	The solution uses the customer's existing Active Directory to authenticate users.
	A centralized solution encrypts all Web-based communication between the user and the solution via 128-bit SSL.
Requirements for administrator interface and functions	The administrative interface is entirely Web-based and doesn't require installing any special software on any workstation that is used to perform administrative functions.
	All activities performed by an administrator are centrally logged, using individual administrator credentials to identify who performed the activity in the log.
	Logging occurs in such a way that it can't be altered, even by an administrator.
	Solution includes a way of specifying which administrators can perform which functions, as a way of delegating responsibilities to a team of administrators and helpdesk personnel.
	Administrators can selectively prevent individual users from logging in to the solution.
	Administrative login allows for strong, two factor authentication via RADIUS.
	If the solution is hardware-based, the solution will permit physical console access in addition to over-the-network console access. All administrative functions will be available via the console.
Administrative and management reporting requirements	The solution exposes statistics database schema to the customer so that the customer can use a standard report-writing product such as Crystal Reports to create its own custom reports.

(continued)

Table B-1 *(continued)*

Category	Requirement
	The vendor will notify the customer immediately if the statistics database schema has changed.
	The vendor will give the customer 30 days notice if the statistics database schema will change. The vendor will also include details of the change in the notification.
	The solution keeps statistics and makes statistical reports available for use in long-term analysis.
	The solution includes a report that shows all unsuccessful login attempts by users and administrators.
	The solution includes a report that shows the date and time for each successful and unsuccessful rules and software update.
	The solution includes a report that shows which users are locked out, including the reason.
	The solution includes a report that shows which users have not logged in for 30 days or more.
	The solution logs all logins, successful and unsuccessful. Log entries include user ID, IP address, log-in time, and log-out time.
Rules and software update requirements	The solution can be configured to pull new rules and software updates from the vendor at will.
	The vendor will push new rules and software updates as soon as they are published.
	The vendor will specify how frequently rules and software are typically updated.
	The vendor will specify how many times rules and software were updated in the prior calendar month.
Security requirements	Audit logs shall be retained for 30 days or longer.
	The centralized solution encrypts all Web-based communication between the administrator and the solution via 128-bit SSL.

Category	Requirement
	Administrators and users cannot alter, remove, or falsify entries in audit logs.
	Users cannot access audit logs.
	If user login is unsuccessful, the solution will not provide details to the user on why the login was unsuccessful.
	The user's account will be administratively locked after three consecutive unsuccessful login attempts.
	If the solution uses its own authentication database, the solution will permit the customer to specify the maximum number of days before a password must be changed; the minimum number of days between password changes; the password history (including a minimum of three prior passwords); and what password complexity settings are available. (*Note to reader:* This is a fallback requirement. You want the solution to use your authentication service, but if it doesn't, you want to assert these requirements on the vendor instead.)
	If a user's account is locked out for any reason, the solution will, upon a login attempt, indicate that the account is locked out, but will not specify why the account is locked out, when the account was locked, or when it will be unlocked.
	No password or any other administrative information will be transmitted to or from the solution in cleartext. SNMP alarms are exempt from this requirement.
Other functional requirements	The solution utilizes NTP to keep its time of day clock accurate.
	The solution permits the administrator to specify which NTP server(s) should be used to obtain the time of day.
Network and alarm management requirements	The solution can send alerts to the customer's network management system.

(continued)

Table B-1 *(continued)*

Category	Requirement
	Administrators can specify which events will be sent to the customer's network management system.
	Events available to be sent to the customer's network management system include shortage of system resources (such as disk space, network bandwidth, or CPU); network connectivity; and excessive time since receipt of any e-mail from the Internet.
	The vendor lists all types of alarms that can be sent to the customer's network management system.
	If the solution is hardware-based, the solution will also produce alarms on physical environment anomalies such as over-temperature and under-temperature.
	In the case of a hardware solution, the vendor will describe how to support hardware failover, including maximum downtime and session failover.
Vendor Business Requirements	*Use the Vendor Business Requirements to eliminate weak players from consideration. Vendors may refuse to answer some questions.*
	The vendor has been producing solutions for at least three years.
	The vendor has annual sales of at least $5 million (U.S. dollars).
	The vendor's sales have been profitable for the current and prior fiscal year.
	The vendor has at least N customers with 100 or more employees.
	The vendor has at least three customers in the *same* industry.
	The vendor has at least one other customer in the local area.
	The vendor has at least three references.

Category	Requirement
Technical Standards	*Technical Standards describe the current and/or future technologies that the customer uses. You want to assert your technical standards so that the solution you implement will integrate easily into your IT infrastructure, running on the hardware you already have, and supporting the services and features you use.* *(Note to reader: Replace the following standards with the appropriate standards for your organization.)*
	Authentication: Active Directory preferred, RADIUS optional, SSL client-side certificate optional.
	Access Control: Active Directory group membership preferred, RADIUS groups optional.
	Alarms: SNMP v2.
	Client workstation: Compaq or HP.
	Client OS: Windows 2000 or Windows XP.
	Client e-mail program: Outlook 2002 or browser.
	Client browser: Internet Explorer 6.0 or Firefox 1.0.
	Client Web browser encryption: 128-bit SSL.
	Client remote access: IPSec VPN, or strongly authenticated 128 bit SSL.
	Client system management: HP Novadigm.
	Client antivirus: Symantec.
	Client anti-spyware: Symantec.
	Client anti-popup: Symantec.
	Client administration: The majority of users do not have administrative privileges on workstations.
	E-mail server: Exchange 2000 for Exchange client or Web-browser client.
	Server hardware: Dell PowerEdge 2650 with U160 RAID controller, 120GB RAID 5 storage.
	Server OS: Windows 2000 or Server 2003.

(continued)

Table B-1 *(continued)*

Category	Requirement
	Firewall: redundant Nokia NG.
	Internet connection: single T-1 from Qwest.
	DNS management: customer self-managed; domain-wide MX record points to internal Exchange server.
Support Requirements	*Support requirements speak to the vendor's responsiveness to problems ranging from end-user questions to complete product failure.*
Service Level Agreements (SLA) define how quickly a vendor responds to a problem	Nomenclature: Severity 1: entire enterprise down Severity 2: more than 20% of users down Severity 3: more than 50 users down Severity 4: individual users down Severity 5: usability issues
	Severity 1 SLA: Live first-tier live-voice support in less than 3 minutes Escalation to second tier in less than 15 minutes without resolution Escalation to engineering in less than 1 hour without resolution Escalation to vendor VP engineer in 2 hours without resolution
	Severity 2 SLA: Live first-tier live-voice support in less than 3 minutes Escalation to second tier in less than 30 minutes without resolution Escalation to engineering in less than 2 hours without resolution Escalation to vendor VP engineer in 4 hours without resolution
	Severity 3 SLA: Live first-tier live-voice support in less than 3 minutes Escalation to second tier in less than 30 minutes without resolution Escalation to engineering in less than 4 hours without resolution Escalation to vendor VP engineer in 6 hours without resolution

Category	Requirement
	Severity 4 SLA: Live first-tier live-voice support in less than 5 minutes Escalation to second tier in less than 30 minutes without resolution Escalation to engineering in less than 8 hours without resolution Escalation to vendor VP engineer in 3 days without resolution
	Severity 5 SLA: Live first-tier live-voice support in less than 30 minutes Escalation to second tier in less than 4 hours without resolution Escalation to engineering in less than 2 days without resolution Vendor will create a written report to customer within 5 days of each Severity 1 and Severity 2 support incident.
	Vendor shall supply upgrade to newest version of product without additional cost, other than a reasonable cost for media and printed manuals.
	Vendor shall supply to customer, at least 30 days prior to general release, a complete Release Notes document. (*Note to reader:* You may want to look at the last Release Notes document to see the quality of the notes you can expect from the vendor.)
Installation Requirements	*Installation requirements will address any special considerations you want the vendor to include.*
	The vendor will provide 4 days on-site architecture and implementation assistance for the solution from vendor's engineering team.

Spam-Specific Requirements

Table B-2 contains requirements that you can use to create you own spam filter project requirements.

Table B-2	Spam-Specific Requirements
Category	*Requirement*
Functional Requirements	*Functional requirements address the core function of the spam filter solution. This is where you define basic features that you require for your business.*
Requirements for the end-user interface and functions	If the solution is centralized, it uses Web-based end-user management of whitelists, blacklists, quarantine, and settings.
	The solution won't require the user to re-authenticate to the solution if the user has already logged in to the customer's e-mail system.
	The solution utilizes Active Directory group membership to determine which users can manage quarantine, whitelists, and blacklists.
	The solution marks all spam messages by prepending an e-mail message subject line with [SPAM].
	The solution delivers all suspected spam messages to end-users who don't have quarantine, whitelist, and blacklist maintenance privileges.
	Users can cut and paste lists of e-mail addresses from current e-mail messages (or any other source) into whitelist and blacklist Add Addresses features.
	Users can specify that e-mail address(es) in an existing incoming or outgoing e-mail message should be added to a whitelist or blacklist.
	Users can specify unmarked messages that should be marked as spam.
	Users can specify marked messages that should not be marked as spam.
	Recipients of a user's e-mail messages are automatically added to the user's whitelist.
	Users can specify how long marked messages remain in the quarantine, up to the site-specified maximum.
	The solution alerts the user when messages in the quarantine will be purged in less than 2 days.
	Users can turn spam filtering off or on at will.

Category	Requirement
	A systray icon change or a change in customer's e-mail interface will indicate whether a user has turned spam filtering on or off.
	When users are managing messages in quarantine, check boxes appear next to each message, enabling users to specify which messages will be the subject of various functions such as delete, report false positive, and add sender to whitelist.
	The solution includes Check All and Clear All features on screens that manage messages in quarantine so that users can easily manage large numbers of messages.
	The Check All and Clear All features select only the messages visible on the current screen, and not the messages on other screens.
	The solution will maintain an audit log that lists each user's activities.
Requirements for administrator interface and functions	Administrators can view messages in an individual user's quarantine. All such accesses shall be logged.
	Administrators can reclassify messages in an individual user's quarantine as spam or not spam.
	Administrators can view and modify an individual user's blacklist and whitelist.
	Administrators can turn spam filtering off and on for individual users.
	Administrators can turn spam filtering off and on for the entire site.
	Administrators can specify which, if any, incoming e-mail addresses should be used to specify all incoming messages as spam. This permits the customer to set up a *spam honey pot* (a set of e-mail addresses which receive nothing but spam and have been exposed to spam harvesting techniques) if and when needed.
	Administrators can specify a site-wide value for the length of time that messages will be kept in quarantine.

(continued)

Table B-2 *(continued)*

Category	Requirement
	Administrators can include any individual user's whitelists or blacklists in the enterprise whitelist or blacklist.
	Whitelist and blacklist entries specify which user(s) added the address to the whitelist or blacklist.
	Whitelist and blacklist entries can be temporarily unchecked instead of being removed.
	The solution reveals to administrators the reason why any individual messages in quarantine have been marked as spam: whitelist, blacklist, keyword, and so on.
	A solution that uses keyword filtering permits administrators to add entries to the keyword list and remove entries from the keyword list.
	If the solution accepts direct incoming SMTP connections, the solution doesn't support SMTP VRFY.
Administrative and management reporting requirements	The solution includes a report that shows the total number of e-mail messages received and how many were filtered.
	The solution includes a report that shows numbers of messages filtered by reason: blacklist, whitelist, keyword, Bayesian, and so on.

Spyware-Specific Requirements

If you're starting a spyware-filtering project, you can use the spyware-specific requirements given in Table B-3 and add more of your own as needed.

Table B-3	Spyware-Specific Requirements
Category	Requirement
Functional Requirements	*Functional requirements address the core function of the spyware filter solution. This is where you define basic features that you require for your business.*

Category	Requirement
Requirements for the end-user interface and functions	If the solution is centralized, it uses a Web-based end-user interface for any end-user management of settings and preferences. All Web-management operations are encrypted by using 128-bit SSL connections.
	The solution maintains lists of known-hostile ActiveX controls.
	The solution maintains lists of known cookies that should be blocked.
	The solution proactively blocks ActiveX controls that appear in list of known-hostile ActiveX controls.
	The solution proactively blocks Java and JavaScript that appear in list of known-hostile Java and JavaScript.
	The solution blocks cookies that appear in the list of known-hostile/unwanted cookies.
	The solution provides a way to scan potentially infected computers and remove all known spyware, adware, and hostile cookies from the hard drive and detect those loaded into memory.
	The solution allows administrative addition of programs and cookies to the known spyware list.
	The solution blocks installation of IE snap-ins.
	The solution blocks installation of "dialers."
	The solution blocks programmatic modification of IE settings.
	The solution blocks modification of the workstation's HOSTS file.
	The product blocks spyware alteration of Windows Registry.
	The solution blocks installation of any executable programs, including but not limited to pl, ade, adp, bas, bat, chm, cmd, com, cpl, crt, dll, eml, exe, hlp, hta, inf, isp, jpg, js, jse, mdb, mde, msc, msi, msp, mst, pcd, pif, reg, scr, sct, shb, url, vb, vbe, vbs, wav, wsc, wsf, wsh, and so on.

(continued)

Table B-3 *(continued)*

Category	Requirement
	The solution logs each spyware-blocking event.
	Users can view the event log.
Requirements for the administrator interface and functions	Administrators can view lists and rules used to filter spyware.
	Administrators can temporarily or permanently direct the product to bypass individual rules.
	The user event log entries are collected centrally.
	The user events are categorized (for example, as high threat, medium threat, or low threat) and event notification is tailored to the category.
	Methods for notification of user events include the following: syslog, e-mail, SNMP traps, and local logging. The notification will be based on the type of event and administrative choice.
Administrative and management reporting requirements	The solution includes a report that shows all spyware-blocking events that can be sorted by time, user, type of object blocked, object blocked, and so on.
	The solution includes a report that details spyware-blocking events and the specific threat that each spyware posed.
	The solution includes a report that shows all known objects that should be blocked.
	The solution includes a report that shows all known installed users.
	The solution includes a report that shows a log of all rules and software updates.
	The solution includes a report that shows all rules and software update errors.

Appendix C

Glossary

Active scripting: Using JavaScript, ActiveX, or VBScript in a Web page to accomplish something on the target machine via the Web browser. While they have their intended benevolent uses, active scripts are often used to deliver spyware by exploiting weaknesses in Microsoft's Internet Explorer Web browser.

ActiveX: A specific kind of binary script that Internet Explorer can download and run. ActiveX has no restrictions regarding what it can do on the client computer, so it's dangerous unless digitally signed by someone you trust.

antivirus software: A program that detects and eliminates computer viruses. Antivirus software can run on desktop systems, servers, and gateways, and in each case watches for files delivered to the system, comparing the file to known viruses or known virus behavior and not allowing the virus to infect.

appliance: A standalone device with one or more dedicated and predefined functions. Spam-filtering appliances are specialized hardware running an OS and software specifically tuned for that purpose. Typically, the operating system and hardware for an appliance are maintained only by the vendor.

Application Service Provider (ASP): A business that supplies clients with access to a specific application, typically off-site. A spam ASP filters the client's spam by directing the client's mail to the ASP's data center, filtering the mail and then sending only the nonspam mail.

architecture: The high-level design and design principals of a computer system or collection of systems.

backup: An archive of all relevant data for a computer system. Backups can be used to restore that system to its former state in the event of a catastrophe. Note that data backups are able to restore information on a system but not the system itself, but system backups can restore the system to a running state.

Bayesian filtering: A method for assigning probabilities to words in an e-mail that describe what category of e-mail an individual word is likely to be in, and then using the cumulative probabilities to determine whether the e-mail is spam. For example, the word *refinance* is a typical spam word and might get a 78 percent probability that it would be in spam mail. If you receive an e-mail with the word *refinance* in it but the rest of the words in your e-mail all get high probabilities that it came from your uncle Bob, the e-mail would not be classified as spam. This filter is loosely based on a work by Thomas Bayes, which was posthumously published in 1763 as "An Essay Toward Solving a Problem in the Doctrine of Chances."

Bayesian poisoning: An attempt to defeat Bayesian filtering by putting a lot of harmless words into obvious spam mail, thereby training the filter that the harmless words are spam related. The result is that the filter learns that okay words are spam and you get lots of false positives. If you get enough false positives, your filter becomes useless.

blacklist: A list of domains and e-mail addresses that a spam filter should always filter as spam. See also *whitelist*.

bot: Any computer, usually a home computer, that has been taken over by a person on the Internet for the purpose of creating a large group of controlled machines that will perform in concert with each other at the controller's behest. Bots are usually used for launching Denial of Service (DoS) attacks, sending large amounts of spam, or causing other types of trouble. Collections of bots are known as *bot armies*.

browser helper object: Executable code that Internet Explorer loads into memory and that has complete access to everything the browser does and displays. BHOs are used by spyware to track what you are doing and where you are going and then to send that information to mama.

browser hijacking: Action taken by spyware that changes browser configuration settings such as home page and search page.

chainsaw math: A method of rough approximation, such as when two estimated figures are multiplied together.

colo: Collocation Facility. A datacenter where the facility operator rents out rack space to companies for computer and communication facilities that they would like to locate off-premises. These facilities typically provide redundant power, Internet connections, and environmental controls.

cookie: A small text file that is created by a Web site and stored on the user's computer by the user's browser. A cookie is used to uniquely identify each user's action and possibly prepare customized pages for the user. See also *session cookie* and *persistent cookie*.

data circuit: A company's physical connection to the Internet, or to another company location. Data circuits come in many shapes and sizes, including T1, T3, DSL, cable modem, and microwave.

Denial of Service attack: Any attack whose primary goal is to prevent users or owners of a service from accessing that service.

directory service attack (DSA): A technique spammers use to harvest e-mail addresses from online sources. This attack takes advantage of the fact that some hosts on the Internet will reveal usernames or e-mail addresses if queried in just the right way. Often, these sorts of attacks make thousands of queries against such a server with a list of common names, using yes or no answers to collect usable addresses.

domain: That part of the name of a host on the Internet that uniquely identifies the organization that the host is a part of. For example, in the host name `www.dummies.com`, `dummies.com` is the domain.

Domain Name Service (DNS): A distributed database that allows computers to find information about systems and domains on the Internet by submitting queries. Although many different information types can be queried via DNS, getting an IP address starting with a name and getting MX records starting with a domain are the most common.

engine: The program logic part of a spam filter. The engine reads and interprets spam-filtering rules, and then applies them to incoming mail. The engine and filter rules are typically separate, so they're upgraded separately.

envelope: The information actually used to execute an SMTP transaction that delivers e-mail. The envelope must describe an actual recipient, but the message headers may forge almost anything, including sender and recipient. After an e-mail is delivered, none of the envelope information is available in the message; only MTA logs retain that.

evaluation: An agreement with a vendor that allows you to install and use the vendor's product for a short period of time in order to determine the product's suitability for your use. Sometimes this is shortened to eval.

false negative: A spam e-mail that the spam filter didn't mark as spam. The filter sends these on to the recipient as normal e-mail.

false positive: An e-mail that has been marked as spam even though it is actually good e-mail. Spam filters treat false positives like spam and dispose of them in whatever way they dispose of spam — usually by putting them into quarantine.

filter: A service, device, or program that removes spam from the incoming mail stream based on rules that describe spam.

filter rule: In spam blocking, a directive that describes a specific thing that will be blocked. For example, a filter rule might say that all mail with more than 10 percent capital letters will be considered spam.

firewall: A device or software that intercepts traffic from trusted hosts to and from the Internet, and only allows traffic through that has been allowed in the firewall rules. Firewalls protect trusted hosts by preventing attacks from the Internet from reaching the trusted hosts.

forgery: See *header forging*.

fully loaded: In accounting terms, this is a cost number that accounts for 100 percent of the actual costs to the company. For example, a salaried employee costs the company wages, benefits, and overhead (such as office, phone, and parking). The fully loaded cost for that employee is all of these items combined.

gateway filter: Any device that performs a filtering function on what passes through it. For example, spam, virus, and spyware appliances would be considered gateway filters.

hash: A computation across a range of data that yields a smaller range of data mostly unique to the original information given. In spam terms, a hash is a number that represents an entire e-mail message. Any two identical e-mails that you run through the same hash function will yield the same number. Note that based on the input data, two completely different messages might also produce the same hash, but a well-designed function and known inputs will make such collisions extremely rare.

hash busting: A technique used by spammers to get past spam filters by inserting strings of nonsense words into spam, which fools filters in two different ways:

- ✔ For filters that collect hashes of spam mail and then compare incoming mail to the known hashes, this makes each new spam unique, so the comparison fails.
- ✔ For Bayesian filters, the nonsense words could increase the percentage of text that the filter hasn't been trained to recognize as spam, allowing the new spam to pass.

header forging: Putting false information into mail headers to either fool the recipient regarding the actual sender or hinder the job of tracing the true sender. Typically, forged headers include the `From:` header (which should be the e-mail address of the person who sent the mail) and the `Received from:` header (which should describe the MTAs that handled the e-mail).

helpdesk: The person or group that typically handles trouble calls from users in an organization. In larger companies, this group has no other tasks but servicing these calls, but in medium to smaller companies, the helpdesk staff may have other duties.

helper object: See *browser helper object*.

HyperText Markup Language (HTML): An encoding scheme that describes text, graphics, and Web browser behavior in a text file typically delivered to Web browsers via the Internet. HTML describes the fonts, layout, color, and multimedia content of Web pages.

Internet Protocol (IP): An OSI layer 3 protocol used for communicating between hosts on a packet switched network. IP is used for all Internet communication.

Joe Job: Causing an innocent Internet user to be targeted by thousands of irate people by fooling the thousands into believing that the innocent person is the source of particularly heinous spam. Methods other than spam can be used as well, such as providing an offensive Web site with the `mailto:` links pointing to the innocent target.

key logger: A type of spyware that records a user's keystrokes (and possibly mouse movements and button clicks) and sends the recorded information back to a central location. The purpose of a key logger is to capture sensitive information, such as financial institution account numbers, user IDs, and passwords.

knowledge base: A database built from information learned while supporting a specific product or system. Support workers use knowledge bases as supplies of information about known problems and solutions so that they can help users.

Mail Exchange record (MX record): A DNS record that indicates where mail for the query key (usually a domain) should be sent. MX records can return multiple mail targets, each with a priority to determine the order in which they should be tried.

`mailto:` **link:** A link on a Web site that includes an address to allow the Web site visitor to send e-mail to someone associated with the site. Spammers scour the Internet with automated tools, looking for these addresses to add to their list of spam victims.

Mail Transfer Agent (MTA): Any host that handles e-mail that's on its way from the sender's mail client to the recipient's mail client. Typical examples include sendmail hosts, Microsoft Exchange servers, and spam-filtering appliances.

malware: Any software that performs unwanted actions on your computer. Items that fall into this category include viruses, worms, Trojan horses, and spyware.

Non-Delivery Receipt (NDR): An e-mail sent from a recipient mail host back to the sender indicating that the intended recipient doesn't exist. Spammers use NDRs by sending huge numbers of e-mails to a target and watching what addresses do *not* generate NDRs to identify what mail addresses actually exist.

persistent cookie: A permanent cookie that is used to identify a unique user from one visit to the next. A persistent cookie is stored on a user's computer until it expires or the user deletes it. See also *cookie* and *session cookie*.

phishing e-mail: E-mail that attempts to get the recipient to divulge her private credentials by tricking the recipient into believing that the mail is from her bank, credit card company, or other financially related entity. The goal of phishing spam is nearly always identity theft and financial fraud.

quarantine: A place where spam is placed so that it can be inspected in the event that a nonspam mail was accidentally filtered as spam. Quarantine typically refers to spam and suspected spam stored on a separate system, but could also refer to local spam folders on the user's machine.

Real-time Blackhole Listing: A system by which mail servers can look up the IP address of the sending host while mail is being delivered and reject an e-mail because the sender is on the list of sending hosts.

redundancy: The practice of having more than one instance of any particular device or program, so that in the case of failure of one, the other is able to take over the functions of the first.

regression testing: A retest of original functionality after changes have been made. This testing is meant to verify that new changes have not had any unintended effects on the system.

relay: A misconfigured mail host used to pass on e-mail from a spammer to the intended target, usually without the cooperation of the owner of the relay. This is also referred to as spam relay. Relays are used to mask the actual origin of the spam.

requirements: The list of conditions that must be satisfied for the new system to perform its business functions.

scumware: Spyware present on a user's computer that is used to substitute banner ads displayed on Web pages with banner ads of its own, thereby depriving the Web page owner or creator of the opportunity to display the intended banner ad.

security patch: Any software update whose principal purpose is to improve the security of the system it's applied to. The word *patch* refers to the nature of this kind of fix; much like gluing a patch to a hole in an inner tube.

session cookie: A temporary cookie that is used to uniquely identify a user's session. A session cookie is deleted when the user closes the Web browser. See also *cookie* and *persistent cookie*.

Simple Mail Transport Protocol (SMTP): The method used to transmit electronic mail on the Internet. Spammers commonly exploit security weaknesses in SMTP to deliver their payloads and discover new addresses to send spam to.

sniffer: Hardware or software that reads all the information on a network and displays it (rather than just displaying the traffic sent to a specific destination).

snowflaking: Using complex HTML tags to help pass through spam filters while still rendering the spam message properly on the target e-mail client. Spammers use this technique to make every e-mail message different from every other in order to make detecting specific mass-mailings more difficult for spam filters.

spam relay: See *relay.*

spoofing: The act of falsifying the origins of an e-mail or e-mail connection, usually in order to get the recipient to read the e-mail and to make it more difficult to determine the true origins of the message or connection. See also *header forgery.*

T1: A 1.54-million-bit-per-second digital data circuit to the Internet. A T1 is actually 24 64,000-bit-per-second channels used as a single pipe. For medium to small companies, this is the most common link type for Internet access.

telco: Shortened form of "telephone company." In information technology speak, the telco is the entity that's supplying the physical link to the Internet or Internet service provider.

Transmission Control Protocol (TCP): TCP is a transport layer protocol that guarantees delivery of packets. By guarantee, I mean that if a packet doesn't arrive and get acknowledged by the recipient, the protocol detects this and notifies the sending application. In practical terms, mail over the Internet uses TCP, and because of that, masking the sender's IP address is difficult.

Trojan horse: A computer program that infiltrates systems by imitating a useful or desirable program, but which actually does something other than what the user expected. Trojan horses are closely related to viruses, but they aren't the same.

trouble ticket: A record of a specific user support issue. The *ticket* part refers to a virtual, serialized ticket that everyone involved may use to refer to the incident.

update: The act of acquiring new filtering rules, typically automated and from the Internet. Update is typically associated with new data for the current engine, unlike an upgrade, which modifies the engine.

upgrade: The act of installing new software to update a previously installed version to the current revision level.

User Datagram Protocol (UDP): A transport layer protocol that does not guarantee delivery. UDP packets can be easily faked, because there is no handshake between the sender and the recipient.

virus: A computer program whose primary purpose is to replicate itself. Viruses may or may not also have a payload, which serves some secondary purpose, such as turning the host computer into a zombie or destroying data.

VRFY: An SMTP command, short for *verify,* that allows an attacker to confirm that a specific address is valid on the mail host being queried. Typically turned off by default on modern mail systems.

vulnerability scanning: The process of examining network devices for security weaknesses that might allow attackers to gain unauthorized access to the device.

whitelist: A list of domains and e-mail addresses that a spam filter should never apply any filter rules to. See *blacklist.*

worm: A malicious program that propagates itself over networks, often disrupting the activities on the computers it infects. Such disruptions are a result of deliberately malicious instructions in the worm or the worm's attempts to locate other potential victim computers. The most "successful" worms are able to propagate without human interaction, and hence can infect thousands of computers in minutes or hours.

zombie: See *bot.*

Index

• *T* •

• U •

● **W** ●

BUSINESS, CAREERS & PERSONAL FINANCE

0-7645-5307-0

0-7645-5331-3 *†

Also available:
- Accounting For Dummies †
  0-7645-5314-3
- Business Plans Kit For Dummies †
  0-7645-5365-8
- Cover Letters For Dummies
  0-7645-5224-4
- Frugal Living For Dummies
  0-7645-5403-4
- Leadership For Dummies
  0-7645-5176-0
- Managing For Dummies
  0-7645-1771-6

- Marketing For Dummies
  0-7645-5600-2
- Personal Finance For Dummies *
  0-7645-2590-5
- Project Management For Dummies
  0-7645-5283-X
- Resumes For Dummies †
  0-7645-5471-9
- Selling For Dummies
  0-7645-5363-1
- Small Business Kit For Dummies *†
  0-7645-5093-4

HOME & BUSINESS COMPUTER BASICS

0-7645-4074-2

0-7645-3758-X

Also available:
- ACT! 6 For Dummies
  0-7645-2645-6
- iLife '04 All-in-One Desk Reference
  For Dummies
  0-7645-7347-0
- iPAQ For Dummies
  0-7645-6769-1
- Mac OS X Panther Timesaving
  Techniques For Dummies
  0-7645-5812-9
- Macs For Dummies
  0-7645-5656-8

- Microsoft Money 2004 For Dummies
  0-7645-4195-1
- Office 2003 All-in-One Desk Reference
  For Dummies
  0-7645-3883-7
- Outlook 2003 For Dummies
  0-7645-3759-8
- PCs For Dummies
  0-7645-4074-2
- TiVo For Dummies
  0-7645-6923-6
- Upgrading and Fixing PCs For Dummies
  0-7645-1665-5
- Windows XP Timesaving Techniques
  For Dummies
  0-7645-3748-2

FOOD, HOME, GARDEN, HOBBIES, MUSIC & PETS

0-7645-5295-3

0-7645-5232-5

Also available:
- Bass Guitar For Dummies
  0-7645-2487-9
- Diabetes Cookbook For Dummies
  0-7645-5230-9
- Gardening For Dummies *
  0-7645-5130-2
- Guitar For Dummies
  0-7645-5106-X
- Holiday Decorating For Dummies
  0-7645-2570-0
- Home Improvement All-in-One
  For Dummies
  0-7645-5680-0

- Knitting For Dummies
  0-7645-5395-X
- Piano For Dummies
  0-7645-5105-1
- Puppies For Dummies
  0-7645-5255-4
- Scrapbooking For Dummies
  0-7645-7208-3
- Senior Dogs For Dummies
  0-7645-5818-8
- Singing For Dummies
  0-7645-2475-5
- 30-Minute Meals For Dummies
  0-7645-2589-1

INTERNET & DIGITAL MEDIA

0-7645-1664-7

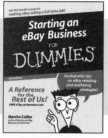

0-7645-6924-4

Also available:
- 2005 Online Shopping Directory
  For Dummies
  0-7645-7495-7
- CD & DVD Recording For Dummies
  0-7645-5956-7
- eBay For Dummies
  0-7645-5654-1
- Fighting Spam For Dummies
  0-7645-5965-6
- Genealogy Online For Dummies
  0-7645-5964-8
- Google For Dummies
  0-7645-4420-9

- Home Recording For Musicians
  For Dummies
  0-7645-1634-5
- The Internet For Dummies
  0-7645-4173-0
- iPod & iTunes For Dummies
  0-7645-7772-7
- Preventing Identity Theft For Dummies
  0-7645-7336-5
- Pro Tools All-in-One Desk Reference
  For Dummies
  0-7645-5714-9
- Roxio Easy Media Creator For Dummies
  0-7645-7131-1

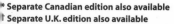

SPORTS, FITNESS, PARENTING, RELIGION & SPIRITUALITY

0-7645-5146-9

0-7645-5418-2

Also available:
- Adoption For Dummies
  0-7645-5488-3
- Basketball For Dummies
  0-7645-5248-1
- The Bible For Dummies
  0-7645-5296-1
- Buddhism For Dummies
  0-7645-5359-3
- Catholicism For Dummies
  0-7645-5391-7
- Hockey For Dummies
  0-7645-5228-7

- Judaism For Dummies
  0-7645-5299-6
- Martial Arts For Dummies
  0-7645-5358-5
- Pilates For Dummies
  0-7645-5397-6
- Religion For Dummies
  0-7645-5264-3
- Teaching Kids to Read For Dummies
  0-7645-4043-2
- Weight Training For Dummies
  0-7645-5168-X
- Yoga For Dummies
  0-7645-5117-5

TRAVEL

0-7645-5438-7

0-7645-5453-0

Also available:
- Alaska For Dummies
  0-7645-1761-9
- Arizona For Dummies
  0-7645-6938-4
- Cancún and the Yucatán For Dummies
  0-7645-2437-2
- Cruise Vacations For Dummies
  0-7645-6941-4
- Europe For Dummies
  0-7645-5456-5
- Ireland For Dummies
  0-7645-5455-7

- Las Vegas For Dummies
  0-7645-5448-4
- London For Dummies
  0-7645-4277-X
- New York City For Dummies
  0-7645-6945-7
- Paris For Dummies
  0-7645-5494-8
- RV Vacations For Dummies
  0-7645-5443-3
- Walt Disney World & Orlando For Dummies
  0-7645-6943-0

GRAPHICS, DESIGN & WEB DEVELOPMENT

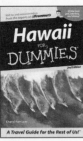

0-7645-4345-8

0-7645-5589-8

Also available:
- Adobe Acrobat 6 PDF For Dummies
  0-7645-3760-1
- Building a Web Site For Dummies
  0-7645-7144-3
- Dreamweaver MX 2004 For Dummies
  0-7645-4342-3
- FrontPage 2003 For Dummies
  0-7645-3882-9
- HTML 4 For Dummies
  0-7645-1995-6
- Illustrator CS For Dummies
  0-7645-4084-X

- Macromedia Flash MX 2004 For Dummies
  0-7645-4358-X
- Photoshop 7 All-in-One Desk Reference For Dummies
  0-7645-1667-1
- Photoshop CS Timesaving Techniques For Dummies
  0-7645-6782-9
- PHP 5 For Dummies
  0-7645-4166-8
- PowerPoint 2003 For Dummies
  0-7645-3908-6
- QuarkXPress 6 For Dummies
  0-7645-2593-X

NETWORKING, SECURITY, PROGRAMMING & DATABASES

0-7645-6852-3

0-7645-5784-X

Also available:
- A+ Certification For Dummies
  0-7645-4187-0
- Access 2003 All-in-One Desk Reference For Dummies
  0-7645-3988-4
- Beginning Programming For Dummies
  0-7645-4997-9
- C For Dummies
  0-7645-7068-4
- Firewalls For Dummies
  0-7645-4048-3
- Home Networking For Dummies
  0-7645-42796

- Network Security For Dummies
  0-7645-1679-5
- Networking For Dummies
  0-7645-1677-9
- TCP/IP For Dummies
  0-7645-1760-0
- VBA For Dummies
  0-7645-3989-2
- Wireless All In-One Desk Reference For Dummies
  0-7645-7496-5
- Wireless Home Networking For Dummies
  0-7645-3910-8